The Making of Persianate Modernity

From the ninth to the nineteenth centuries, Persian was the preeminent language of learning far beyond Iran, stretching from the Balkans to China. In this book, Alexander Jabbari explores what became of this vast Persian literary heritage in the nineteenth and twentieth centuries in Iran and South Asia, as nationalism took hold and the Persianate world fractured into nation-states. He shows how Iranians and South Asians drew from their shared past to produce a "Persianate modernity" and create a modern genre: literary history. Drawing from both Persian and Urdu sources, Jabbari reveals the important role that South Asian Muslims played in developing Iranian intellectual and literary trends. Highlighting cultural exchange in the region and the agency of Asian modernizers, Jabbari charts a new way forward for area studies and opens exciting possibilities for thinking about language and literature.

ALEXANDER JABBARI is Assistant Professor in the Department of Asian and Middle Eastern Studies at the University of Minnesota. He is a literary historian working on the literature, history, and philology of the Middle East and South Asia. His research has been published in *Iranian Studies, Journal of Middle East Women's Studies, Journal of Persianate Studies, International Journal of Islam in Asia, Comparative Studies of South Asia, Africa, and the Middle East,* and elsewhere.

The Global Middle East

General Editors

Arshin Adib-Moghaddam, *SOAS, University of London*
Ali Mirsepassi, *New York University*

Editorial Advisory Board

Faisal Devji, *University of Oxford*
John Hobson, *University of Sheffield*
Firoozeh Kashani-Sabet, *University of Pennsylvania*
Madawi Al-Rasheed, *London School of Economics and Political Science*
David Ryan, *University College Cork, Ireland*

The Global Middle East series seeks to broaden and deconstruct the geographical boundaries of the "Middle East" as a concept to include North Africa, Central and South Asia, and diaspora communities in Western Europe and North America. The series features fresh scholarship that employs theoretically rigorous and innovative methodological frameworks resonating across relevant disciplines in the humanities and the social sciences. In particular, the general editors welcome approaches that focus on mobility, the erosion of nation-state structures, travelling ideas and theories, transcendental techno-politics, the decentralization of grand narratives, and the dislocation of ideologies inspired by popular movements. The series will also consider translations of works by authors in these regions whose ideas are salient to global scholarly trends but have yet to be introduced to the Anglophone academy.

Other books in the series:

1. *Transnationalism in Iranian Political Thought: The Life and Times of Ahmad Fardid*, Ali Mirsepassi
2. *Psycho-nationalism: Global Thought, Iranian Imaginations*, Arshin Adib-Moghaddam
3. *Iranian Cosmopolitanism: A Cinematic History*, Golbarg Rekabtalaei

The Making of Persianate Modernity

Language and Literary History between Iran and India

ALEXANDER JABBARI

University of Minnesota

CAMBRIDGE
UNIVERSITY PRESS

Shaftesbury Road, Cambridge CB2 8EA, United Kingdom

One Liberty Plaza, 20th Floor, New York, NY 10006, USA

477 Williamstown Road, Port Melbourne, VIC 3207, Australia

314–321, 3rd Floor, Plot 3, Splendor Forum, Jasola District Centre,
New Delhi – 110025, India

103 Penang Road, #05–06/07, Visioncrest Commercial, Singapore 238467

Cambridge University Press is part of Cambridge University Press & Assessment,
a department of the University of Cambridge.

We share the University's mission to contribute to society through the pursuit of
education, learning and research at the highest international levels of excellence.

www.cambridge.org
Information on this title: www.cambridge.org/9781009320863

DOI: 10.1017/9781009320825

First published 2023

A catalogue record for this publication is available from the British Library.

Library of Congress Cataloging-in-Publication Data
Names: Jabbari, Alexander, author.
Title: The making of Persianate modernity : language and literary history between
  Iran and India / Alexander Jabbari.
Description: Cambridge ; New York, NY : Cambridge University Press, 2023. |
  Series: The global Middle East | Includes bibliographical references and index.
Identifiers: LCCN 2022050175 (print) | LCCN 2022050176 (ebook) | ISBN 9781009320863
  (hardback) | ISBN 9781009320818 (paperback) ISBN 9781009320825 (epub)
Subjects: LCSH: Persian literature–Iran–History and criticism. | Persian literature–India–
  History and criticism. | Modernism (Literature)–Iran. | Modernism (Literature)–India. |
  Persian language–Iran–History. | Persian language–India–History. | Iran–Relations–India. |
  India–Relations–Iran. | Iran–Intellectual life–19th century. | India–Intellectual life–19th
  century.
Classification: LCC PK6412.M63 J33 2023 (print) | LCC PK6412.M63 (ebook) |
  DDC 891/.55–dc23/eng/20221207
LC record available at https://lccn.loc.gov/2022050175
LC ebook record available at https://lccn.loc.gov/2022050176

ISBN 978-1-009-32086-3 Hardback

For my parents.

Contents

Figures

Acknowledgments

This book is the product of a lifelong obsession with language. I am indebted, above all, to those who taught me Persian and Urdu language, literature, and philology and would like to acknowledge them first: Shayan Afshar, Safineh Tahmassebi, Leili Vatani, Hasmik Giragosian, Victoria Arakelova, Sheba Iftikhar, Shahnaz Ahmad, Basharat Husain Khan, Ahtesham Ahmad Khan, Fahmida Bano, and Ghulam Nabi Ahmad.

The project began at the University of California, Irvine (UCI), where Nasrin Rahimieh encouraged and supported me as I found my way in academia. Touraj Daryaee was one of my first guides in Early New Persian and in the field of Iranian Studies. Jane O. Newman, Kavita Philip, Ngugi wa Thiong'o, and R. Radhakrishnan engaged generously with my work. It pains me that Aijaz Ahmad did not live to see the final manuscript. He remains my model of a true intellectual, and I will forever be grateful for his comradeship. At UCI, grants from the Zarrinkelk family, the Center for Asian Studies, the School of Humanities, and the University of California Humanities Research Institute made my archival research and writing possible. I also benefited greatly from support from the American Institute of Indian Studies.

A stint cataloging Urdu print works at UCLA provided me with a rich source of research materials. I would like to thank Sharon Benamou and David Hirsch for their support in that position. Dan Sheffield helped me gain access to countless sources over the years. Zahra Sabri and Sajjad Rizvi were also generous in sharing sources and insights. Karen B. Leonard kindly shared her personal collection of periodicals from Hyderabad. I am grateful to the late Yasmin Rashed Hassan for sharing her father N. M. Rashed's private letters with me. I would also like to thank Pasha M. Khan for sharing materials from

McGill's Noon Meem Rashed Archive, as well as for lively and knowledgeable discussions on Urdu philology. At the University of Cambridge, Yasmin Faghihi helped me access the archives of E. G. Browne's diaries. Shaista Wahab and Abby Cape offered great assistance in accessing the Arthur Paul Afghanistan Collection at the University of Nebraska, Omaha. I would also like to thank the Tehran Museum of Contemporary Art for granting permission to use the image on this book's cover.

I was fortunate to benefit from the insights and mentorship of Afshin Marashi, Paul Losensky, Frank Lewis, Nile Green, and Sunil Sharma, who read my work and helped me formulate my ideas from early on in the project. I owe a special debt of gratitude to Mana Kia's intellectual generosity. Several scholars were kind to read and comment on the manuscript. Kathryn Babayan and Domenico Ingenito offered incisive feedback on the "Erotics" chapter, and I am grateful for their thoughtful, critical engagement. Adam Benkato helped me understand the historical development of Iranian languages, taught me Middle Persian, and offered comments on the "Origin Myths" chapter. Austin O'Malley and Matt Miller gave helpful feedback on several points throughout the manuscript. Kevin L. Schwartz, Sam Hodgkin, Paul Losensky, Fran Pritchett, Mana Kia, Afshin Marashi, and Sunil Sharma all read the entire manuscript and gave extensive, edifying feedback, which greatly improved the final book.

At the University of Oklahoma, my friends and colleagues Afshin Marashi and Manata Hashemi offered indispensable support and advice throughout the entire process of writing this book. Afshin Marashi and Kathleen Kelly were great mentors at the stages of research, writing, and publishing. Manata Hashemi and Farzan Mahmoudzadeh were my lifeline during my years in Oklahoma; their friendship is invaluable to me. I wish to thank all those who welcomed me to the University of Minnesota and helped me create an intellectual home there, especially Christine Marran, Travis Workman, and Nida Sajid.

Other scholars and friends who shared advice and encouragement over the years, and to whom I am grateful, include Kamran Scot Aghaie, Meraj Ahmed, Muzaffar Alam, Samad Alavi, Andrew Amstutz, Anjali Arondekar, Blake Atwood, Hunter Bandy, Kaveh Bassiri, Theo Beers, Ainsley Boe, Max Bruce, Fatima Burney, Palita Chunsaengchan, Ferenc Csirkés, Cam Cross, Subah Dayal, Purnima Dhavan, Iskandar Ding, Emily Drumsta, Jennifer Dubrow, Arthur Dudney, Esmat Elhalaby, Joe Farag, Sheer Ganor, Mohsen Goudarzi, Sara Hakeem Grewal, Carol Hakim, Aaron Hall, Kaveh Hemmat, Suleiman Hodali, Ahmet Karamustafa, Ahmad Karimi-Hakkak, Fatemeh Keshavarz, Prashant Keshavmurthy, Hassaan Zia Khan, Bilal Nasir, Sravanthi Kollu, Hajnalka Kovacs, Mikiya Koyagi, Selim Kuru, Justine Landau, Waleed Mahdi, Nabil Matar, Jason McGrath, Ali Altaf Mian, Jane Mikkelson, Martha Mockus, Ghada Mourad, Josh Mugler, Marcia Ochoa, Tyson Patros, Zozan Pehlivan, Yao Pei, Baryon Posadas, Sholeh Quinn, Anandi Rao, Julia Rubanovich, Samer Shehata, Suvadip Sinha, Shaden Tageldin, Mohamad Tavakoli-Targhi, Levi Thompson, Tiffany Tsai, Katrien Vanpee, Yuhan Sohrab-Dinshaw Vevaina, and Anand Yang.

I often discussed my ideas with Shahla Farghadani, and I owe much to her encyclopedic knowledge of Persian literature, her assistance with locating manuscripts, and her critical feedback. Aria Fani was also a constant interlocutor throughout the project, and I am thankful for his camaraderie and insights. Sina Salessi and Tahereh Aghdasifar shared the gift of their friendship. Without them in my life, I could not imagine having written this book. The love of my parents and my brother and their pride in my success were great sources of inspiration throughout the process of writing.

Shir Alon brilliantly untangled every knot I struggled with in writing this book. She offered suggestions on the entire manuscript with endless patience and generosity, improving it enormously in the process, and her love made the entire effort achievable.

I wrote this book in a time of historic disruptions and uncertainty, when it was often difficult to remember why such scholarship mattered. In addition to the support of my dearest friends and family, what helped me see the project through to completion was a stubborn determination in spite of the material conditions, or, to paraphrase Gramsci in Islamic terms: Ashʿarism of the intellect but Muʿtazilism of the will.

Note on Transliteration and Dates

When I have occasionally made use of an English translation, I have cited both the original and the translation; otherwise, all translations are my own.

I have followed the *International Journal of Middle East Studies* (*IJMES*) transliteration scheme, without diacritics, when transliterating Persian, Arabic, and Ottoman Turkish sources. I have also adapted the *IJMES* scheme to the extent possible when transliterating Urdu while striving to remain faithful to Urdu phonology; as a consequence, the *izafah* has been rendered differently in Urdu than in Persian (e.g., *taranah-i hindi* in Urdu but *taranah-yi hindi* in Persian).

I distinguish between Gregorian calendar dates (CE, common era), Islamic lunar calendar (AH, for *anno hegirae*), and Islamic solar calendar (HS, for *hijri shamsi*) when necessary. Because the Gregorian and Islamic calendars do not line up evenly, Gregorian dates are provided as ranges. For example, the year 1300 HS corresponds to 1921–2 CE, depending on the month of the original date. When I was able to ascertain the month of Islamic calendar dates and, therefore, perform a more precise conversion, I have given the exact year on the Gregorian calendar rather than a range. When only one date is given, it should be assumed to be Gregorian.

Key Figures and Texts

Siraj al-Din ʿAli Khan-i **Arzu** (1689–1756). Indian Muslim litterateur, poet, and scholar. His important works discussed in this book include *Musmir* (*Fruitful*, n.d.), a philological treatise that addressed the historical development of the Persian language; a substantial *tazkirah* (biographical anthology) titled *Majmaʿ al-Nafaʾis* (*Assembly of Subtleties*, 1751), which was an early source of Persian literary criticism; and *Tanbih al-Ghafilin* (*Admonition to the Heedless*, ca. 1744), a polemic work of poetic criticism.

Sadid al-Din Muhammad ʿ**Awfi** (fl. 1204–58). Born in Bukhara and studied there before settling in Sindh, where he compiled his Persian-language *Lubab al-Albab* (*The Piths of Intellects*, 1221). This is the earliest extant *tazkirah*, and it served as an important model and reference for later texts.

Abuʾl Kalam **Azad** (1888–1958). Indian nationalist, Islamic scholar, leader of the Indian National Congress, intimate companion of Shibli Nuʿmani. No relation to Muhammad Husayn Azad.

Muhammad Husayn **Azad** (1830–1910). Indian scholar whose *Ab-i Hayat*, or *Water of Life* (1880), was an influential study of Urdu literature and important transitional text between the *tazkirah* genre and modern literary history. Other relevant works include *Sayr-i Iran* (*Travels in Iran*, 1886); a collection of lectures on Persian philology, *Sukhandan-i Fars* (*[On the] Poets of Persia*, 1907); and *Nigaristan-i Fars* (*Picture-Gallery of Persia*, 1922), on Persian poetry. No relation to Abuʾl Kalam Azad.

"Malik al-Shuʿara" Muhammad-Taqi **Bahar** (1886–1951). Iranian poet laureate, literary scholar, constitutionalist, and politician. His *Sabkshinasi, ya Tarikh-i Tatavvur-i Nasr-i Farsi* (*Stylistics, or the History of the Evolution of Persian Prose*, 1942) was commissioned as a textbook for the University of Tehran's inaugural doctoral program in Persian literature.

Edward Granville **Browne**, also referred to as **E. G. Browne** (1862–1926). British Orientalist, professor at the University of Cambridge, supporter of Iran's Constitutional Revolution. His *Literary History of Persia* was published in four volumes between 1902 to 1924 and covers Persian literary history from 226 to 1924.

Dawlatshah Samarqandi (ca. 1438–94 or 1507). Timurid poet and litterateur. His Persian *Tazkirat al-Shu'ara'* (*Memorial of the Poets*, 1487) is the second earliest surviving *tazkirah* and, as such, is highly influential. Dawlatshah was unaware of 'Awfi's *Lubab al-Albab*.

Muhammad-'Ali **Furughi** "Zuka' al-Mulk" (1877–1924). Prime minister of Iran, Persian litterateur, and son of Muhammad-Husayn Furughi, from whom he inherited his title. He wrote an influential introduction to European thought, *Sayr-i Hikmat dar Urupa* (*The Development of Philosophy in Europe*, 1931–41), and helped compile his father's lecture notes for publication.

Muhammad-Husayn **Furughi** "Zuka' al-Mulk" (1839–1907). Iranian litterateur and journalist who taught Persian literature at Tehran's School of Political Science. Father of Muhammad-'Ali Furughi. His untitled lecture notes were completed posthumously by his sons and lithographed in 1917.

Badi' al-Zaman **Furuzanfar** (1903–70). Iranian literary scholar who taught at some of Iran's first modern institutions of higher learning, including the Dar al-Funun and later the University of Tehran. His literary histories include *Sukhan va Sukhanvaran* (*Poetry and Poets*, 1933) and *Tarikh-i Adabiyat-i Iran* (*History of Iranian Literature*, 1938).

Riza-Quli Khan **Hidayat** (1800–71). Poet, administrator, and man of letters in the Qajar court. His *Majma' al-Fusaha'* (*Assembly of the Eloquent*, 1871) was produced at Iran's first modern educational institution, the Dar al-Funun in Tehran. It was a comprehensive, universal *tazkirah* that served as an important source for modern literary histories.

Jalal al-Din **Huma'i** (1900–80). Iranian litterateur and author of *Tarikh-i Adabiyat-i Iran* (*History of the Literature of Iran*, 1929).

Sir Muhammad **Iqbal** (1877–1938). Indian Muslim thinker and poet in Persian and Urdu. Considered Pakistan's national poet, he was an important philosopher of Islamic modernity and became a symbol of Indo-Muslim identity.

Muhammad **Shibli** Nu'mani (1857–1914). Indian Muslim scholar, educator, and reformer who taught at various institutions in India. His Urdu-language *Shi'r al-'Ajam* (*Poetry of the Persians*), published in volumes between 1908 and 1918, was an influential work of Persian literary history.

N. M. **Rashid**, also Rashed (1910–75), pen name of Urdu poet Nazar Muhammad Rashid. Served the British Army in public relations at Radio Tehran during the Allied occupation 1944–6. He authored *Jadid Farsi Sha'iri* (*Modern Persian Poetry*, 1969), as well as numerous collections of modern Urdu poetry, including *Iran mein Ajnabi aur Dusri Nazmen* (*A Stranger in Iran and Other Poems*, 1957).

Introduction

You have plucked roses from the garden of the Persians
witnessed the new spring of India and Iran
Now taste a little of the heat of the desert
drink the old wine of the date!

(Muhammad Iqbal, 1877–1938)[1]

In April 2019, Pakistani prime minister Imran Khan made his first official visit to neighboring Iran. Speaking at a joint press conference in Tehran, he prefaced his talks with Iranian president Hassan Rouhani by claiming in English that "had the British not come into India in the 1800s, you would not need an interpreter because we all used to speak Farsi [Persian]; the court language for 600 years in India was Farsi [Persian]."[2] Though an oversimplification, Imran Khan's statement was not far from the truth. From roughly the ninth to the nineteenth centuries, Persian was a preeminent literary language throughout a broad region consisting not only of Iran, but reaching from the Balkans in the west to China in the east, and from Siberia in the north to India in the south.[3] Those societies where Persian was used as a language of learning, whether or not people actually spoke Persian in their daily lives, are collectively referred to as the Persianate world. India became one of the centers of Persian as various ruling dynasties in the subcontinent patronized the language, outpacing even Iran in sheer volume of Persian literary production.

---

[1] *"Az chaman-zar-i 'ajam gul chidah'i / naw-bahar-i hind u iran didah'i / andaki az garmi-yi sahra bikhvur / badah-yi dirinah az khurma bikhvur"* (Iqbal, *Asrar-i Khvudi*). Adapted from Nicholson.
[2] Khabarguzari-yi IRNA.   [3] Green, "Frontiers."

Many might assume the influence of Persian in the subcontinent had something to do with India being subsumed into a "Persian empire," ruled from somewhere in Iran and governed by native Persian speakers. In fact, Persian's status as a Eurasian lingua franca had little to do with Iran. The language had served to link different peoples and societies together in a Persianate cosmopolis through a shared idiom and texts and common aesthetic, social, and political forms. The term "cosmopolis" need not suggest an idealized zone free of hierarchies, as scholars like Nile Green rightly warn against romanticizing the Persianate past.[4] But the Persianate was cosmopolitan in the sense that Persian learning was not the purview of one religious or ethnic community, but rather the common language of varied groups, allowing for connections across a highly diverse region without a single geographic core or center.[5]

Persian was spread to the subcontinent by Turks and Pashtuns – not groups we would today call "native Persian speakers" – and patronized by everyone from Sikhs to Bengalis. Rather than a "mother tongue" learned without effort in infancy, Persian was the language of literacy, acquired through education. Historically, Persianate lands lacked a concept of a single "native" or "mother tongue," a neologism (*zaban-i madari* in Persian, *madari zaban* in Urdu) introduced to Urdu under the influence of English in the mid-nineteenth century, which also emerged in Iranian nationalist discourse in the early twentieth century.[6] Instead, different languages could fulfill different social functions, and one's language of education played a much more

---

[4] Green, "Introduction: The Frontiers of the Persianate World," 2.

[5] Eaton, "The Persian Cosmopolis."

[6] According to the *Urdu Lughat* (a comprehensive project equivalent to the *Oxford English Dictionary*, issued by Pakistan's Taraqqi-i Urdu Board), the first recorded instance of *madari zaban* is in Nazir Ahmad's 1885 novel *Fasanah-i Mubtala* ("Madari Zaban"). On the emergence of *zaban-i madari* in Persian, see Najmabadi, *Women with Mustaches*, 124, and Tavakoli-Targhi, *Refashioning Iran*, 137. Earlier developments in the early modern period made the "mother tongue" thinkable in the Persianate; see Dudney, "Going Native" and Pellò, "A Linguistic Conversion." On the similar absence of "native" speech see Pollock, *Language of the Gods*, 505–11, also discussed in Gould, "How Newness Enters the World," 546–7.

important role than the language spoken at home.[7] Many of the most celebrated Persian poets had learned literary Persian as what we would now call a "second language." Some lived in parts of the Persianate world where other languages were used in daily life, like Mirza ʿAbd al-Qadir Bidil in northern India, or Fuzuli in what is today Iraq. Iran itself has never been monolingual, and Persian has always coexisted with other vernaculars there. Many Iranian poets, like Saʾib Tabrizi, spoke Turkic languages before learning Persian. Even poets like Hafiz and Saʿdi who lie at the heart of the modern Iranian canon, and are today thought of as "ethnically Persian," did not write as they spoke. Like most "Persian speakers" living before the standardization efforts of the Pahlavi state (r. 1925–79), the languages of their daily lives were local dialects that were mutually unintelligible and highly divergent from written Persian, attested to in the "dialect poetry" they also left behind.[8]

With the rise of nationalism in the nineteenth century, "vernacular" languages outside of Iran officially replaced Persian, and the interconnected Persianate world began to fracture into nation-states. Colonial India was no exception, as the British replaced Persian as a state language with idioms deemed "local," like Urdu, especially after the anti-colonial revolt of 1857. But Imran Khan may have overstated the effects of that policy. While it is true that he and Hassan Rouhani did not share a language, Persian – and the Persianate tradition – did not simply die out in South Asia after 1857, but instead found new forms and new homes. What became of the vast Persianate literary heritage after Persian was no longer the lingua franca of a far-reaching cosmopolitan milieu? And how did Iranians, who now saw Persian as a national language, and South Asians, who now saw

---

[7] Kia, *Persianate Selves*, 19–20. On the global advent of the "mother tongue" concept, see Mitchell, *Language, Emotion, and Politics in South India*, 19–24.

[8] Windfuhr, "FĀRS viii. Dialects;" Browne, "Some Notes on the Poetry of the Persian Dialects." On the unsuitability of "ethnicity" for the Iranian context, see Elling, *Minorities in Iran*, 15–28 and 41–4.

Persian as a foreign idiom, make sense of the corpus of Persian literature produced in India?

This book answers these questions by examining how Iranians and Indians alike adapted the premodern Persianate tradition to produce a modern genre, that of literary history. While other modern genres of writing – the novel, free verse poetry, the short story, and others – have received a great deal of scholarly attention, far less attention has been paid to literary history as a genre.[9] Yet literary history is a modern genre par excellence; this book captures how the genre participated in many of modernity's most salient features in Iran and India. In particular, *The Making of Persianate Modernity* shows how, from the late nineteenth to the mid-twentieth centuries, modernizing literary scholars brought together transformations in understandings of nation, history, sexuality, and technology in producing the first modern literary histories of Persian. Challenging the nationalist narrative of Persian literary singularity, the book argues that Persian literary history emerged out of collaboration between Indians and Iranians; drawing from Urdu-language sources as well as Persian, it demonstrates the crucial role of Urdu for literary modernizers in both Iran and South Asia.

Rather than a book about the premodern Persianate cosmopolis, this is a book about Persianate modernity. What happens to the Persianate in the age of nationalism and print? *The Making of Persianate Modernity* uses the emergence of literary history to elucidate the role of Indo-Iranian connections in the process of modernization from the late nineteenth to the mid-twentieth centuries. While scholars have often considered the nineteenth century as the end of the Persianate, I argue that it endures much later than typically thought.[10] Mohamad Tavakoli-Targhi first articulated "Persianate modernity" in his groundbreaking work. Following Michel Foucault, he treated modernity less as an epoch than an ethos,

---

[9] On poetry see Karimi-Hakkak, *Recasting Persian Poetry*. For travelogues see Rastegar, *Literary Modernity*, 77–100. For other prose genres see Meisami, "Iran."

[10] For examples of such claims see Arjomand, "From the Editor," 3; Spooner, "Epilogue," 303.

a way of positioning oneself against the present, which he located in the early modern Persian-language texts of India and Iran.[11] Tavakoli-Targhi left his coinage largely undefined, inviting "other historians of Persianate modernity" to further pursue the project.[12]

Persianate modernity, as I use it here, is a discourse involving shared texts and concepts, in which Iranians, Indians, and European Orientalists participated from the late nineteenth century to the middle of the twentieth. To be modern was to participate in that discourse, to valorize the present moment as a break with tradition. In order to see the present as discontinuous with the past, one must first consolidate the "tradition" against which the "modern" is defined. Indian Muslims and Iranians alike were often invested in the same literary heritage: the poetry of the premodern Persianate world. This book shows how modernizers made use of (and generated) tradition in the making of a new genre, that of national literary history. Nationalism – here, more a particular logic or way of seeing the world than a political movement – has been central to Persianate modernity. With apologies to Stuart Hall, I would argue that the nation-state is the modality through which modernity is experienced.

Persianate modernity is also an era: the period of time during which this discourse unfolded, as modernizers reworked the raw material of the past into national literary culture. The period which I call "Persianate modernity" that this book covers was bracketed between two texts, one often considered the last Persian *tazkirah* (a genre of biographical anthology) and the other seen as the hallmark of modern Persian literary history. Riza-Quli Khan Hidayat's *Majma' al-Fusaha'* (*Assembly of the Eloquent*, 1871), produced at Iran's first modern educational institution, the Dar al-Funun, was a comprehensive, universal *tazkirah*. It served as an important starting point for later modernizers in Iran, India, and Europe, who all cited it, responded to it, and defined their modernizing projects against it.

---

[11] Tavakoli-Targhi, *Refashioning Iran*, 1–17; Foucault, "What Is Enlightenment?"
[12] Tavakoli-Targhi, *Refashioning Iran*, 143.

The process of reworking the *tazkirah* into literary history culminated in the institutionalization of the latter genre with the 1942 publication of Muhammad-Taqi Bahar's *Sabkshinasi* (*Stylistics*), the first textbook for the nascent doctoral program in Persian literature at the University of Tehran. The works of Hidayat and Bahar serve as meaningful bookends to a process of literary modernization. They also roughly correspond chronologically to the period between revolt and partition (1857–1947) in South Asia, or between the reigns of Nasir al-Din Shah and Riza Shah (1848–1941) in Iran.

This timeline challenges established chronologies of the Persianate. Earlier scholarship averred that the Persianate began to decline in the nineteenth century, and eventually dissipated.[13] The "late Persianate" period following this supposed decline was neglected, as many scholars took for granted that the rise of nationalism and colonialism did away with the shared Persianate sphere. The latest scholarship, however, has extended the "late Persianate" period into the twentieth century.[14] This book responds to the question posed by Mana Kia and Afshin Marashi: "are the nineteenth and twentieth centuries between Iran and India, indeed, after the Persianate?"[15] The Persianate was always a living tradition; its core texts and concepts were not static over time, remaining in motion from the ninth century to the fifteenth and up to the nineteenth. As Marashi argues, "as the early modern Persianate system of thought began to fray during the nineteenth century, its component elements

---

[13] This idea dates back at least as early as Hodgson, who coined the term "Persianate" (first introduced in *The Venture of Islam*, 1:40, and defined in ibid., 2:293–4). Hodgson connected the decline of the Persianate to modernization and the rise of nationalism (see ibid., 3:237). The term "late Persianate" – which still lacks much currency in academia – was applied to earlier centuries, ending before the nineteenth and twentieth centuries.

[14] Examples include Amanat, "From Peshawar to Tehran;" Fani, "Becoming Literature;" Hodgkin, "Lāhūtī;" Hodgkin, "Revolutionary Springtimes;" Marashi, *Exile and the Nation*. This attention to the "late Persianate" is by no means ubiquitous; Richard Eaton's recent, and excellent, *India in the Persianate Age* ends in 1765.

[15] Kia and Marashi, "Introduction: After the Persianate."

did not disappear or melt away, but were in many cases reconfigured, empowered, and enabled to operate as the basis of modernist projects of culture and politics."[16] While Marashi's focus is on Indo-Iranian neoclassicism, I show how the shared Persianate tradition was reshaped once again by modernizers to develop a shared Persianate modernity with a common set of references and modern conventions. As the cultural logics underpinning the Persianate shifted, modernity and nationalism did not simply bring an end to Persianate affiliations; instead, such historical ties endured – now strengthened by new physical infrastructure like drivable roads linking India and Iran – and even played an essential role in generating national identities and national heritage.[17] Modernizers reworked the Persianate textual tradition, producing a Persianate modernity which drew on the connections that the earlier cosmopolis had engendered.[18] Yet, simultaneously, this Persianate modernity sought to cover its tracks, erasing the traces of its cosmopolitan connections so as to present an image of national heritage that appeared to be *sui generis*, independent, self-contained.[19] In other words, what I term "Persianate modernity" is the form the Persianate takes after the transformations around the turn of the century. It is the connected framework left over from the bygone cosmopolis that enabled intellectuals from Iran and India to learn from each other in their modernizing projects, and to rework the literary texts of the earlier tradition into national heritage.[20]

---

[16] Marashi, *Exile and the Nation*, 15.

[17] I draw from Fredric Jameson's understanding of a "dominant cultural logic" as "the force field in which very different types of cultural impulses ... must make their way" (Jameson, *Postmodernism*, 6). On the physical infrastructure see Green, "New Histories" and Koyagi, "Drivers across the Desert."

[18] As Eric Lewis Beverley suggests, cosmopolitan languages like Persian "provided templates whose elements could be disaggregated and recombined into new systems" (Beverley, "Documenting the World," 1051–2).

[19] Tavakoli-Targhi describes a similar dynamic in which the contributions of Persianate native informants were erased from European Orientalism's self-narrative, producing what he terms a "genesis amnesia" (Tavakoli-Targhi, *Refashioning Iran*, 18–34).

[20] Kia also argues for Persianate culture as "the basis for a modern self" produced through Indo-Iranian dialogue (see Kia, "Indian Friends.")

The nineteenth and twentieth centuries were a time of tremendous social and political change in the Persianate world, including India and Iran. For centuries, Persian had been "the most widely used language for governance across South Asia,"[21] and it continued to be used as such under British East India Company rule. However, British support for Persian learning in India began to erode in Bombay and Madras Presidencies in 1832, and further in 1837 with Act XXIX in the Bengal Presidency, which dispensed with the requirement to use Persian in judicial proceedings.[22] Persian's status changed even more dramatically after the failed 1857 revolt against Company rule. The British, for their part, violently suppressed the rebellion, and reconsidered their colonial approach in its aftermath. Preoccupied with their failure to comprehend "native Indian religious and social belief" and prevent the bloody uprising, the British shifted focus from rule through the Persian written tradition to vernacular languages like Urdu.[23] The language policy first implemented in particular administrative units two decades earlier became universalized throughout British India.[24] As the British saw it, vernaculars were authentically "native" languages, grounded in the reality of Indian daily life, as opposed to literary languages like Persian, which they understood as belonging to Iran and therefore foreign to India (though Indians literate in Persian had historically had few such qualms). As a result, patronage for the Persian literary tradition in India declined, though as I show in this book, reports of its demise are greatly exaggerated. Persian never fully disappeared from the subcontinent.

---

[21] Eaton, *India in the Persianate Age*, 17.

[22] King, *One Language, Two Scripts*, 54–9; Mir, "Imperial Policy."

[23] Mamdani, *Define and Rule*, 8–10.

[24] Persian maintained official status in the several of the princely states until much later. It was described as the common language of Kashmir, uniting linguistically diverse Kashmiris, as late as 1941, and was still taught in Jammu and Kashmir in the 1950s even as Urdu became the sole official language (Zutshi, *Languages of Belonging*, 272, 319). In Chitral (now part of Pakistan), Persian was the only language of writing and government until 1953 (Bashir, "Indo-Iranian Frontier Languages.")

Colonialism and revolution impacted the place of Persian in Iran as well. European colonial powers had swallowed up neighboring territories like India, and Iran had suffered devastating territorial losses to the Russian empire during the Russo-Persian wars. Iranian intellectuals developed a modernizing, proto-nationalist discourse in response, which culminated in the Constitutional Revolution of 1905–11. Nationalists, intellectuals, and revolutionaries transformed Persian into a national language and "mother tongue." Consequently, Persian literature became understood as national heritage. As the modern, nationalist state developed institutions like the university, it remade *adab* (belles-lettres and proper comportment), into *adabiyat*, "literature" in the modern, institutional sense.[25] Literature as a modern institution was supported by several pillars, including dictionaries, canons, academic departments, and, as I argue here, literary history.

Modern literary history emerged out of engagement with the *tazkirah*, a Persianate prose genre that flourished from the fifteenth century until the end of the nineteenth century. *Tazkirah*s were anthologies of poetry, typically consisting of relatively short biographical notices about the poets followed by selections of their poetry. While Persianate modernizers understood literary history to be something different from the structure, internal logic, and genre conventions found in *tazkirah*s, *tazkirah*s were nevertheless a crucial source of material that was refashioned according to the modernizers' expectations. *Tazkirah* production peaked in the eighteenth and nineteenth centuries, during the politically tumultuous final years of the genre's lifespan, but rather than simply fading away, literary history ascended to take its place as a genre that performed similar functions under – and in response to – changing epistemic conditions. As

---

[25] On *adab* see Ahmed, *What Is Islam*, 380–1; Kia, "*Adab* as Ethics of Literary Form," 282, 288; *Persianate Selves*, 199–200; Mayeur-Jaouen, "Introduction;" Metcalf, *Moral Conduct and Authority*. On the transformation of *adab* into *adabiyat* see Allan, *In the Shadow of World Literature*, chapter 4, and Fani, "Becoming Literature," chapter 1.

commemorative texts, *tazkirahs* were particularly important in times of disorder and disruption, as litterateurs strived to memorialize communities in their *tazkirahs* which were disrupted in real life.[26] If *tazkirahs* preserved the memory of moral communities during times when turmoil threatened morality in the seventeenth and eighteenth centuries, as Kia contends, literary histories commemorated national communities, both generated and suppressed by colonial modernity, in the nineteenth and twentieth centuries.

Literary history offered narratives of the nation's history through the lens of what the British Orientalist Edward Granville Browne (1862–1926) called the "manifestation of the national genius" – that is, national literature.[27] Significantly, literary history was nationally defined. Unlike the anthological structure of *tazkirahs*, with their entries on individual poets loosely organized by criteria such as profession or pen name, literary history assumed a progressive chronology, with poets grouped together in poetic movements which developed in relation to national conditions. Literary history was structured by nineteenth-century historiography's positivist assumptions of a recuperable past. These assumptions made it possible to trace a genealogy of Persian literature, and indeed of the Iranian national spirit.[28]

The hitherto unexplored archive of Persian literary histories offers a unique way of telling a connected South–South history of modernizing Iran and South Asia. Each chapter of this book is about significant aspects of the new literary histories, which reflect intellectual developments in Persianate notions of historiography, sexuality, nationalism, and print culture. Through the literary histories, we encounter some of the most influential and colorful

---

[26] Kia, *Persianate Selves*, 165. On the peak in *tazkirah* production see Schwartz, *Remapping Persian Literary History*, 178–9.

[27] Browne, *Literary History of Persia*, passim.

[28] On the genre's origins and development in Europe – relevant for our purposes as European literary histories were influential models for Persian literary history – see Perkins, *Is Literary History Possible*, chapter 1.

intellectuals of the era. Far from the obscure scholars we might imagine, obsessing over esoteric literary minutiae, many literary historians were deeply involved in the political and cultural affairs of their time, from pan-Islamists like Shibli Nuʿmani (1857–1914) of India to constitutionalist revolutionaries like Muhammad-Taqi Bahar (1886–1951) from Iran. Shibli was a brilliant scholar whose Urdu-language *Shiʿr al-ʿAjam (Poetry of the Persians)* was a landmark in literary history, while his *Sirat al-Nabi (The Life of the Prophet)* remains one of the most influential biographies of the prophet Muhammad. He traveled throughout the Ottoman empire, taught at modern institutions all over South Asia, and corresponded with some of the greatest minds of his day, from Englishmen to Egyptians. He also accidentally shot his own leg off, feuded with as many scholars as he befriended, and may have had a homoerotic love affair with Abu'l Kalam Azad (1888–1958), who would go on to lead independence efforts as president of the Indian National Congress.[29] Bahar was no less brilliant a scholar, and his life was no less adventurous. A prolific poet throughout his lifetime, at age eighteen he became the last writer in Iran to ever hold the title of poet laureate (*malik al-shuʿara*'), which employed him at the shrine of the eighth Shiʿite imam Riza in Mashhad. In the years that followed he joined the Constitutional Revolution, was elected to the parliament (*majlis*), survived an assassination attempt, endured multiple stints in prison and in exile, and eventually taught at the University of Tehran, where his *Sabkshinasi (Stylistics)* served as the textbook for the country's first doctoral program in Persian literature.[30]

Examining these literary histories gives us insight into the modernization of education in several Persianate institutions.

---

[29] For Shibli's travels, see Shibli, *Safarnamah*, translated as *Turkey, Egypt, and Syria: A Travelogue*; for his accident, see Bhajiwalla, *Maulana Shibli*, 30–2. I discuss his relationship with Azad in Chapter 2, "Erotics."

[30] Loraine, "Bahār in the Context of Persian Constitutional Revolution;" Katouzian, "The Poet-Laureate Bahar in the Constitutional Era;" Loraine and Matīnī, "Bahār, Moḥammad-Taqī;" Smith, "Literary Courage;" ʿIrfani, *Sharh-i Ahval va Asar*.

*Tazkirah*s were often produced with court patronage, but literary histories were in most cases associated with a new institution: the university. The rise of literary history is closely tied to the rise of modern university campuses, which sprung up across the Persianate world (and beyond) in the nineteenth century. The Dar al-Funun polytechnic college (est. 1851) and the School of Political Science (*madrasah-yi 'ulum-i siyasi*, est. 1899 and incorporated into the University of Tehran upon the latter's inauguration in 1935), were both important institutional patrons of some of the earliest literary histories in Iran, while Aligarh Muslim University (est. 1875 as the Muhammadan Anglo-Oriental College) and Dar al-'Ulum Nadwat al-'Ulama (est. 1894) played similar roles in India.

Literary history responded to the uncertainty wrought by colonialism and political upheaval by attempting to impose order. Early modern *tazkirah*s were often attempts to organize and order knowledge in the face of disruption, but as epistemic conditions changed, so did what constituted "order." In other words, order was conventional. Literary history dealt with historiography and sexuality as scientific enterprises, as Chapters 1 and 2 detail, while treating literature as a living organism that underwent evolution over time, explored in Chapter 3. Such order was enabled by the standardization of writing and its mass reproduction through print, the subject of Chapter 4.

Many of the differences between *tazkirah*s and literary histories were conventional. The two genres had different sets of literary conventions, such as absence or presence of narrative structure, representations of sexuality, or even the way text appeared on the page. These conventions were not simply passive reflections of the changing political and material circumstances of the Persianate world and the emergence of the modern state in Iran and India. Instead, the material conditions and the conventions existed in a dialectical relationship, each affecting the other, albeit unevenly.[31] The conventions themselves

---

[31] Following Raymond Williams, I recognize a dialectical relationship between the base (material conditions) and superstructure (here, literature) rather than the more

did work, functioning as a modernizing technology and guiding decisions taken by the state. In other words, modernization did not merely beget new conventions; the new conventions *were* modernization.

An illustrative example of this can be found in the court of Muhammad Rahim Khan II (1847–1910), the ruler of Khiva, in what is now Uzbekistan. In 1874, a year after the territory was annexed by the Russian Empire, Muhammad Rahim invited an expert from Iran to establish a palace printing press, which was the first lithographic publishing house in Central Asia. Though the Khiva press was actively used, creating lithographed editions of hundreds of works of the Persian, Arabic, and Turkic classical literary tradition, literacy was exceedingly limited in the region, and the produced works did not circulate outside the court.[32] Unlike Benedict Anderson's classic account of nationalist modernity emerging organically out of a print culture that was connecting people for the first time, here the desire for modernization preceded print, and the printing press was unconnected to mass circulation, at least initially.[33] Muhammad Rahim must have understood the printing press as a technology of modernity, something he needed to have if he wished to be modern, and a tool to be used not simply to break with tradition, but also to protect it. Like Muhammad Rahim, modernizers across the Persianate world feared European domination, and sought to harness new technologies in order to reform, strengthen, and revitalize aspects of tradition, and thus ensure its survival. As Persianate intellectuals encountered modern European genres of writing such as the genre of literary history, they understood these genres in much the same way as Muhammad Rahim understood his printing press. Like the press, literary history was a kind of modern technology, the very use of which marked one as modern.

mechanical materialist view of a "determining base and a determined superstructure" (Williams, *Marxism and Literature*, 75–82; see also Eagleton, *Marxism and Literary Criticism*, 9–16).

[32] Toutant, "De-Persifying Court Culture," 251–4.

[33] Anderson, *Imagined Communities*.

One of the major arguments of this book is that Persianate modernity had its own set of genre conventions, and it is vital that we understand and pay attention to them. Premodern Persianate literature was highly conventional, and its literary forms, among them the *tazkirah*, maintained a great deal of formal consistency even as they evolved over time. While modern writing breaks with many of those conventions, it adheres to its own set of rules. This book demonstrates how modernizers reworked their Persianate literary heritage and developed new, modern conventions. Modernizers in both Iran and South Asia shared new understandings of history which animated their appropriations of the *tazkirah* genre. They labored together to replace the homoerotic, frank sexuality of premodern Persianate literature with bashful, Victorian-inspired mores. Influenced by Orientalist philology, they introduced new concerns with origins into their narratives of literary history. As the manuscript tradition gave way to print, formal conventions of type, orthography, and punctuation emerged.

I.I   IRAN, INDIA, AND THE PROBLEM OF AREA STUDIES

In most North American universities today, Iran and India as well as Persian and Urdu are studied in separate departments. Iran and the Persian language are generally covered by Middle East Studies, whereas India, Pakistan, and Urdu are taught in South Asian Studies. The two were not always studied separately, however. Earlier European Orientalism had considered both countries part of the nebulously defined "Orient," and faculties of Oriental Studies could encompass everything from Anatolia to Japan. The Persianist E. G. Browne's language studies at Cambridge at the end of the nineteenth century (which included Turkish, Arabic, and Persian alongside Hindustani and Sanskrit) were by no means unusual. The rise of Area Studies after World War II, with its discretely bounded fields of Middle East Studies, East Asian Studies, and so on, inherited this model from what began as a British distinction between its colonial possessions in South Asia on the one hand, and the strategically important lands between London and Delhi; hence the terms "Near East" (nearer to London than the "Far East") and its synonymous successor "Middle East" (in the middle of the metropole and India).[34]

One of the goals of this book is to introduce Middle East Studies to paradigms that already exist in other Area Studies fields and to challenge conventional thinking around the question of influence. Middle East Studies has privileged trajectories of language that are rarely transgressed. It is understood and accepted that Arabic influenced Persian, and therefore learning Arabic is an important part of any Persianist's training, especially in the field of literary studies. There is a rich scholarly literature on literary transmission from Arabic into Persian, whether classical or modern.[35] Studies of Persian influence on Arabic are far rarer and usually limited to linguistics rather than literature or intellectual history.[36] Similarly, the influence of Persian on Urdu is widely acknowledged. Just as Arabic literacy is an important component of training in classical Persian literature, Urdu scholars in training typically study some Persian. Yet the reverse is even more scarce, as Iran scholars tend to be trained in departments that teach Persian alongside Arabic and Turkish but not Urdu. As a result, scholars have failed to recognize bilateral exchange between Persian and Urdu rather than unilateral "influence."[37]

Yet this hierarchy of languages is not endemic to all Area Studies disciplines. In East Asian Studies, for example, scholars of Japanese history and literature must know classical Chinese, which exerted tremendous influence over the Japanese language and provided literary models much like how we understand the influence of Persian on Urdu. But scholars of China often learn Japanese as well.

---

[34] On the origins of the terms "Near East" and "Middle East" see Yilmaz, "The Eastern Question;" on the emergence of Area Studies, see Lockman, *Field Notes*.

[35] For classical literature, see Elwell-Sutton, "ARABIC LANGUAGE iii;" de Bruijn, "Arabic Influences;" for modern literature, see Rastegar, *Literary Modernity*.

[36] Recent scholarship has only begun to challenge this pattern; see for example Thompson, "Re-Orienting Modernism;" Key, "Translation of Poetry."

[37] This parallels earlier trends in comparative scholarship on India and the Malay archipelago, in which cultural transmission was seen as unidirectionally originating in India; see Ricci, *Islam Translated*, 11.

Much of the modern and nationalist vocabulary of Chinese was forged in Japanese.[38] Just as importantly, there is an incredibly rich and vibrant secondary literature on Chinese Studies written in Japanese, which scholars of China would be remiss to not acknowledge and draw from.[39] The East Asian Studies model is more applicable to Middle East Studies than may be apparent. Similar to the relevance of Japanese for Chinese Studies, India has been a uniquely important site for studies of Iranian nationalism and modernization.

Just like the role of Japan for Chinese modernizers, India was a crucial site of Iranian nationalist and intellectual activity. The first Persian-language printing press was established in Calcutta in the late eighteenth century; at the end of the following century, Iranian nationalist newspapers in Persian cropped up from Bombay to Bengal.[40] In 1933, *Dukhtar-i Lur* (*The Lor Girl*), the first Persian-language "talkie" (sound film), was produced in India, the result of cooperation between Iranians and Parsis (Indian Zoroastrians), and screened in both India and Iran.[41] As Mohamad Tavakoli-Targhi has argued, for Iranians at the turn of the twentieth century, India was a heterotopia – an alternative space through which other possibilities could be imagined.[42] Indians had to grapple with colonial modernity earlier, and in some ways more directly, than their peers in Iran, putting them at the forefront of efforts to modernize the Persianate. Consequently, some of the developments I detail in this book – the transition from writing *tazkirah*s to literary history, the emergence of Victorian-inspired sexual aesthetics, and the introduction of Persian

---

[38] Chung, "Some Returned Loans."

[39] On the other hand, the Korea historian Bruce Cumings laments how "to be in 'Korean studies' is to study Korea and not China or Japan" (Cumings, "Seeing Like an Area Specialist," 93). As an outsider to East Asian Studies, perhaps I view the field with rose-tinted glasses.

[40] Floor, "ČĀP."

[41] Naficy, *A Social History of Iranian Cinema*, 1:231–45; Fish, "The Bombay Interlude;" Rekabtalaei, *Iranian Cosmopolitanism*, 105–10. The director, Ardeshir Irani (1886–1969), was also responsible for the first Indian sound film, the Urdu-language *'Alam Ara* (*The Ornament of the World*, 1931).

[42] Tavakoli-Targhi, *Refashioning Iran*, 1–4.

movable type – occurred in India before Iran. South Asia features prominently in classical Persian poetry, not only by Indian poets or those who traveled to India, but in poetry from the Iranian heartland as well; everyone knows Hafiz's widely quoted lines about his beloved's "Hindu mole" or the "Persian sugar-candy which goes to Bengal." Less widely recognized are the South Asian characters who dot the literary and cinematic landscape of modern Iran as well, featured in various celebrated novels from Sadiq Hidayat's *Buf-i Kur* (*The Blind Owl*, 1936) to Iraj Pizishkzad's *Da'i Jan Napil'un* (*Dear Uncle Napoleon*, 1973) or Simin Danishvar's *Savushun* (1969), and in films from *Dukhtar-i Lur* to *Ganj-i Qarun* (*Qarun's Treasure*, 1965).

There is also an expansive, and often highly sophisticated, secondary literature on Persian literature and Iran written in Urdu, which Persian Studies scholars outside of South Asia are wholly unaware of. While ancient India captured the interest of Iran scholars from the beginning of the twentieth century, Iranian Studies has largely ignored modern India and Pakistan, and as a result, it has overlooked valuable scholarship in Urdu. By the same token, South Asian Studies has too often considered Iran outside of its bailiwick and has therefore failed to adequately account for the salience of South Asian litterateurs in modern Iran.[43]

Over the past two decades, a new wave of scholarship has started to break down the divide between Iranian Studies and South Asian Studies, as Iranian Studies has paid increasing attention to modern Indo-Iranian connections. Some have focused on exchange between Iranians and Parsis,[44] while others have located the roots of

---

[43] Scholarship on the early modern period, especially studies of the Deccan, has paid close attention to Indo-Iranian connections. However, the field has not yet addressed South Asians in nineteenth- and twentieth-century Iran. Notable exceptions include Pue, *I Too Have Some Dreams*; Fuchs, *In a Pure Muslim Land*; and much of Nile Green's work such as *Bombay Islam*.

[44] Grigor, "Persian Architectural Revivals;" Ringer, *Pious Citizens*; Marashi, *Exile and the Nation*; Sheffield, "Iran, the Mark of Paradise."

Iranian nationalism and modernization projects in India.[45] These scholars laid important ground in critically analyzing Iranian nationalism and uncovering its origins in India, challenging nationalist paradigms that had long defined Iranian Studies. At the same time, however, in their focus on Parsis and Iranian émigrés and exiles in India, they have continued to focus on people who claim Iranian origins, whether historical or recent; the important role of South Asian Muslims in Iranian modernity has generally been overlooked. This is due in no small part to Area Studies training, which results in most Iranian Studies scholars being unable to engage with Urdu-language materials. By not examining Urdu sources, this "Persianate turn" in Iranian Studies has essentially been limited to studying figures who had some ostensible genealogical connection to Iran, whether Iranian migrants and travelers writing in Persian, or Parsis, writing in English or Persian, who considered Iran their ancestral homeland.[46]

Yet considering the Urdu-language contributions to Persian literary history allows us to see that South Asian Muslims did indeed play an important role alongside Parsis and Iranian émigrés. Some, like Muhammad Husayn Azad (1830–1910), claimed Iranian ancestry like their Parsi compatriots, but others had no such ties and did not form their Indo-Iranian ties on the basis of an (imagined) shared genealogy. Shibli Nuʿmani saw Persian literature as part of the Islamic heritage that pertained to him as a Muslim with no familial link to Iran, while the poet N. M. Rashid understood Indo-Iranian connections in terms of their shared experience of colonialism, in what A. Sean Pue has termed "position without identity."[47] South Asian Studies has neglected these connections as well. With the exception of Pue's *I Too Have Some Dreams: N.M. Rashed and*

---

[45] Tavakoli-Targhi, *Refashioning Iran*; Marashi, *Nationalizing Iran*; Adib-Moghaddam, *Psycho-nationalism*.

[46] On the "Persianate turn" see Khazeni, *The City and the Wilderness*, 3; Hemmat, "Completing the Persianate Turn."

[47] Pue, *I Too Have Some Dreams*, chapter 2.

Modernism in Urdu Poetry, Iran has not featured in works on Urdu literary modernity. Islamic religious networks connecting modern Iran and South Asia have received some scholarly attention,[48] but literary and intellectual connections between the two have been all but entirely ignored by South Asianists.

Reassessing the link between modern Urdu and Persian offers a new perspective on Mohamad Tavakoli-Targhi's notion of "homeless texts" of Persianate modernity.[49] "Homeless texts," for Tavakoli-Targhi, are those Persian works produced in India in which can be found an early modern ethos, yet which have "fallen between the cracks of area studies" and similarly not featured into Indian or Iranian accounts of modernity, being understood as not Indian (by virtue of being in Persian) and not Iranian (by virtue of being from India), and therefore "homeless."[50] As we have seen, Tavakoli-Targhi is right to consider these texts as disciplinarily lost between Middle East Studies and South Asian Studies. It is certainly true that most of these texts did not feature into Iranian accounts of modernity and were, in fact, largely unknown in Iran until the final decades of the twentieth century; it is also true that they were not the texts secular nationalist Indians turned to in making claims of an indigenous modernity. For example, among the "homeless texts" he discusses are the works of Siraj al-Din ʿAli Khan-i Arzu, an early modern Persianate litterateur, philologist, and literary critic of eighteenth-century India. As Tavakoli-Targhi discusses, Arzu explored the relationship between Sanskrit and Persian decades before Europeans like Sir William Jones took up the subject. Tavakoli-Targhi laments that Arzu's contributions were ignored; indeed, Bahar was scantly aware of Arzu, referring to the Indian litterateur only twice

---

[48] Green, *Bombay Islam*; Fuchs, *In a Pure Muslim Land*, and several essays in Jaffrelot and Louër, *Pan-Islamic Connections*.

[49] Tavakoli-Targhi, "The Homeless Texts of Persianate Modernity;" Tavakoli-Targhi, *Refashioning Iran*, 8–17.

[50] Tavakoli-Targhi, *Refashioning Iran*, x.

throughout his works.[51] In Bahar's time, Arzu was barely known in Iran; in 1960, the *Dihkhuda* dictionary still described him as merely "one of the poets of India. His poetry is frequently cited in the *Anandraj* dictionary," with no mention of his philological oeuvre; indeed, this deficient definition is still found in contemporary editions of the encyclopedic *Dihkhuda* dictionary.[52]

This book locates a home for Tavakoli-Targhi's "homeless texts of Persianate modernity" in Urdu scholarship. Shibli Nu'mani's *Shi'r al-'Ajam*, for example, relies on Arzu's linguistic treatises and his important *tazkirah* of Persian poetry, *Majma' al-Nafa'is* (*Assembly of Subtleties*). Muhammad Husayn Azad drew even more extensively on Arzu, translating entire chapters of Arzu's philological work *Musmir* (*Fruitful*) into Urdu, celebrating him as the father of all Urdu speakers, and lauding Arzu's poetry in his *Nigaristan-i Fars* (*Picture-Gallery of Persia*).[53] There was never a time when the works of Arzu, among other supposedly "homeless" Persian-language works of the subcontinent, ceased to be read and commented on in India, first in Persian and later in Urdu. Literacy, we must recall, had always been a rarefied phenomenon; even at the height of the Persianate cosmopolis, just a miniscule fraction of society was literate enough

---

[51] In one article Bahar points dismissively to the many "errors" of the "spurious" (*ja'li*) books of Arzu and others (*Bahar va Adab* 2:408). The article, "*Ta'lim-i Zaban-i Farsi va Kitab-ha-yi kih Lazim Darim*," originally appeared in *Majallah-yi Ta'lim va Tarbiyat* in 1938. Bahar's mentioning (and dismissing) Arzu alongside works like the *Farhang-i Jahangiri, Burhan-i Qati', Dasatir, Namah-yi Khusruvan*, and other *dasatiri* or neo-Zoroastrian texts, and italicizing Arzu's name as he does the titles of these other works, could indicate that Bahar was referring to Arzu's dictionary *Chiragh-i Hidayat* and that he had not actually seen the dictionary himself but had only read about it in other works. Later, in his *Sabkshinasi*, Bahar briefly mentions "the dictionary *Chiragh-i Hidayat* written by the great scholar [*fazil-i 'alimaqam*] Khan-i Arzu" (*Sabkshinasi* 3:290.) Bahar's paucity of references to Arzu, and the inconsistency between them, suggest that he was most likely unfamiliar with Arzu's works, which is unsurprising given their rarity in Iran until much later.

[52] Dihkhuda, *Lughat-Namah*, 55:155. *Anandraj* refers to a late nineteenth-century Persian dictionary from the Deccan.

[53] On Azad's engagement with Arzu, see Kovacs, "The Role of Persian Language and Literature" and Dudney, *India in the Persian World*, 193–8, 245–8; on Arzu as the father of all Urdu speakers, see Azad, *Ab-i Hayat*, 115–17; on Arzu's poetry, see Azad, *Nigaristan-i Fars*, 220–4.

to access such texts directly.[54] Therefore, precolonial Persian texts
would have had only a very small number of readers – comparable to
the elite of the Urdu literati today who continue to read and engage
with Persian literature. In absolute numbers, it is less the case that
Persian literacy decreased in South Asia so much as it was over-
shadowed by the explosion of new literacy in Urdu, Hindi, English,
and other languages; classes of people who would have generally been
unlettered in the past are now often literate in "vernacular" languages. There was no radical break with the Persianate tradition; it
did not disappear but instead shifted – albeit with some transformations – in the written medium of Urdu, in the works of Indian
Muslim modernizers like Shibli and Azad.[55]

I.2   CIRCULATION, NETWORKS, EXCHANGE

The history of Persian influence on Urdu is well-documented and
widely acknowledged, with Urdu deriving its writing system and
much of its vocabulary and literary forms from Persian.[56] For the most
part, Iranians had been ignorant of Urdu, with the exception of some
Iranian travelers to South Asia in the Mughal era. However, in the
time of Persianate modernity, this dynamic was no longer so clear-
cut. Indian scholars belonging to the Persianate tradition were
attempting to bridge the gap between traditional forms of knowledge
and writing and what they saw as modern, European approaches to
science and historiography. Urdu writers like Shibli Nuʿmani were
seeking native models which could be used to reform, revitalize, and
preserve the Persianate or Islamicate heritage and make it compatible
with colonial modernity. This approach was very much in line with
the goals of many literary scholars and intellectual reformers across
the border in Iran, and the efforts of these Urdu writers did not go

---

[54] Spooner and Hanaway, "Siyaq;" Cole, "Iranian Culture and South Asia," 18.

[55] Spooner and Hanaway describe Urdu as a "successor Persianate [language] of
literacy" (ibid., 434).

[56] Matthews, "URDU;" Syed, "Role of Persian;" Sadiq, *A History of Urdu Literature*,
14–49; Faruqi, *Early Urdu Literary Culture*, 109–26.

unnoticed. As Iranians and Indians became part of shared social and intellectual networks, their ideas cross-pollinated. Shibli Nu'mani's lengthy Urdu-language work on Persian poetry, *Shi'r al-'Ajam*, which was an important milestone in refashioning the traditional genre of *tazkirah* writing into modern European-style literary history (taken up in detail in Chapter 1, "Histories"), influenced Iranian literary scholars like Muhammad-Taqi Bahar and Zayn al-'Abidin Mu'taman (1914–2005).[57]

Bahar was unable to read Urdu himself, but made many favorable references to Shibli's work. He may have read the Persian translation of *Shi'r al-'Ajam* commissioned by the Afghan Ministry of Education in 1925. However, this translation, published in Afghanistan, had very limited circulation in Iran.[58] More likely, Bahar learned about Shibli through his social circle, which was full of Urdu-speaking South Asian and Iranian litterateurs. While textual influence tends more often to be one-sided (more Urdu speakers read Persian texts than the reverse, and more Iranian intellectuals read French texts than vice versa), the conversation between Bahar and his South Asian colleagues provides insight into a different dynamic, one of reciprocal networks and mutual exchange. This same dynamic can be witnessed in the relationship between Orientalist scholars and their Asian friends and tutors; for example, Shibli received his exposure to European thought and writing primarily through his friendship with the British Orientalist T. W. Arnold (1864–1930). Their friendship was based on mutual exchange, as they tutored one another in Arabic and French, respectively. Browne had a similar dynamic with his Iranian friends and Indian students, though he was also capable of reading Persian and Urdu himself.[59]

---

[57] Mu'taman discusses this in the unnumbered preface to his *Shi'r va Adab-i Farsi* (1953).

[58] Shibli [Gilani translation], *Shi'r al-'Ajam*, 3:ha-vav. It was later translated again into Persian, this time by an Iranian, Muhammad-Taqi Fakhr-i Da'i Gilani, and published in Iran in 1948.

[59] This is also discussed in Vejdani, "Indo-Iranian," 442–8.

Shibli's *Shi'r al-'Ajam* is a text whose influence stretched far beyond the borders of Urdu, leaving an impression on Iranian literary scholars as well as European Orientalists like Browne, as well as elsewhere in the Persianate world.[60] It is also an illustrative example of the long afterlife of Persian in the subcontinent. Published in multiple volumes between 1908 and 1918, it, like many other such Urdu texts, continues the developments and debates that had previously been taking place in Persian. The shift to Urdu from Persian does not necessarily represent a break with the tradition of Persian learning. Long after the supposed decline of Persian in the subcontinent, *tazkirah*s and histories of Persian literature, like Shibli's, continued to be written in Urdu (rather than in Persian) alongside commentaries (*sharh*) on the core texts of the Persianate tradition like the *Gulistan* (*Rose Garden*) of Sa'di or the *Masnavi* of Mawlana Rumi.[61] Even today, Persian language and literature remain fundamental aspects of a traditional religious education in South Asia, and secular newspapers serialize Urdu translations and commentaries on Persian texts like the *Gulistan*.[62] In earlier times Persian was taught to Indian learners using Persian-language texts which had very convoluted, highly specific discussions of Persian grammar and related minutiae. It was incumbent on the teacher to help students understand these principal texts by breaking them down and explaining them orally, typically in a vernacular language like Urdu.[63] Later Persian grammars, prosody manuals, and the like, began to be written in Urdu, or sometimes in Persian with interlinear Urdu translation. These grammars of Persian written in Urdu are a continuation of the

---

[60] It also became an important part of the Persian literary curriculum in Afghanistan and Tajikistan, though these countries are beyond the scope of this book. For a Tajik example, see Toirov et al., *Adabiyoti Tojik*, 81.

[61] For a fascinating study of an Urdu commentary on the *divan* of Hafiz, see Mian, "Surviving Desire."

[62] For a few examples see "Bicchu ki Paida'ish;" "Hikayat-i Sa'di;" "Mashriqiyat;" Zaheer, "Hikayat-i Sa'di;" Zehra, "Hikayat-i Sa'di."

[63] This dynamic is comparable to that of a contemporary graduate seminar at an anglophone institution, where the class may discuss a foreign-language text in English.

tradition of orally teaching Persian grammar through Urdu. The link to Persian literary traditions and texts has not been lost; it is now mediated through Urdu.[64]

The context in which Indo-Iranian exchange took place must be considered. It is not only the shared Persianate heritage, but also the shared experience of colonial modernity that made these connections possible, as the Urdu poet N. M. Rashid (1910–75) suggested through his poetry collection *Iran mein Ajnabi* (*A Stranger in Iran*).[65] Simply celebrating exchange risks overlooking the power structure that enabled it in the first place, as the historian Sebastian Conrad cautions.[66] Iranians and South Asians both faced similar conditions in the time of Persianate modernity, particularly in the colonial encounter with Britain, which came to a head as Britain invaded Iran and occupied Iranian territory with the help of the British Indian Army during both world wars. The Allied occupation of Iran from 1941–6, in which the Indian Army played a cultural role in addition to its military function, was an especially decisive time for Indo-Iranian exchange. Rashid himself was a conduit for such exchange; conscripted into the British Indian Army, he served the army in public relations at Radio Tehran under the British occupation. As a litterateur fluent in both Urdu and Persian, with a social circle that included many of Tehran's most prominent intellectuals and literati, Rashid was a living link between the two countries. Cultural connections continued after the war, especially between Iran and newly independent Pakistan, both US-aligned modernizing Asian states during the Cold War.

---

[64] Urdu has even become a vehicle for the Persian tradition in some regions of South Asia where Urdu is not natively spoken, especially the Punjab, resulting in *madrasa* settings where Punjabi-speaking pupils learn Urdu to understand instruction about Persian and Arabic texts. See Rahman, *From Hindi to Urdu*, 112–33. For a fascinating parallel in northern Nigeria, where Kanuri-speaking Muslims study Qur'anic Arabic through the medium of a third language, Old Kanembu, see Dmitry Bondarev, "Qur'anic Exegesis in Old Kanembu" and Bondarev and Tijani, "Performance of Multilayered Literacy."

[65] Pue, *I Too Have Some Dreams*.   [66] Conrad, *What Is Global History?* 71, 127.

The Making of Persianate Modernity is a comparative history that examines how different nationalist narratives developed in Iran and South Asia, offering comparative readings of Persian and Urdu literary histories. Comparison is useful because it can challenge such narratives, revealing them to be historically contingent. The literary theorist Susan Stanford Friedman reminds us that "comparison across cultures defamiliarizes what one takes as natural in any given culture."[67] As intellectuals in India and Iran reworked their shared Persianate heritage into modern literary histories, they developed radically different national narratives. Juxtaposing the different "origin stories" exposes their historical contingency. As Chapters 3 and 4 further demonstrate, the historical development of Persian and Urdu, and the linguistic relationship of each to other languages like Arabic, were similar in many ways. Yet due to their different relationships to Orientalist philology, Iranian and South Asian modernizers gave completely different accounts of their respective languages' histories. Iranian nationalists, with their emphasis on nativism, stressed the continuity of the Persian language before and after the advent of Islam, seeing it as a single trajectory not broken by the introduction of Arabic. In contrast, Urdu speakers believed the coming of Islam (and of Arabic and Persian) to the subcontinent to be a fundamental rupture with the past which birthed Urdu. By comparing these two narratives, we understand that neither account is natural or inevitable; each could have followed the path traced by the other.

This book offers not only comparison, but also a connected history.[68] *The Making of Persianate Modernity* traces the exchanges and interaction between Iranians and South Asians in the production of modern literary history. In doing so, it joins an emerging body of scholarship on "South–South" intellectual and literary connections which has begun to focus on the interactions between Asian

---

[67] Friedman, "Why Not Compare?" 756.
[68] I draw methodological inspiration from Sanjay Subrahmanyam's scholarship on the connected Indian Ocean world in the early modern period. See Subrahmanyam, "Connected Histories."

modernizers, unmediated by Europe.[69] Urdu, I argue, is vital to the story of the emergence of Persian literary history. I demonstrate how India's Persianate tradition continued in Urdu, and how ideas and conventions traveled between Urdu and Persian, moving in both directions.

I.3   OUTLINE

The chapters of this book are organized thematically rather than chronologically, each examining a different aspect of the making of Persianate modernity. The book's first section, "Connections," maps the connections between modern Iranian and South Asian litterateurs. This Indo-Iranian exchange had a crucial impact on intellectuals modernizing the Persianate heritage. The intellectual networks they formed facilitated the exchange of ideas and scholarship, making possible the shared project of Persianate modernity described in the following chapters. This preliminary section demonstrates that South Asians were well-integrated into Iranian intellectual and literary circles. Readers more interested in the impact of such connections on the emerging genre of literary history can skip ahead to the first chapter.

Chapter 1, "Histories," shows how Persian literary histories emerged from modernizing historiographers' engagement with the *tazkirah*, a premodern Persianate genre of literary anthology. The contradictions the *tazkirah*s posed served as an invitation to produce literary history, in opposition to what modernizers saw as deficiencies in the premodern *tazkirah* tradition. These contradictions and deficiencies included the fact that *tazkirah* writers did not see history as linear, progressive, and teleological, nor was historical accuracy necessarily a concern of theirs. This chapter examines how

---

[69] Recent works in intellectual and literary history include Amstutz, "Finding a Home for Urdu;" Elhalaby, "The Arab Rediscovery of India;" Fani, "Becoming Literature;" Leese, "Longing for Salmá and Hind;" Thompson, "Re-Orienting Modernism." These works complement connected histories of the Indian Ocean world such as Marashi, *Exile and the Nation*; Kia, *Persianate Selves*; Green, *Bombay Islam*.

modernizing intellectuals changed conceptions of "history," turned premodern Persian literature into national heritage, and transformed premodern scholars into national heroes.

Chapter 2, "Erotics" engages questions of homoeroticism and bawdy poetry, two interconnected themes that appear throughout the Persianate literary heritage and the *tazkirah* tradition but pose problems for modern literary historiographers. While pre-nineteenth-century Persianate writing abounds in frank, unabashed depictions of homoerotic sexuality – the dominant literary convention for depicting love – modernizers of Persianate literature adopt a Victorian-influenced approach that emphasized bashful silence about sexuality, particularly homoeroticism. As Persian literary historians were faced with making sense of the ribald erotic poetry at the heart of the tradition they wrote about, homoerotic conventions coalesced as objects of scorn and relics of the premodern world against which modernizing historiographers positioned themselves.

Chapter 3, "Origin Myths," explores how literary historians narrated the origins of Persian and Urdu languages and literary traditions. I challenge the nationalist narratives around these traditions, of Iranian continuity and Indo-Muslim rupture, which remain dominant today. Tracing the reception of evolutionary theories and Orientalist philology in Iran and India, I analyze fundamental differences in nationalist thought in the two contexts. Iranians articulated a vision of linear language history, emphasizing continuity with pre-Islamic precursors to modern Persian which the addition of an Arabic element did not fundamentally change. On the other hand, Indian Muslims offered a contrary account of Urdu's origins, emphasizing rupture with the pre-Islamic past and the constitutive role of Persian, Arabic, and Turkish in Urdu's formation. Through a comparative reading of these "origin myths" I demonstrate how historically contingent the dominant narratives around Persian and Urdu were.

Chapter 4, "Print" analyzes the transition from manuscript to print culture and the formal conventions of modern Persianate writing. I trace the emergence and standardization of standard typography, orthography, and punctuation. Questioning the assumption that these aspects of print culture arose organically from the material conditions of modernization, I argue that they were fetishized as a kind of modernizing technology in and of themselves, and understood as productive of – rather than products of – modernization. In other words, Iranian and Indian literary scholars sought to modernize their prose by abandoning certain formal conventions of the Persianate manuscript tradition and adopting the conventions of European print: type rather than calligraphy, standardized spelling, and a new set of punctuation marks. The transition from manuscripts to a standardized print culture is typically presented as pragmatic, but it was shaped by various networks of affective attachments.

Far from modernity marking a definitive rupture with the Persianate past, then, this book demonstrates how Persianate connections and literary heritage were vital to nationalist, modernizing projects in Iran and India from the middle of the nineteenth to the middle of the twentieth century. The Persianate modernity produced through Indo-Iranian exchange was not uniform across the two countries, but it shared its repository of literary heritage as well as its structuring logic of nationalism. The Conclusion carries the book's arguments forward in time, considering what became of Persianate modernity in the second half of the twentieth century. It is an invitation for scholars of regions and time periods beyond the scope of this book to take up Persianate modernity as a useful framework for analyzing the role of the Persianate heritage in the making of modernity, not only in Iran and South Asia, but in Afghanistan, the erstwhile Ottoman territories, Central Asia, and elsewhere.

Connections

Iran and India have deep historic ties. Many Iranians sought patronage in the lavish courts of the Mughals in northern India or various sultanates in the Deccan.[1] South Asians have also been frequent visitors to Iran, especially in modern times. Many worked in Iran for long periods of time and were integrated into many facets of Iranian daily life. Thousands of Sikh migrants played important roles in developing transportation infrastructure in southeastern Iran during the 1920s and 1930s, while thousands more Indian migrants filled skilled and semi-skilled positions in Iran's oil industry in Abadan in the first half of the twentieth century.[2] More importantly for literary history, South Asian intellectuals were intimately embedded in Iranian literary circles; countless modern Iranian litterateurs had South Asian friends and acquaintances. This section outlines religious, political, intellectual, and literary connections between Iranians and South Asians, offering context for the Indo-Iranian exchange of ideas in the following chapters. Readers more interested in the consequences and outcomes of these connections can skip ahead to Chapter 1.

A great many Iranian intellectuals – from the reformist politician Sayyid Hasan Taqizadah to the writer and critic Jalal Al-i

---

[1] Ahmad, "Ṣafawid Poets and India;" Bandy, "Building a Mountain of Light;" Dayal, "Vernacular Conquest;" Dudney, "Going Native;" Fischel, *Local States*; Flatt, *The Courts of the Deccan Sultanates*, chapter 2; Haneda, "Emigration of Iranian Elites;" Khan, "What Storytellers Were Worth;" Mikkelson, "Of Parrots and Crows;" Overton, *Iran and the Deccan*; Shafieioun, "Some Critical Remarks;" Sharma, *Mughal Arcadia*, 22–7; Subrahmanyam, "Iranians Abroad."

[2] Koyagi, "Drivers across the Desert;" Atabaki, "Indian Migrant Workers." Mikiya Koyagi also demonstrates how Baluchis maintained networks that traversed the Indo-Iranian border. Koyagi, "Tribes and Smugglers."

Ahmad – began their education in the *hawzah* or Shiʿite seminaries. Studying alongside them were large numbers of South Asian Shiʿites. As Simon Fuchs describes, when these religious scholars returned to South Asia, they "acted as brokers between texts written in Arabic and Persian and the vernacular medium of Urdu."[3] In other words, they were able to orally translate knowledge they acquired in Arabic and Persian into a language their communities understood: Urdu. I suggest that the reverse is also true. South Asian intellectuals worked, studied, and socialized alongside Iranians. As they did so, they shared what they had learned from Urdu scholarship, translating it orally into Persian for their Iranian friends.

Indian Ocean circuits ensured that people flowed in all directions. South Asians and Iranians rubbed shoulders with one another in the shrine cities of Iran and Iraq – figuratively, as they studied with the same teachers in the seminaries – and literally, as they jostled inside crammed shrines.[4] Iranians also visited South Asia, seeking refuge from political or religious persecution in Iran, engaging in missionary work, or spending extended layovers (sometimes stretching for months) in Bombay en route to Mecca.[5] Like South Asian intellectuals in Iran, Iranians who had learned Urdu in India, such as Daʿi al-Islam Isfahani and Fakhr-i Daʿi Gilani, served as translators for their friends and colleagues when they returned home.[6] In this way, knowledge traveled along vernacular routes that are harder to trace, and thus less understood, than textual connections.

The Indian literary historian and philologist Muhammad Husayn Azad traveled by steamship to Iran in 1885 in order to acquire books and gather materials for a comprehensive Persian dictionary he planned but never completed.[7] Along the way, he encountered Iranian

---

[3] Fuchs, *In a Pure Muslim Land*, 5.   [4] Shams, "Politics of South Asian Pilgrimage."
[5] Green, *Bombay Islam*, 3–4.
[6] On Fakhr-i Daʿi Gilani and his translations see Jabbari, "From Persianate Cosmopolis to Persianate Modernity."
[7] Azad, *Sayr-i Iran*; Sharma, "Redrawing the Boundaries," 58–9; Kovacs, "The Role of Persian Language and Literature." Azad's grandson Agha Muhammad Tahir edited

merchants who had lived much of their lives in British India, from Madras to Rangoon.[8] In Iran, Azad met with prominent intellectuals, litterateurs, and political figures. These included Mukhbir al-Dawlah, then Minister of Education and son of Qajar litterateur Riza-Quli Khan Hidayat; the literary historian Muhammad-Husayn Furughi; and the script reformer Mirza Riza Khan Afshar Bakishughlu. While in Tehran, Azad moved in reformist circles, spending time with Manikji Limji Hataria, a Parsi reformer from India and visiting Iran's first modern institute of higher learning, the Dar al-Funun.[9]

Azad was not a unique figure in this regard; the late nineteenth and early twentieth century was a time of growing Indo-Iranian political solidarities. United by their shared opposition to British colonialism, Indians and Iranians formed international anti-imperialist networks around the time of the Constitutional Revolution, and Iranian reformers based in India worked closely with Indian nationalists, including Muslim nationalists like the All-India Muslim League. Several Indian nationalist activists also took refuge in Iran, where they connected with Iranian Constitutionalists. Among these refugees were the editors of an Urdu newspaper, *Peshva* (*The Leader*). Itinerant pan-Islamists like Jamal al-Din al-Afghani moved between India, Iran, and elsewhere. Iranian reformers like Taqizadah forged bonds with militants of India's revolutionary anticolonial Ghadar party. As Iranian nationalists formed associations and newspapers in India, their Indian counterparts did the same in Iran.[10]

In World War I, the British invaded Iran, deploying thousands of Indian soldiers. At the onset of World War II, Riza Shah declared Iran neutral, and in 1941 the British invaded Iran again, together with

---

Azad's notes and the dictionary was published posthumously as *Lughat-i Azad* (Lahore: Karimi Press, 1924).

[8] Azad, *Sayr-i Iran*, 67.

[9] Ibid., 25, 30–1. Hataria was the emissary to Iran of the Bombay-based Society for the Amelioration of the Conditions of Zoroastrians in Persia. See Kotwal et al., "Hataria, Manekji Limji;" Boyce, "Maneckji Limji Hataria in Iran;" Zia-Ebrahimi, "An Emissary of the Golden Age;" Marashi, *Nationalizing Iran*, 61–3.

[10] Bonakdarian, "Iranian Nationalism and Global Solidarity Networks."

Soviet forces. The British occupation, which endured through the end of the war, relied heavily on Indian troops; by 1944 there were 100,000 or more Indians in the Persia and Iraq Command, a British Army formation occupying Iran and neighboring Iraq.[11] These Indian soldiers would remain in Iranian cultural memory long after the war was over, featuring conspicuously in Persian novels set during the occupation like Danishvar's *Savushun* or Pizishkzad's *Da'i Jan Napil'un* (*Dear Uncle Napoleon*).

During the Allied occupation of Iran in the 1940s, Indians served not only on the battlefield, but in cultural and diplomatic positions as well. South Asian cultural workers like the Urdu poet N. M. Rashid, assigned to Radio Tehran, or the scholar 'Abd al-Hamid 'Irfani, posted to the British Consulate in Mashhad, were at the center of Iranian literary circles. Here I trace these social circles in order to demonstrate the kinds of connections that facilitated intellectual exchange between Indians and Iranians. These networks must have informed literary historians in Iran and India, as they were active just as literary history was coming into its own as a genre in Persian and Urdu. The connections sometimes arose in unexpected circumstances; in the case of Rashid and 'Irfani, the British use of Indians to occupy Iran during World War II helped forge new connections and anticolonial solidarities between Iran and India.

Nazar Muhammad Rashid, more commonly known by his initials N. M. Rashid, was one of Urdu poetry's premier modernist poets, sometimes compared to the Iranian modernist poet Nima Yushij.[12] Deployed to Iran during the British occupation, Rashid was at the center of an intellectual milieu where Iranians and Indians mingled. Serving in the British Indian Army as a public relations officer with

---

[11] Motter, *The Persian Corridor*, 10; Jackson, *Persian Gulf Command*, 277, 292. See also Raghavan, *India's War*, 142–9. On the relationship between Riza Shah and Nazi Germany see Jenkins, "Iran in the Nazi New Order."

[12] Rashid himself made one such comparison, albeit with tongue in cheek. Passing by the home of Nima Yushij in Tehran, a friend pointed it out and remarked that Nima had ruined Persian poetry. "Then I can be counted alongside him," Rashid reportedly retorted, "for I have ruined Urdu poetry."

the Inter-Service Public Relations Directorate from 1943 to 1947, Rashid was posted to a number of locales across the Middle East and South Asia, including Tehran. From 1944 to 1946, by then a captain in the army, he worked at Radio Tehran. Having studied Persian literature at Punjab University, he perfected his spoken Persian in Iran. Rashid's fluency in Persian, keen insights into Persian literature, and solidarity with Iranians – not to mention his cultural work in the country – all help explain how he found himself at the center of literary circles in Iran, where he could introduce Iranians to developments and debates that had taken place in Urdu. His connections with the Iranian literati impacted his Urdu poetry, and likely influenced Iranian literary history as well. Through the letters he sent home to his wife Safiyah, we learn of Rashid's friendships with the same figures who went on to shape modern Persian literary studies in Iran.

Rashid wrote to Safiyah, wanting to introduce her to his female coworkers at Radio Tehran such as Fatimah Sayyah (1902–47), founder of the discipline of Comparative Literature in Iran, and the country's first woman professor.[13] Another was Furugh al-Saltanah Hikmat, sister of ʿAli-Asghar Hikmat (who served variously as Iran's Minister of Education and Minister of Foreign Affairs under Riza Shah). She was married to Nizam al-Din Khan Hikmat "Mushar al-Dawlah," a representative of the Ministry of Education. Furugh al-Saltanah was also a classmate of the famed novelist Simin Danishvar; both women completed doctoral degrees in Persian literature at the University of Tehran, in addition to working for Radio Tehran.[14]

Rashid also worked with Iran Banu, daughter of Sayyid Muhammad-ʿAli Daʿi al-Islam. Rashid was close with Daʿi al-Islam (1878–1951), who had spent years as a professor of Persian at Nizam

---

[13] Letter from N. M. Rashid dated July 3, 1944. Personal collection of Yasmin Rashed Hassan. On Sayyah, see Anushiravani, "Comparative Literature in Iran."

[14] Rastigar Fasaʾi, "ʿAli-Asghar Khan Hikmat Mard-i Farhang," 8. Danishvar's doctoral advisor was Fatimah Sayyah. Furugh al-Saltanah is virtually unknown in Iranian Studies scholarship. Only by considering Urdu-language sources – here, Rashid's letters to his wife – do we learn some of these details about her life and work.

College (part of Osmania University) in Hyderabad, Deccan. Da'i al-Islam edited religious newspapers including *Da'vat al-Islam* (*Invitation to Islam*), published in Bombay.[15] He was also a lexicographer and compiled the *Farhang-i Nizam*, an influential Persian dictionary.[16] Rashid had great respect for the professor as well as his daughter. "They're wonderful people," Rashid wrote to his wife. "When I'm in their home, it feels like I'm with my own brothers and sisters."[17] Iran Banu was also involved in religious journalism, translating articles from the Urdu newspaper *Intikhab*, based in Hyderabad, for the Iranian weekly magazine *A'in-i Islam*.[18]

On October 2, 1945, Rashid attended the unveiling of a statue of the eleventh-century Persian poet Firdawsi in Tehran, along with Minister of Education 'Isa Sadiq.[19] The statue was donated by the Zoroastrian Society of India.[20] This ceremonious event captures the coming together of multiple groups – Iranian nationalists, Parsis, and South Asian Muslims – who all contributed to the making of Persianate modernity. Urdu-speaking Muslims of India like Rashid were often key figures in multinational and multiconfessional circles, and they played an important role in modernizing and nationalizing Iran, even as they wrote themselves out of the story (as we shall see in Chapter 3).

Charged with organizing soirées for Iranian elites and intellectuals, Rashid was well-connected to the Iranian literati. He was familiar with and versed in contemporary Persian poetry, and knew many of the poets personally. In his study of the subject, *Jadid Farsi Sha'iri* (*Modern Persian Poetry*, 1969), Rashid notes the strange coincidence

---

[15] Browne, *Press and Poetry*, 41, 85–6.   [16] Storey, *Persian Literature*, 3 part 1:53–4.

[17] Letter from N. M. Rashid dated July 3, 1944. Personal collection of Yasmin Rashed Hassan.

[18] Iran Banu, "Din-i Babi va Hajji Husayn-Quli," *A'in-i Islam* 17 (25 Shahrivar 1328/ September 16, 1949), 4. Many Iranian newspapers reported on India at the time, reflecting public interest. See Ahanchi, "Reflections of the Indian Independence Movement in the Iranian Press."

[19] Noon Meem Rashed archive, McGill University. Sadiq had also met Tagore in Iran; see Marashi, *Nationalizing Iran*, 123.

[20] Grigor, *Building Iran*, 71–2.

of new poetic movements in Urdu (1931–2) and Persian (1935). Acknowledging the influence of European literature in both cases, he argues that an even greater influence was the similar political, economic, and social conditions affecting poets in both traditions.[21] Rashid saw the shared experience of colonialism as the basis for Indo-Iranian commonality, rather than Persianate heritage or Islamic identity, a view he later developed in his poetry collection *A Stranger in Iran and Other Poems* (*Iran mein Ajnabi aur Dusri Nazmen*, 1957).[22] The British ruled India and occupied Iran; small wonder, then, that both Indian and Iranian poets responded in similar ways to the literary challenges of colonial modernity. Rashid's letters sent home to his wife indicate his sensitivity to his complicity, however unwilling, in a colonial, occupying force; he lamented that some of the hotels in Tehran where he organized events did not ordinarily allow entrance to Iranians, barring their doors to all but the British and other foreign elites.[23]

The eminent Iranian poet and literary historian Muhammad-Taqi Bahar, a central figure in this book, maintained a social circle every bit as international as Rashid's. An important interlocutor for Bahar was Khwajah 'Abd al-Hamid 'Irfani (1907–90). 'Irfani completed masters of arts degrees in Persian and English and taught both languages at Government College in Quetta, India before serving as a liaison officer of education in the British Consulate in Mashhad, Iran. After the Partition, 'Irfani became Pakistan's first cultural and press attaché at its embassy in Tehran, where he served from 1949 to 1955. He later completed a PhD in Persian Language and Literature at the University of Punjab, Lahore, and wrote his dissertation on the life and works of Bahar.[24] 'Irfani had met Bahar only a few months after his arrival in Iran in 1949, and they quickly became close friends.

---

[21] Rashid, *Jadid Farsi Sha'iri*, 1.   [22] Pue, *I Too Have Some Dreams*, 42–64.
[23] Letter from N. M. Rashid. Personal collection of Yasmin Rashed Hassan.
[24] Bukhari, "Obituary;" Rizvi, *Farsi-guyan-i Pakistan*, 522–6.

'Irfani would drop in on Bahar unannounced, who received him "like a member of his own family." As Bahar's health declined towards the end of his life, 'Irfani visited him at home two or three times a week. Bahar wrote a *qit'ah* (fragmentary poem) in honor of his friendship with 'Irfani: "An angel dressed as a man / came to visit my sickbed last night / I asked him, what is your name? He replied / Khwajah 'Abd al-Hamid 'Irfani."[25] The two of them often discussed the poet Muhammad Iqbal (1877–1938), as well as Iranian-Pakistani relations. 'Irfani translated Iqbal's Urdu-language poetry collection *Zarb-i Kalim* (*The Rod of Moses*, 1936) into Persian. In their conversations, 'Irfani was keen to prove that Pakistan had more in common with Iran than with India. He claims these discussions on South Asia had a deep impact on Bahar. Indeed, Bahar showed keen interest in the subcontinent. He indicated in a letter that he wished to visit South Asia; unable to do so, in 1945 he sent his son Hushang to study in India, where he learned Urdu.[26]

Bahar mentioned a speech he gave at the Teachers' Training College (*danishsaray-i 'ali*) in which he had predicted the future independence of Hindustan and spoke of India's Persian-speakers (*parsi-guyan-i hind*). "To the utmost sorrow and regret, the natural relation and connection between Iran and its Hindustani brothers was severed for more than a century because of the expansion of colonialist policies," he lamented. He went on to add that with the establishment of Pakistan, it was as if an enormous curtain which had been drawn between Iran and "our brothers" (*baradaran-i ma*) for 150 years was suddenly removed, a curtain which had not been able to reduce even one iota of the feelings of solidarity, consanguinity, shared faith, and shared language. Bahar likened Iqbal – the "inventor and founder

---

[25] Bahar, *Divan*, 2:532. The phrase "an angel dressed as a man" (*malaki dar libas-i insani*) is borrowed from Hafiz. Bahar also wrote a *du-bayti* (double couplet poem) in praise of E. G. Browne.

[26] 'Irfani, *Sharh-i Ahval*, 5. Hushang Bahar studied at the Indian Forest College, now the Indira Gandhi National Forest Academy.

of Pakistan" – to Firdawsi, the "inventor and founder of Islamic Iran."[27] His lecture was printed in both Iran and in India.

Scholarship on Bahar has often treated him as single-mindedly chauvinist in his Iranian nationalism. While this was indeed an element of his thought, it also oversimplifies his more complex attitudes about Iran's neighboring Others, namely the Arabs and the Indians. By all evidence, Bahar was a nativist, not a supremacist. His literary criticism of what he famously termed the "Indian Style" (*sabk-i hindi*) of Persian poetry was nationalist, but not, as some have argued, motivated by racial animus against Indians.[28] He described Iran and India as "brothers," united by Aryan lineage (*nasl-i ariya*) in a *qasidah* titled "India and Iran" (*hind u iran*) written in celebration of India's independence.[29] Another, "Bahar's Memorial to Pakistan" (*yadgar-i bahar bah pakistan*), celebrates Pakistan on the basis of its Islamic identity before adding that "the nation [*millat*] of Iran is not, and must not be, separate / from the nature and essence of Pakistan / Do not suppose that anyone on earth / loves Pakistan more than the Iranians … Bahar loves the culture, customs, and etiquette [*adab*] / which strengthen the warp and weft of Pakistan."[30] After Bahar's death, his daughter Parvanah would recite this poem at Iqbal commemorations organized by Pakistani embassies in Tehran and Washington, DC.[31]

---

[27] Bahar, *Bahar va Adab*, 2:323–5.
[28] See for example Kinra, "Make It Fresh," 15–16. Matthew C. Smith's excellent dissertation on Bahar takes a more nuanced view, noting that he "did not carry his literary preferences into the realm of racial prejudice," but sees Bahar's admiration of India as based solely in Aryanism, overlooking his attachment to Pakistan articulated on Islamic grounds (Smith, "Literary Courage," 56–7). For an English translation of the introduction to his *Sabkshinasi*, wherein he lays out his tripartite periodization of Persian poetry, see Jabbari, "Bahar's *Sabkshenāsi*."
[29] Bahar, *Divan*, 1:772–3.
[30] Ibid., 1:794–6. This *qasidah* was written on the occasion of Muhammad-Riza Shah's first state visit to Pakistan. The Shah traveled together with ʿAli-Asghar Hikmat and ʿIsa Sadiq. A Persian hemistich well-known in the subcontinent, "*ay amadanat ba ʿis-i abadi-yi ma*" (O, your arrival is cause for our flourishing), was recited in the Shah's honor ("Safar-i Shahanshah ba-Pakistan"). Bahar also wrote an additional ode to Pakistan upon its independence; see Bahar, *Divan*, 1:762–3.
[31] Bahar, *Murgh-i Sahar*, 146.

Bahar's poetry found an audience in Pakistan even during the poet's lifetime.[32] He met with Pakistani ambassador Ghazanfar 'Ali Khan.[33] On 'Irfani's invitation, Bahar led an event celebrating Iqbal at the Pakistani embassy in Iran in April 1950, where a number of the Iranian literati (including Bahar himself) read poetry they had composed in honor of Iqbal.[34] Bahar admired Iqbal deeply and shared his ardent anticolonialism. He had planned to write additional volumes of his magnum opus *Sabkshinasi* (*Stylistics*) that would deal with poetic style, and according to 'Irfani, Bahar intended to dedicate a chapter to the style of Iqbal. However, he passed away before he could undertake this project.[35] 'Irfani was one of the last people to visit Bahar, only two weeks before the latter's passing.[36]

Bahar's network included many other Indians, like Adib Pishavari, a Pashtun from Peshawar and accomplished poet in Persian whose "heart throbbed for his childhood homeland" of India.[37] Bahar wrote a lengthy *qasidah* in response to one of Adib's world-renouncing ascetic poems.[38] He was also friends with the literary historian Muhammad Ishaq of Calcutta, who, like Rashid, wrote about contemporary Iranian poetry.[39] The Iranian Constitutionalist poet and editor of *Nasim-i Shimal* newspaper Sayyid Ashraf al-Din Husayni Qazvini (Ashraf Gilani, 1870–1934) composed a poem in Ishaq's honor:

> Lighting up the land, the torch of Hindustan / An ocean of
> knowledge and perfection, Muhammad Ishaq Khan / The First
> Teacher, in his knowledge of history / Goes down in history as an

---

[32] Mu'azzini and Fazli-Darzi, "Maqam-i Shamikh-i Bahar dar Pakistan."

[33] Bahar, *Murgh-i Sahar*, 265. The ambassador is misidentified in the text as Liyaqat 'Ali Khan.

[34] Ibid., 131.   [35] 'Irfani, *Sharh-i Ahval*, 2–3.   [36] Ibid., 142–4; ibid., 7–8.

[37] Amanat, "From Peshawar to Tehran," 293. See also Sinha, *Iqbal: The Poet and His Message*, 128–9.

[38] Bahar, *Divan*, 1:536–40. For Adib Pishavari's *qasidah* which prompted Bahar's response, see Pishavari, *Divan*, 13–15. See also Aryanpur, *Az Saba ta Nima*, 2:317–22.

[39] See Ishaque, *Sukhanvaran-i Iran* and *Modern Persian Poetry*.

ingenious historian / Worthy of the pride of India in these times / As he has made his home in Calcutta / The night he came to see Ashraf al-Din in Tehran / My home became the envy of the garden of paradise with his presence.[40]

In addition to his South Asian associates, Iranians like Da'i al-Islam who had spent time in India were also important sources of Bahar's knowledge about Urdu literature.[41] Tracing out Bahar's social circle shows that he was surrounded by South Asian intellectuals as well as Iranians with knowledge of Urdu. While he never met some of the Indian literary historians like Muhammad Husayn Azad or Shibli Nu'mani, Bahar was nevertheless connected to their work through his Urdu-literate colleagues.

Bahar's peers and literary compatriots were equally integrated into Iranian-Indian circles. Sayyid Muhammad-'Ali Jamalzadah (1892–1997), a pioneering figure in the history of Persian prose fiction, kept company with Indian nationalists and revolutionaries.[42] Ghulam-Riza Rashid Yasami (1896–1951) was a similarly influential Iranian litterateur, and a link between Bahar and N. M. Rashid.[43] Together with Bahar and 'Ali-Asghar Hikmat, among others, Yasami was a founding member of the literary journal *Danishkadah* and the Persian Language Academy (*Farhangistan*, Iran's equivalent of the Académie Française). He taught at the University of Tehran, and wrote a contemporary rather than comprehensive literary history (*Adabiyat-i Mu'asir*, 1937). Yasami edited the *divan* of Mas'ud Sa'd Salman, considered the first major Persian poet of the Indian subcontinent, and translated the fourth volume of Browne's *Literary History*

---

[40] *Indo-Iranica* 23 (1970), 35. On Ashraf Gilani see Rahman, "AŠRAF GĪLĀNĪ;" on his role as a historian, see Vejdani, *Making History in Iran*, 50–2.

[41] Bahar, *Bahar va Adab*, 2:139.

[42] Bonakdarian, "Iranian Nationalism and Global Solidarity Networks," 93.

[43] Letter from N. M. Rashid dated July 17, 1945. Personal collection of Yasmin Rashed Hassan. Yasami also met Tagore during the Indian poet's visit to Iran; see Marashi, *Exile and the Nation*, 126. For Yasami's Parsi connections see ibid., 56, 222.

(1316 HS/1937–8 CE).[44] Like Bahar and his other contemporaries, Yasami composed poems celebrating India and Indo-Iranian relations.[45] From February 26 to May 6, 1944, he visited India as part of an Iranian cultural delegation led by ʿAli-Asghar Hikmat and along with Ibrahim Purdavud.[46]

Even Iranian prime minister Muhammad-ʿAli Furughi (1877–1942) spent time in India and later surrounded himself with Indian friends and acquaintances. Indian connections ran in the family; his father, Muhammad-Husayn Furughi, composed one of the earliest literary histories of Persian in Iran, and had met the Indian scholar Muhammad Husayn Azad, author of literary histories of Persian and Urdu. The younger Furughi edited his father's literary history. His grandfather, Muhammad-Mahdi Arbab Isfahani, had been involved in commerce and publishing in India, and regaled his grandson with tales of his many years spent working in Bombay.[47]

During his time attending the Paris Peace Conference as a member of Iran's delegation (December 1918–August 1920), Muhammad-ʿAli Furughi's circles included Iranians who lived in India.[48] While in Paris he received a Persian letter from Shibli Nuʿmani's protégé Sayyid Sulayman Nadvi, who was an active promoter of Shibli's work. Nadvi learned of Furughi through E. G. Browne, whom he had previously met in London.[49] Furughi and the Iranian literary scholar Muhammad Qazvini agreed to meet Nadvi and his delegation – "the Indians" (hindi-ha) as Furughi referred to them in his diaries. They met twice. During these meetings, Nadvi pleaded the cause of pan-Islamism and supporting the Ottoman

---

[44] Rahman, *Encyclopedia of Islam* 2, "Rashīd Yāsimī," 448; Yasami, *Divan*, chahar.

[45] Yasami, *Divan*, 55–6 and 75–6.

[46] Hikmat, *Rah-Avard-i Hikmat*, 1:235–338. Hikmat translated the third volume of Browne's *Literary History* into Persian. He also admired Iqbal and remarked on the impact of Prakrit vocabulary on Persian, even in Iran. See Hikmat, *Naqsh-i Parsi bar Ahjar-i Hind*, 1–6.

[47] Furughi, *Khatirat 1293–1320*. [48] Furughi, *Yaddasht-ha-yi Ruzanah*, 227, 327.

[49] Green, "Spacetime and the Muslim Journey West," 410.

caliph, but his words fell on deaf ears; Furughi described Nadvi's call to "set aside nationality – forget being Iranian, Turk, Arab, or Indian" as "brainless [bi-maghz] and contradictory," but he and Qazvini nevertheless agreed to attend a banquet hosted by the Indians two days later, and to meet with them the following day.[50] Thus, ideas developed in Urdu reached Iranians via verbal routes; while Furughi could not read the Urdu works of someone like Shibli, he could still learn of Shibli's ideas through conversation with Nadvi.

As we have seen, Iranians and South Asians interacted a great deal during the period of Persianate modernity, from studying together in the Shi'ite seminaries of Qom and Najaf, to working alongside one another in cultural and political institutions in Tehran and Mashhad. South Asians who could speak Persian, like 'Abd al-Hamid 'Irfani or N. M. Rashid, served as vernacular translators between Urdu and Persian knowledge, as did multilingual Iranians like Da'i al-Islam or Fakhr-i Da'i Gilani. In the following chapters, we will explore the outcome of these international connections: a shared project of modernizing the Persianate literary heritage and developing the genre of literary history.

These connections also reveal the relevance of Urdu sources for Iranian Studies scholarship. As this book demonstrates, Urdu is a useful language beyond the borders of the subcontinent, valuable not only for investigating the afterlife of Persian texts in South Asia, where they continue to be commented on (now in Urdu rather than in Persian), but also as a source for studying modern Iran. Reading across national and disciplinary divisions allows us to consider Iranian and South Asian modernizing projects as part of a shared Persianate modernity, as Persian- and Urdu-speakers worked together to refashion their literary heritage even as new identities and borders drew them apart.

---

[50] Furughi, *Yaddasht-ha-yi Ruzanah*, 386, 388–9.

I Histories

From Tazkirah *to Literary History*

> O you who do not know yourself, what is history? / Is it a story, a tale, a fable?
>
> It is what makes you aware of yourself, / guides you and shows you the way.
>
> (Muhammad Iqbal[1])

Beginning in the nineteenth century and gaining momentum in the early twentieth century, there was a proliferation of publications in a new genre calling itself Persian literary history. Writing the history of Persian literature was not solely an Iranian project – at least, not yet. These first literary histories appeared not only in Persian but also in German, Italian, English, Urdu, and other languages. Writing the preface to one such book, Shibli Nu'mani's Urdu-language *Shi'r al-'Ajam* (*Poetry of the Persians*, 1920), the author's protégé Sayyid Sulayman Nadvi expressed his surprise at the publication of two other Persian literary histories nearly contemporaneous with *Shi'r al-'Ajam* – Muhammad Husayn Azad's *Sukhandan-i Fars* ([*On the*] *Poets of Persia*, 1907) in Urdu, and the second volume of E. G. Browne's *Literary History of Persia* (1902, 1906) in English. Shibli, the author, concluded that Azad's *Sukhandan-i Fars* "did not even touch" his *Shi'r al-'Ajam* and dismissed Browne's work in even stronger terms: "Without exaggeration or embellishment, I say that I felt great regret upon seeing Browne's book. It is extremely common and plebeian."[2]

---

[1] "*Chist tarikh ay zi khvud biganah'i / dastani qissah'i afsanah'i / in tura az khvishtan agah kunad / ashina-yi kar u mard rah kunad.*" Iqbal, *Rumuz-i Bikhvudi*.

[2] Nu'mani, *Shi'r al-'Ajam*, 5:2–3. Nadvi met with Browne in London in 1920 and may have discussed the latter's book, *A Literary History of Persia*, in person. See Green, "Spacetime," 410–11.

Amidst the boasting and opprobrium, these literary historians were engaged in a shared project, drawing on the same sources and responding to one another's work. The early literary historians responded in particular to *Majma' al-Fusaha'* (*Assembly of the Eloquent*), a Persian biographical anthology or *tazkirah* by the Iranian courtly litterateur Riza-Quli Khan Hidayat, completed in 1871. They relied on this *tazkirah* as a source yet were critical of it; its innovations opened up new possibilities, while its shortcomings invited correction and response. Iranians, Indians, and Europeans alike developed literary history through both appropriating this text and distancing themselves from it.

A model for this kind of exchange can be found in Persian poetry in the form of *javab-gu'i*, which Paul Losensky translates as "speaking in reply," where one poet may respond to a poem by another poet, retaining some of the original's structure but reworking its theme, for example. As Losensky explains, in *javab-gu'i* "the model poem becomes a question that calls for an answer or a problem that demands solution .... Instead of an antagonistic opposition [between the model poem and its response], we now have the image of a careful and reasoned debate across time."[3] This chapter shows how Persian literary histories emerged through modernizers speaking in reply to the *tazkirah*, a premodern genre of biographical anthology. The contradictions posed by using *tazkirah*s served as an invitation for modernizers to produce modern prose through literary history, in opposition to what they saw as deficiencies in the premodern tradition. Modernizing literary historians were transforming under-standings of history's enterprise. Building on the changing notions of nation and identity explored in the Introduction, this chapter examines how premodern Persian literature is made national and indeed appropriated in the service of nationalism, and how the "great men" of history are transformed through modern literary histories into national figures.

---

[3] Losensky, *Welcoming Fighani*, 112.

Considering literary history as an important and overlooked site for the modernization of literature, I treat Persianate modernity as a shared discourse produced through scholarly exchange between Iranians and Indians reworking their shared literary heritage. I examine how these figures used premodern materials – namely *tazkirah*s – for their modernizing projects and make an argument for a verbal as well as textual discourse of modernization shared between early twentieth-century Iranian and Indian intellectuals. In this way, Persian literary histories in the early twentieth century can be brought into larger debates about literary modernization.

Foucault offers a useful way of conceptualizing modernity: not (only) as an epoch, but as an attitude, an ethos, which sets one apart from the contemporary.[4] It is a discourse about what it means to be modern, which, for early twentieth-century Iranian and Indian modernizers, often included what the modernizers thought of as the adoption of scientific principles and their application to tasks such as the writing of history, as well as a set of moral and aesthetic considerations about sexuality, which are dealt with in the following chapter. In other words, *modernization* as it is used here means quite simply participating in that discourse and considering oneself modern. As Henri Lefebvre put it, modernity involves continually repeating the old and refashioning it as "new," which describes how twentieth-century litterateurs refashioned the premodern *tazkirah* genre into modern literary history (*tarikh-i adabiyat*)[5] and repurposed Firdawsi's epic eleventh-century poem, the *Shahnamah*, into a source for modern historiography.[6]

---

[4] Foucault, "What Is Enlightenment?" 39–40. Here I am largely in agreement with the historian Frederick Cooper's argument that the language of modernity is best understood "as a claim-making device" (*Colonialism in Question*, 146).

[5] As I argue below, the term (and concept of) *tarikh-i adabiyat* appears in Persian as a calque of the English literary history or French *histoire littéraire*. I have therefore opted to refer throughout this chapter to *tarikh-i adabiyat* using the English term "literary history" while referring to the indigenous *tazkirah* genre using the untranslated Persian term.

[6] See the discussion in Lefebvre, *Introduction to Modernity*, 168–238.

   As Iranians writing in Persian and Indians writing in Urdu
began to write for emergent national and communal readerships,
respectively, they drew on the past in similar ways, seeking local
models like *tazkirah*s or the *Shahnamah* that could be used to
reform, revitalize, and preserve heritage, whether "national" heritage
in Iran or "Islamic" heritage in India. This modernizing process of
appropriating the past and reforming it ultimately produced modern
literary history. It involved engagement with the *tazkirah* tradition,
inclusion of extraliterary "national" figures alongside poets, and use of
a shared set of Orientalist references and Persianate sources. This was
not a uniform process across different contexts; Iranians and Indians
differed in the importance they gave to the so-called great men of
history, as it became important for nationalist reasons for Iranians to
attach them to Persian literary history, but irrelevant to the writing of
Persian literary history in India. At the same time, this chapter challenges nationalist assumptions that treat modernization in Iran and
India as separate, revealing them to be even more intimately connected
than scholarship has heretofore acknowledged. This chapter examines
the emergence of some of the earliest literary histories of Persian, from
Shibli Nu'mani's pioneering efforts in Urdu, to E. G. Browne's influential contributions in English, and, ultimately, to the first textbook for
the doctoral program in Persian literature at the University of Tehran,
by Muhammad-Taqi Bahar. All of these figures were speaking in reply
to each other and to the "last" Persian *tazkirah*, *Majma' al-Fusaha'*
(*Assembly of the Eloquent*), by Riza-Quli Khan Hidayat.

1.1   *TAZKIRAH*S AND LITERARY HISTORY

Modernizing litterateurs found a useful genre that could be reworked
into literary history in the *tazkirah* tradition. The *tazkirah*, akin to a
biographical dictionary or anthology, was often supported by and
produced through courtly patronage.[7] The earliest Persian *tazkirah*s
were collections of hagiographies of prominent Sufis, or biographical

---

[7] For an overview of the *tazkirah* genre, see Losensky, "Biographical Writing."

notices about princes, scholars ('*ulama*'), or poets. The latter consisted of short biographies of various poets along with selections of their poetry. Seminal early *tazkirah*s, such as Muhammad 'Awfi's *Lubab al-Albab* (*The Piths of Intellects*, 1221) and Dawlatshah Samarqandi's *Tazkirat al-Shu'ara'* (*Memorial of the Poets*, 1487), were largely uncritical, whereas later *tazkirah*s written in the Indian subcontinent during the Mughal era, such as Siraj al-Din 'Ali Khan-i Arzu's *Majma' al-Nafa'is* (*Assembly of Subtleties*, 1751) and Azad Bilgrami's *Khazanah-yi 'Amirah* (*Royal Treasury*, 1763), followed the same biographical anthology format, but also contained poetic criticism and analysis. Such criticism is limited and typically does not identify itself as such; instead, sprinkled throughout biographical descriptions of poets, the modern reader can find poetic judgments and comments on taste that can be categorized as literary criticism. Criticism was otherwise relegated to separate genres of writing outside of the *tazkirah* tradition. For example, in addition to his *tazkirah* titled *Majma' al-Nafa'is*, Arzu offered literary criticism *avant la lettre* in *Tanbih al-Ghafilin* (*Admonition to the Heedless*, ca. 1744), his treatise on the poetic works of Hazin Lahiji. Whereas Iranian *tazkirah*s of the period were far less critical than those produced in India, the abovementioned early modern *tazkirah*s from India remained largely unknown in Iran until the latter part of the twentieth century.

Generally, premodern *tazkirah* writers arranged the poets they discussed alphabetically, geographically, chronologically, or according to other factors; some of the chronologically ordered *tazkirah*s grouped poets into ancient (*mutaqaddimin*), middle (*mutavassitin*), and later (*muta'akhkhirin*) periods, but beyond that, the narrative about the historical development of Persian poetry was quite limited.[8]

---

[8] This becomes less true of *tazkirah*s written in the early modern period under the Safavids and Mughals. On early modern Persian *tazkirah*s, see Losensky, *Welcoming Fighani*, 26–55; Schwartz, *Remapping Persian Literary History*; Sharma, "Redrawing the Boundaries"; and Kia, *Persianate Selves*. For the development of what scholars now identify as literary criticism in early modern Persian *tazkirah*s and other genres, see also Losensky, *Welcoming Fighani*, 17–55; Farghadani, "A History of Style"; Shamisa and Farghadani, "Tahlil-i Didgah"; and Dudney, "Sabk-e Hendi."

In some *tazkirah*s, entries for individual poets did not even mention when the poet lived. Differing from modern European literary histories, the premodern *tazkirah*s also restricted their literary scope. The latter genre limited itself to those poets deemed to belong to the nation-state, whereas the boundaries of *tazkirah*s were not necessarily political and, instead, could cover only those poets known to the author, those the author considered significant, or those selected through a variety of other sensibilities and arrangements. Beginning in the mid-eighteenth century, some *tazkirah*s from the Indian subcontinent began to cover Urdu poetry as well, first in Persian-language works dedicated primarily to Persian poetry; later, in the nineteenth century, Urdu grew in importance as a prose language, and Urdu-language *tazkirah*s emerged, which solely addressed Urdu poetry.

Modern literary history writing was not simply invented in Europe and then exported to Asia, where it was imitated by local scholars. Instead, the genre of literary history – in particular Persian literary history (regardless of the language in which it is written) – developed through Persianate litterateurs and European Orientalists speaking in reply to one another.[9] That developmental process begins with the earliest Persian *tazkirah*s, which merely functioned as hagiographies and biographical anthologies, as discussed previously. Later *tazkirah*s, especially those produced in India under the Mughals, introduced some elements of literary criticism, namely expressions of taste and stylistics. In the nineteenth century, European Orientalists wrote the first texts intended as "literary histories" of Persian, though, by necessity, they relied heavily on *tazkirah*s as sources. For example, the Austrian Orientalist Joseph von Hammer-Purgstall (1774–1856) based his *Geschichte der schönen Redekünste Persiens* (*History of the Beautiful Oratory of Persia*, 1818) on Dawlatshah Samarqandi's fifteenth-century *Tazkirat al-Shu'ara'*.[10] Like the

---

[9] For other studies of the relationship between Persianate intellectuals and European Orientalists, see Vejdani, "Indo-Iranian," and Tavakoli-Targhi, *Refashioning Iran*.

[10] Browne, *Literary History*, 3:436.

coeval *tazkirah*s of the eighteenth and nineteenth centuries, early literary histories introduced ,elements of literary criticism in their prefaces. Although the early European literary histories do not diverge significantly from the format of the *tazkirah*, they attempt to treat all of Persian literature as a single, continuous whole structured by a sense of time that is particular to capitalist modernity. Unlike the earlier *tazkirah* writers, the European Orientalists understood time as a linear chain, continually impacted by political developments and human agency rather than cosmic machinations, and literature as a product of its particular temporal circumstances.[11]

Elements of the premodern tradition as well as new innovations can both be observed in what is often identified as the last Persian *tazkirah*: Riza-Quli Khan Hidayat's *Majma' al-Fusaha'*, which was commissioned first by Muhammad Shah and later by Nasir al-Din Shah. Hidayat (1800–71) was a poet, administrator, and man of letters in the Qajar court. His life, like his *tazkirah*, bridged the gap between the court and the modern educational institution. Hidayat had been an important fixture in Qajar courts, tutoring shahs and crown princes and composing poetry for important occasions. In addition to these traditional roles, he was made principal (*nazim*) of Iran's first modern educational institution, the polytechnic college Dar al-Funun.

Consider this entry for the thirteenth-century Persian poet Sa'di in *Majma' al-Fusaha'*:

> **Sa'di Shirazi** (may God have mercy upon him)
>   And he is Shaykh Sharaf al-Din Muslih, some have recorded [his name as] Muslih al-Din bin 'Abdullah al-Sa'di. He was [descendant] from generations of pious men and *'ulama*. He appeared in the time of the Atabak dynasties of Fars, and was a contemporary and panegyrist of the chief administrator and of Sa'd Zangi, to whom his pen name is attributed. The author of *Sullam al-Samawat* has

---

[11] For a discussion of nonlinear, premodern understandings of time in the Iranian context, see Tavakoli-Targhi, "Tarikh-pardazi," and Babayan, *Mystics, Monarchs, and Messiahs*, 9–45.

written that [Saʿdi's] origin is in [the city of] Kazirun, and they say
he was close to ʿAllamah Shirazi. They say he lived for 102 or 112
years: thirty years studying, thirty years traveling, and thirty years
dwelling [in one place]. In the year 791 [*sic*] he bade farewell to the
world. He had met many of the shaykhs of the era, such as Shaykh
ʿAbd al-Qadir Jilani and Ibn Jawzi and others. He was a disciple of
Shaykh Shahab al-Din Suhravardi and had met and corresponded
with Mawlana Jalal al-Din Muhammad Mawlavi Maʿnavi in Rum
[Anatolia]. Amir Khusraw Dihlavi hosted him in Delhi and praised
him. Most of his life circumstances are known from his writings,
and the foundation of his taste and preaching can be understood
from his verse and prose. Among the *ghazal*-writers no poet is more
eloquent than him or Mawlavi Rumi. The Shaykh's collected works
are famous all around the world and enjoyed by all classes of
humanity. Truly he is without peer and has no need for
description.[12]

The biographical entry is followed by forty pages of samples of
Saʿdi's poetry. Hidayat provides copious biographical details about
Saʿdi, though not all of them are accurate. Entries on lesser poets
could sometimes be as short as a single line, followed by a sample of
their work in the form of a couplet or two of poetry. For Hidayat, like
other *tazkirah* writers, important details included Saʿdi's lineage, his
contemporaries, and stories of his travels and experiences. Absent
from this biography is historical time – the sense of Saʿdi's place in a
historical chronology, or the idea that Saʿdi's poetry reflects developments in a poetic continuum that precedes as well as follows him.

While Hidayat did not depart from the *tazkirah* tradition struc-
turally – that is to say, he adhered to the same biographical dictionary
format as that of all of his predecessors – he was innovative in introducing pre-Islamic Iranian languages to the *tazkirah* tradition through
his preface to *Majmaʿ al-Fusahaʾ*. It is here that a sense of linear,

---

[12] Hidayat, *Majmaʿ al-Fusahaʾ*, 2:1001–2.

progressive time made it possible to introduce and apply Orientalist philology (connecting the New Persian language and literature to its Middle Persian predecessor, for example), something that was without precedent in premodern *tazkirah*s. Traditionally, Persian *tazkirah*s had only addressed New Persian (i.e., post-Islamic) literature, but Hidayat was exposed to nascent Orientalist philology that had demonstrated the relationship between New Persian and pre-Islamic languages. As elaborated in Chapter 3, Orientalist philologists considered these languages to be part of a single trajectory extending over thousands of years, including the language of the Achaemenids (ca. 700–330 BCE, described as "Old Persian"), the Middle Persian languages associated with the Sasanian era (224–650 CE), and the post-Islamic Persian language ("New Persian"). Though a tradition of philology and lexicology also existed in the premodern Persianate context, these subjects were considered in works belonging to separate genres, like dictionaries and linguistic treatises, rather than being addressed within *tazkirah*s. For example, over a century before Hidayat, the Indian litterateur Siraj al-Din 'Ali Khan-i Arzu had written about the connections between Persian and its predecessors in his linguistic treatise *Musmir* (*Fruitful*), yet he did not address pre-Islamic languages at all in his later *tazkirah*, *Majma' al-Nafa'is*.[13] Hidayat's innovation, therefore, was dealing with pre-Islamic literature within the *tazkirah* genre.

Hidayat's discussion of pre-Islamic Iranian literature is limited to the preface of *Majma' al-Fusaha'* and the rest of the work concerns only New Persian poets, yet this preface paves the way for the later writing of modern, nationalist literary histories. Modern literary history was generically unprecedented in Persianate writing by engaging literary criticism, philology, and lexicology alongside literary history and biography in the same text. Notably, these literary

---

[13] On Arzu's linguistic discoveries see Dudney, *India in the Persian World*, chapter 2, and Tavakoli-Targhi, *Refashioning Iran*, 18–34.

histories construct an Iranian literary canon, wherein Old, Middle, and New Persian literatures came to be understood as belonging to a singular, "Iranian" trajectory. Indian and Iranian litterateurs both adopted the paradigm of an Iranian national literature, including Avestan and Middle Persian. Interestingly, the Indian litterateurs did not challenge this Iran-centric model of Persian literary history, nor did they suggest an Indian national literature in which Persian could be included, but instead elevated Iran's place in their literary histories. In fact, they sometimes even shared and underscored their Iranian contemporaries' prejudices against the Persian literature of South Asia.[14] The Indian scholars Muhammad Husayn Azad and Shibli Nuʿmani both wrote Iran-centric accounts of Persian poetry, which followed their Iranian counterparts in disparaging the Persian poetry of India. Azad's *tazkirah* of Persian poets, titled *Nigaristan-i Fars* (*Picture-Gallery of Persia*, 1922), was published posthumously and received scant attention, but Shibli's *Shiʿr al-ʿAjam* (*Poetry of the Persians*) was influential and circulated widely. Like many of the Persian literary histories written across the border from Shibli in Iran, *Shiʿr al-ʿAjam* was written as a textbook for new educational institutions, but Shibli had a communal readership (Muslims) rather than a national one (Iranians) in mind.[15]

The first known Persian *tazkirah*, *Lubab al-Albab*, was written in Sindh in the thirteenth century, so perhaps it is fitting – however coincidental – that the first literary histories should also emerge in South Asia, more than half a millennium after *Lubab al-Albab*. Frances Pritchett calls Muhammad Husayn Azad's *Ab-i Hayat*, or

---

[14] Shamsur Rahman Faruqi describes this tendency among Indians as a "loss of self-confidence, or a surge of self-hatred" ("Unprivileged Power," 11).

[15] Unlike the Iranians writing for national institutions such as the University of Tehran, Shibli composed *Shiʿr al-ʿAjam* during his time as an educator at the Islamic seminary Nadwat al-ʿUlama in Lucknow. Writing in Urdu, he anticipated an Indian Muslim readership. In Shibli's time, Urdu was acquiring a communal identity as a Muslim language. See Rahman, *From Hindi to Urdu*, 98–135.

Water of Life, published in 1880, both "the last *tazkira* and the first literary history" of Urdu poetry.[16] *Ab-i Hayat* takes up the task of *tazkirah* writing, that is, providing a biographical anthology of Urdu poets and their poetry, but, under the mostly indirect influence of English writing, it brings a narrative structure and a sense of time that were unprecedented for a *tazkirah*.[17] In its more than five hundred pages it covers a wide expanse of Urdu poetry from Vali Dakkani in the seventeenth century to Azad's in the late nineteenth century. Shibli Nu'mani's *Shi'r al-'Ajam* also can be understood with the framework Pritchett used for conceptualizing *Ab-i Hayat*, as a text that has both elements of *tazkirah* and of literary history, straddling the divide between the two genres.

Shi'r al-'Ajam is a monumental work on Persian poetry spanning over 1,500 pages, written in Urdu and published in five volumes between the years 1908 and 1918. It was translated into Persian on two separate occasions, first by a series of Afghan translators in Kabul, beginning in 1925, and later by Fakhr-i Da'i Gilani (d. 1964) in Tehran, completed in 1948. Shibli was an Islamic scholar, educator, and reformer from Azamgarh, India. Like Hidayat in Iran's Dar al-Funun, Shibli played an important role in some of South Asia's earliest modern Urdu-language educational institutions: the Muhammadan Anglo-Oriental College (now Aligarh Muslim University) in Aligarh, Osmania University in Hyderabad, and Nadwat al-'Ulama seminary in Lucknow. His life's work was to develop Islamic education in South Asia – and ultimately develop an approach to Islam – that could be compatible with colonial modernity, using the new European methodologies to revitalize Islam.[18]

---

[16] Pritchett, "Long History," 866. A comparable and contemporary figure to Azad can be found in Mirza Fath 'Ali Akhundzadah, an influential proponent of Iranian nationalism, on whom see Marashi, *Nationalizing Iran*, 66–75.

[17] Pritchett, "Long History," 902.

[18] Shibli was not alone in this endeavor; see also Guimbretière, "Āzād," on Shibli's disciple Abu'l Kalam Azad, for example. I address the relationship between Shibli and Abu'l Kalam Azad in the following chapter, "Erotics."

Shibli was straightforward in his assessment of historical methodology. Explaining why he considered Turkish historical writing superior to Arabic, he noted that:

> Arabic histories have been nothing more than collections of simple facts and events, and [where] effort and care [is taken], it is only related to the principles of narrative transmission. In contrast, Turkish histories are written in accordance with the principles and rules of historical philosophy, *and on the basis of which Europe has taken this science* [fann] *to the peak of perfection.*[19]

Shibli saw Europeans as having perfected historiography, and admired the Turks for mastering European methods and applying them to the writing of Islamic history. Shibli's own writings included scholarly biographies of the early Muslim jurist Abu Hanifa, the caliph 'Umar, and the prophet Muhammad; his extensive biography of the latter, titled *Sirat al-Nabi* (*The Life of the Prophet*), is his best-known work. The late scholar of Islam Sheila McDonough described Shibli's methodology in writing these religious biographies: "Historical method he understands to mean careful scrutiny of primary sources, sifting of materials for anachronisms and other improbable forms of evidence, and in general moving away from the hagiographical qualities of the medieval biographies."[20] In writing *Shi'r al-'Ajam*, he employed the same methodology, making careful and meticulous use of all the sources at his disposal, such as Persian *tazkirah*s and *divan*s. Unlike later Iranian nationalist literary historians such as the poet laureate Muhammad-Taqi Bahar, who almost exclusively made use of Iranian *tazkirah*s, Shibli did not discriminate in his use of *tazkirah*s produced in Iran and those produced in South Asia. He also acknowledged Orientalist scholarship, claiming that the Europeans have given more attention (*i'tina*) to Persian literature than Muslims,

---

[19] Shibli, *Safarnamah*, 69, emphasis added. Adapted from Bruce's translation in Shibli, *Turkey, Egypt, and Syria*, 72.
[20] McDonough, "Shibli Nu'mani," 569.

and lamented the latter's utter ignorance of pre-Islamic Iranian languages such as Avestan.[21] *Ab-i Hayat* had already become extraordin-
arily popular, widely read, and circulated by the time Shibli was
writing *Shi'r al-'Ajam*. For this reason, it is highly likely that Shibli
succumbed to what Pritchett called "the all-pervasive influence of
Ab-e hayat, with its naive and ruthlessly Westernizing notions of
literary history."[22]

The first three volumes of *Shi'r al-'Ajam* resemble the format of
the majority of *Ab-i Hayat*, as well as the older Persian *tazkirah*s. In
these volumes, Shibli outlines periods of Persian poetry, offering biographies of the major poets of each period and selections of their poetry.
His entry on Sa'di, for example, begins quite similarly to the entries in
Hidayat's *Majma' al-Fusaha'* or in other representative *tazkirah*s:

Shaykh Muslih al-Din Sa'di Shirazi

[His] epithet [*laqab*] was Muslih al-Din and [his] pen name
[*takhallus*] was Sa'di, his father was a servant of Atabak Sa'd bin
Zangi, the King [*badshah*] of Shiraz. For this reason the Shaykh
chose **Sa'di** as his pen name. The year of his birth is unknown; with
regard to his death, all agree that it happened in 691 AH. In general
*tazkirah*s wrote the length of his life as 102 years; based on that, the
year of his birth would be 589 AH. The Shaykh [Sa'di] has clarified
that he was a disciple of Abu al-Faraj ibn Jawzi ... Ibn Jawzi died in
597 AH; if we were to accept that the Shaykh was born in 589 AH,
then by the time of Ibn Jawzi's death he would have been nine years
old, and this is in no way correct.[23]

The entry goes on to cover more of the same ground as in Hidayat's
Majma' al-Fusaha, but in much greater detail; where Hidayat spent a
single paragraph providing biography, Shibli elaborated and penned
fifteen pages, interspersed with biographical details about other

---

[21] Nu'mani, *Shi'r al-'Ajam*, 1:6–7. Shibli shared this interest in pre-Islamic Iran with
European Orientalists as well as Iranian intellectuals of the time.
[22] Pritchett, "Long History," 905. [23] Shibli, *Shi'r al-'Ajam*, 2:29.

figures pertinent to the life of Saʿdi. The difference is not merely one of length, however. In his critical discussion of the alleged dates of Saʿdi's birth and death, Shibli applied the logic and reason he had mastered in his studies of the Islamic rational sciences to the task of historiography. Ever critical, he goes on to question other claims about Saʿdi found in *tazkirah*s, and offers a biography of the poet as a figure grounded in, and responding to, the political and historical circumstances of his time.

The fourth and fifth volumes of *Shiʿr al-ʿAjam* offer literary history and criticism of a kind that cannot be found in the *tazkirah* genre. Moving entirely beyond the biographical anthology format which is still intact in the first three volumes, the fourth volume is divided into three main sections: "the reality and nature of poetry" (*shaʿiri ki haqiqat aur mahiyat*), "a general history of Persian poetry and the influence of civilization and other factors" (*farsi shaʿiri ki ʿam tarikh aur tamaddun aur digar asbab ka asar*), and "praise and criticism" (*taqriz va tanqid*). The fifth volume deals exclusively with the development of poetic forms (*qasidah* and *ghazal*) and of poetic genres or themes, covering romantic, Sufi, ethical, and philosophical poetry. Particularly in the last two volumes, Shibli provides an account of Persian poetry guided by a continuous, progressive sense of time. Rather than merely discussing a series of individual poets, each discretely bound within separate biographical entries as in traditional *tazkirah*s, in the fourth and fifth volumes of *Shiʿr al-ʿAjam* Shibli discusses poetic movements which build on literary and historical developments that precede them.[24]

Shibli's innovations indicate that *Shiʿr al-ʿAjam*, like *Ab-i Hayat* before it, should be seen as a hybrid, transitional text between the *tazkirah* and the modern European-style literary history. While much of the format, especially of the first three volumes, belongs to

---

[24] It should be noted that while *tazkirah*s generally treated individual poets within separate entries, *tazkirah*-writers nevertheless sometimes traced out networks of poetic affiliation within a single entry. See Losensky, *Welcoming Fighani*, 17–55.

the *tazkirah* genre, its critical methodology, engagement with Orientalist scholarship, and sense of linear time set it apart. Notably, the title pages of various editions of *Shi'r al-'Ajam* reflect this ambiguity, as it seems that publishers were unsure of how to label the text: *tazkirah*, or *tarikh* (history). The change of terms is especially interesting given that *tarikh* in fact predates *tazkirah* as a genre and has its own long history of generic conventions; yet it appears that by the early twentieth century the word *tarikh* had come to be understood as the direct equivalent of the word *history* in English and its equivalents in other European languages, thus connoting modern European-style historiography, with its secular, linear chronology.[25]

In a 1920 edition of *Shi'r al-'Ajam*, both *tarikh-i 'ajam* (history of the Persians) and *tazkirah* appear on the title page, though not on the same line. A Persian advertisement from 1936 describes it as an "unparalleled" book on "the philosophy of Iranian literary history" (*dar falsafah-yi tarikh-i adabiyat-i iran*).[26] A 1940 edition classifies the work *tazkirah-i Shi'r al-'Ajam* without the word *tarikh*, whereas a 1947 edition omits the word *tazkirah* and adds a clarifying subtitle: *ya'ni farsi sha'iri ki tarikh* (that is to say, the *history* of Persian poetry). Various editions of the Persian translations are also similarly divided between identifying the text as a *tazkirah* or *tarikh*.[27]

By the early twentieth century, publications in the new genre of Persian literary history proliferate. In his preface to the fifth volume of *Shi'r al-'Ajam*, republished in 1920, Shibli's protégé Sayyid Sulayman Nadvi (1884–1953) registers his surprise at the publication of two other Persian literary histories nearly contemporaneous with *Shi'r al-'Ajam*: E. G. Browne's *Literary History of Persia* in England (1902, 1906), and Muhammad Husayn Azad's *Sukhandan-i Fars* in Lahore (1907).

---

[25] On the traditional *tarikh* genre see Meisami, *Persian Historiography*.
[26] This advertisement appeared on the back of Fakhr-i Da'i Gilani's Persian translation of another of Shibli's works. See Shibli, *Kitabkhanah-yi Iskandariyyah*, back matter.
[27] Jennifer Dubrow notes a similar confusion of multiple terms for the emerging genre of the novel in Urdu (Dubrow, *Cosmopolitan Dreams*, 36–7).

Shibli's work emerges in parallel to these early European national literary histories rather than in response to them. The majority of his exposure to English literature was through indirect means such as translation, and while Shibli was well aware of the contemporary Orientalist scholarship on Persian literature, much of it – such as the pioneering works on Persian literary history in German and Italian – was inaccessible to him.[28] To a certain extent, Shibli used similar sources and employed similar methodology to those of the European Orientalists, and thus it is no surprise that their works are so similar. The genre of Persian literary history continued to develop with the publication of E. G. Browne's *Literary History of Persia* which appeared in English from 1902 to 1924 and in Persian and Urdu translations in the following decade.[29]

Browne was in many ways an English equivalent of his Iranian and Indian counterparts. While Hidayat and Shibli received traditional Muslim educations but came to be involved in European-style modern institutions, Browne was a Cambridge-educated Orientalist who mastered Persian poetry and the traditional literary sciences. If Azad, the "ruthless Westernizer," was a South Asian Victorian, Browne was an Iranian nationalist who happened to be a Victorian Englishman. He was a great supporter of the Constitutionalist movement in Iran, and often deferred to his Iranian friends on matters of literary taste.[30]

Browne's *Literary History* did not share the generic ambiguity of Shibli's *Shiʿr al-ʿAjam*; Browne envisioned his book from the start as a national literary history. While he was aware of earlier European histories of Persian literature, namely Hammer-Purgstall's *Geschichte der schönen Redekünste Persiens* (1818, itself based

---

[28] Such works include Hammer-Purgstall, *Geschichte der schönen Redekünste Persiens*, and Pizzi, *Storia della poesia persiana*.

[29] The earliest partial translations into Persian appeared starting in 1932; in Urdu, the first volume was translated as *Tarikh-i Adabiyat-i Iran* by Sayyid Sajjad Husayn, Jamiʿah ʿUsmaniyya, Hyderabad, 1932, under the auspices of the Anjuman-i Taraqqi-i Urdu.

[30] On Browne's support for the Constitutionalist movement see Bonakdarian, "Edward G. Browne."

closely on a fifteenth-century Persian *tazkirah*) and the Italian
Orientalist Italo Pizzi's *Manuale di letteratura persiana* (1887) and
Storia della poesia persiana (1894), these were not important models
for Browne.[31] Having been invited to contribute to the publisher
T. Fisher Unwin's series *The Library of Literary History*, he modeled
his *A Literary History of Persia* on the earlier volumes in the series,
especially Jean Jules Jusserand's *A Literary History of the English
People* (1893), as well as another national history, John Richard
Green's *A Short History of the English People* (1874). As Jusserand
described his task, the book is not "a 'History of English Literature,'
but rather a 'Literary History of the English People.'"[32] Following
these models, Browne wrote a literary history of the Persians, not just
of poets who wrote in Persian – he was interested in religion, philosophy, and science as much as in literature, and he included Iranians
who wrote in other languages while excluding Indians who wrote in
Persian from the scope of his book. Like Jusserand, Browne relates a
story in which the protagonist is the nation, unlike *tazkirah*s which
treat each poet separately through independently bounded entries. In
modern, national literary histories like Browne's, the nation is an
autonomous entity, developing as it moves through linear time.

Consider Browne's section on Saʿdi, which comes from a chapter discussing ʿAttar, Rumi and Saʿdi as "Three Great Mystical Poets"
of the earlier Mongol period:

> We come now to Saʿdí of Shíráz, the third of the great poets of this
> epoch ... He is a poet of quite a different type from the two already
> discussed in this chapter, and represents on the whole the astute,
> half-pious, half-worldly side of the Persian character, as the other
> two represent the passionately devout and mystical.[33]

---

[31] Browne refers only rarely to Hammer-Purgstall (e.g., Browne, *Literary History*,
3:436), and never to Pizzi, aside from mentioning in his bibliography that the latter
"has published (in Italian) an excellent little sketch of Persian Literature from the
earliest times" (*Literary History*, 1:492).

[32] Jusserand, *A Literary History of the English People*, ix.

[33] Browne, *Literary History*, 2:525–6.

Browne does, of course, also provide the biographical details about Sa'di which could be found in the *tazkirah* tradition, including his lineage and patronage, the dates of his birth and death, and so on. However, like Shibli, Browne grounds his analysis of Sa'di in historical and political circumstances. Going beyond the biography of an individual poet, he describes Sa'di's position in the Iranian nation, as well as in the poetic trends of his era and his influence on later poets. Browne identifies several verses where Hafiz quotes from Sa'di through *tazmin* ("insertion" or "inclusion" of another poet's verse in one's poem), another form of poetic response related to speaking in reply.

Browne himself was developing the genre of literary history and synthesizing the nationalist model of Jusserand and Green with the source criticism of Shibli. He cited *Shi'r al-'Ajam* numerous times and expressed his admiration and respect for Shibli's work; later Orientalists such as Jan Rypka (1886–1968) also made use of *Shi'r al-'Ajam*.[34] Thus, Shibli's text not only reflects European influence, but also influences European literary thought and contributes significantly to the development of Persian literary history.[35] Browne, in turn, influences later Iranian literary historians like Muhammad-Taqi Bahar, thereby passing some of Shibli's ideas and approach on to Iranians. These new literary histories relied heavily on *tazkirah*s as sources – just as the earlier *tazkirah*s had often cribbed or borrowed directly from one another – and responded directly to them. Some have considered *tazkirah*s and literary histories to belong to the same tradition, if not the same genre.[36] I suggest instead that the *tazkirah*

---

[34] Rypka relies on *Shi'r al-'Ajam* throughout his "History of Persian Literature up to the Beginning of the 20th Century" in *History of Iranian Literature*.

[35] Farzin Vejdani notes this relationship between Browne and Shibli as well; see Vejdani, *Making History*, 149. He makes a similar argument about what he terms a "Persian 'Republic of Letters'" in ibid., 145–66.

[36] For example, one author simply conflates the two, using *tazkirah* and *literary history* seemingly interchangeably in his work (Ali, *Persian Tadkira Writing*, 5). The Encyclopedia of Islam entry claims that "it cannot be denied that the *tadhkira*s [*tazkirah*s] constitute the only form of literary history created by the tradition itself" (Stewart-Robinson, "Tadhkira," 54).

tradition provided early twentieth-century literary historians with a useful local form they could repurpose, and ultimately transform, for use in their modernizing projects.

I.2 THE LAST PERSIAN *TAZKIRAH*

One Persian *tazkirah* that was used ubiquitously as a source by literary historians, whether in Iran, India, or Europe, was Hidayat's *Majma' al-Fusaha'*. Its preface, bridging the gap between pre-Islamic languages and New Persian literature as previously discussed, is not the text's only innovative feature; Hidayat's biographical entries are also worthy of note. Some of Hidayat's biographies of poets are unique, such as his claim that Hafiz authored a commentary (*tafsir*) on the Qur'an, a claim most likely not repeated elsewhere, and one that Browne tactfully described as "of doubtful authenticity."[37] It is unclear where this claim originates, and quite possible that Hidayat simply fabricated it to add some flavor to his entry on Hafiz, or to emphasize the poet's piety. Of especial relevance to the present study is another of Hidayat's seemingly eccentric stories: his account of the origins of Abu al-Qasim Firdawsi's eleventh-century epic poem, the *Shahnamah* (*Book of Kings*). Hidayat begins by stating that the *Shahnamah* originated long before the time of Firdawsi as a history of the ancient kings of Iran, continuing until the reign of Yazdgird III (d. 651), but here Hidayat's account starts to diverge wildly with what can be observed elsewhere in the traditional accounts of the *Shahnamah* found in other *tazkirah* sources.[38] Hidayat claims that at the time of the Arab-Islamic conquest of Iran, the *Shahnamah* fell into the hands of the Arabs, and as Iran's bounties were being divided up the book made its way to Abyssinia (*habashah*), where it was translated into "Abyssinian" (*habashi*). According to Hidayat's account, it then traveled from Abyssinia to the Deccan and

---

[37] Hidayat, *Majma' al-Fusaha'*, 2:36–7; Browne, *Literary History*, 2:274.
[38] There is nothing to this effect in *tazkirahs* like *Lubab al-Albab*, *Tazkirat al-Shu'ara'*, *Haft Iqlim*, *Majma' al-Nafa'is*, *Riyaz al-Shu'ara'*, *'Arafat al-'Ashiqin*, or *Atashkadah*, for example.

Hindustan, where it circulated until Ya'qub-i Lays Saffar (840–79), the founder of the Saffarid dynasty, sent someone to Hindustan to bring the manuscript to Firdawsi's native Khurasan.

Though he does not specifically cite his Firdawsi sources, it seems likely that Hidayat's story comes from the preface to the Baysunghuri *Shahnamah* manuscript, an illuminated, gilded manuscript of the *Shahnamah* which was commissioned under the Timurid dynasty in the fifteenth century.[39] The Baysunghuri *Shahnamah* is one of the lengthiest extant *Shahnamah* manuscripts due to the number of extra verses and other details added to it. Its preface contains a strikingly similar story about the history of the *Shahnamah*, not to mention a good detail of other historical inaccuracies about the text, its author, and other relevant figures.[40] Qajar prince Farhad Mirza Mu'tamad al-Dawlah owned this manuscript, and since it is known that he inherited some of his other manuscripts from Hidayat (such as a treatise by 'Abd al-Rahman Jami), it seems likely that either the Baysunghuri manuscript was originally in Hidayat's possession, or that Hidayat was at least able to access Mu'tamad al-Dawlah's copy. According to the Iranian literary scholar Ahmad Gulchin-Ma'ani, Hidayat had the only manuscript of Taqi Awhadi's *'Arafat al-'Ashiqin* in Iran, and Gulchin-Ma'ani criticizes him for "plagiarizing" from this earlier *tazkirah* without citing his source, so it is not at all unlikely that Hidayat would borrow from the Baysunghuri *Shahnamah* without citing it, despite the fact that he does sometimes cite his sources elsewhere.[41]

What is noteworthy in Hidayat's account of the history of the *Shahnamah* is not that it is historically inaccurate, but that it is unique; other *tazkirah* writers, many of whom likely did not have access to the Baysunghuri manuscript, do not include these details in

---

[39] The preface to the Baysunghuri *Shahnamah* is also the source of much information in Arthur George Warner and Edmond Warner's English translation of the *Shahnamah*, 1905–25. See Firdawsi, *Shahnamah-yi Firdawsi*, 10.

[40] Khaleghi Motlagh and Lentz, "BĀYSONĞORĪ ŠĀH-NĀMA."

[41] Gulchin-i Ma'ani, *Tarikh-i Tazkirah-ha*, 2:147.

their biographies of Firdawsi. Hidayat can thus be credited for introducing this story from the Baysunghuri *Shahnamah;* however falla-
cious it might have been, it became something that later literary
historians would have to engage with, even if only to negate it. For
example, the story is reproduced in full in the 1911 edition of the
Encyclopedia Britannica's entry on Firdawsi, which concludes by
noting that this story "is rejected by modern scholars."[42]

Browne, one such modern scholar, wrote that *tazkirah*s "contain few trustworthy biographical details, and consist for the most
part of anecdotes connected with certain verses of ... poems, and
probably in most cases, if not all, invented to explain or illustrate
them."[43] Browne's contemporary, the German Orientalist Hermann
Ethé (1844–1917) similarly warned in his *Neupersische Literatur*
(New-Persian Literature) that the Persians have "no special love of
truth" and that the greatest caution must be exercised when reading
*tazkirah*s.[44] He then went on to list fifty "indispensable" Persian
*tazkirah*s in chronological order, ending with *Majma' al-Fusaha'*.
Despite his warning, he called this source "the latest, but in every
respect richest and most valuable of all the general *tazkirah*s."[45] Ethé
explained that Hidayat had consulted all the relevant works, from
'Awfi's *Lubab al-Albab* (a rare manuscript) to contemporary sources,
and this made *Majma' al-Fusaha'* a valuable resource. Indeed, it is for
this very reason that Hidayat's work earned its stature, such that later
literary historians and Orientalists – European, Iranian, and Indian
alike – had no choice but to use it as a source even as some grumbled
about its inaccuracies and exaggerations.

As one of the latest *tazkirah*s in the genre's history, *Majma' al-
Fusaha'* contains a wealth of information about Hidayat's contemporaries, Qajar-era poets who were not covered by earlier sources. It was
not only by virtue of being the latest great *tazkirah* that *Majma' al-
Fusaha'* gained its particular value as a source on Qajar poetry, but

---

[42] "Firdousī."   [43] Browne, *Literary History*, 3:271–2.
[44] Ethé, "Neupersische Litteratur," 213.   [45] Ibid., 216.

also thanks to Hidayat's stature as poet and administrator which put him into personal contact with a great number of his literary contemporaries. Abbas Amanat repeats the clichés that *Majma' al-Fusaha'* was "the last and most comprehensive *tadhkera* [*tazkirah*] in the long tradition of Persian biographical dictionaries," yet "suffer[ed] from ... inaccuracies and distortions," and describes it as promoting the literary revival in Persian poetry contemporary to the author, and Qajar cultural renewal more generally. In this way, Amanat argues, Hidayat makes a place for Qajar-era poetry in the millennium-old Persian literary tradition.[46]

Later literary histories all seem to agree that *Majma' al-Fusaha'*, despite being the most comprehensive and latest *tazkirah*, was riddled with inaccuracies, errors, and embellishments. Why, then, did it become such a ubiquitous source? Perhaps it was such a popular source not in spite of its errors, but partly because of them. Its great expanse as a comprehensive general *tazkirah* (as opposed to the more specific *tazkirah*s which narrowed their focus to a particular region, time period, or the like) made it a model worthy of appropriation for modern literary histories with their universal scope. Working through its many errors and contradictions proved to be a productive exercise, with the faults of *Majma' al-Fusaha'* serving for later scholars as a kind of invitation to comment and assert corrective narratives. Like poets replying to one another through response poems (*javab*), modernizing literary scholars found in *Majma' al-Fusaha'* an entry point where they could insert themselves into a conversation by correcting Hidayat's mistakes, without writing his work off altogether.

The Iranian literary scholar Jalal al-Din Huma'i (1900–80), who like Hidayat was affiliated with the Dar al-Funun in Tehran, was perhaps the best example of this: an entire book of nearly 300 pages was compiled and published from Huma'i's notes in the margins of *Majma' al-Fusaha'* on Hidayat's errors, as well as poets Hidayat left

---

[46] Amanat, "Legend, Legitimacy, and Making a National Narrative," 318.

out; yet in his book's introduction Huma'i praises *Majma' al-Fusaha'* and says that if he has stumbled upon anything worthwhile, it is all because of Hidayat (a double entendre as *hidayat* means "guidance"). After acknowledging that to err is human, and only God does not make mistakes, Huma'i defends Hidayat, saying "if a learned man like Hidayat in this work suffers from mistakes, it should not come as a surprise at all" and says that those who would dismiss his work on the basis of such errors are very short-sighted and unfair.[47]

I.3   EXPANDING THE SCOPE OF LITERATURE

A development peculiar to the modern Persian literary histories produced in Iran was the expansion of scope from poets (the subject of *tazkirah*s) to writers of all genres, including scientists, who were not traditionally considered belletristic writers.[48] This may appear on first blush to be a minor innovation of little consequence, but it is in fact indicative of the broadening scope required by Persian literary histories changing to accommodate a burgeoning Iranian national identity. While premodern *tazkirah*s also included extraliterary figures for a variety of reasons, those figures were still integrated on the basis of their Persian poetry. Mana Kia provides the example of the entry on Safavid Shah Isma'il I in Azar Baygdili's *Atashkadah* (*Fire Temple*, 1760), suggesting that "this shah is most important for who he was, rather than his poetry, most of which was written in Turkish."[49] Yet even this Safavid shah appears under his poetic nom de plume "Khata'i," and his brief biography is followed by one of his Persian couplets, indicating that despite the shah's great importance, he still must qualify as a poet to be included in a *tazkirah*. The modern logic of nationalism, however, made possible the inclusion in literary histories of scientists who had little or no literary significance, especially as Persian poets; they could be integrated instead on the basis of their status as national heroes. The absence of this development among the

---

[47] Huma'i, *Yaddasht-ha-yi Ustad*, 1:22, 119.   [48] Vejdani, *Making History*, 161.
[49] Kia, "Imagining Iran," 101.

Persian literary histories from India is therefore understandable, as writing Persian literary history had a more nationalist valence in Iran than in India. As Farzin Vejdani illustrates, modern Iranian "history textbooks were a nationalist genre par excellence," written for modern educational institutions that strove to promote a national canon of Iranian, rather than Persian, literature.[50] Kia argues that eighteenth-century *tazkirah*s functioned to produce a cultural community of litterateurs, comprising past and present poets.[51] Her reading demonstrates how modern literary histories are at once continuous with the older *tazkirah* tradition and distinct from it: continuous in that literary histories also imagined a community comprising figures from across time, but distinct in that the basis for inclusion in the community became ethnicity rather than poetry. Notably, the treatment of Ibn Sina and ʿUmar Khayyam in Persian literary histories exemplifies this point.

Scientists, in particular, became especially important for inclusion in literary histories. One such scientist was Abu ʿAli ibn Sina (henceforth "Ibn Sina"), or "Avicenna" (980–1037), a polymath known primarily for his works on medicine and philosophy.[52] He was traditionally known as a scholar rather than a poet (though of course the two categories are not mutually exclusive) and he wrote mainly in Arabic rather than Persian. Ibn Sina was from Bukhara, located in today's Uzbekistan, but he later settled in what is present-day Iran. The earliest known Persian *tazkirah*s, *Lubab al-Albab* and *Tazkirat al-Shuʿara*, do not mention Ibn Sina at all. Hidayat includes Ibn Sina and attributes some poetry to him in his *Majmaʿ al-Fusaha*, which is generally considered to be the last *tazkirah* produced in Iran, as

---

[50] Vejdani, *Making History*, 37. Vejdani examines this point in greater detail in ibid., 156–66.

[51] Kia, *Persianate Selves*, chapter 7.

[52] For the remaking of Ibn Sina from Muslim polymath to Iranian national figure in the first half of the twentieth century, see Grigor, *Building Iran*, 112–43. By Bahar's time he was widely considered by Iranians as their compatriot, a view that remains dominant today, despite the fact that he is also currently claimed as a national figure in Uzbekistan, Tajikistan, and Afghanistan.

previously discussed. Like most *tazkirah*s that precede it, the entry on Ibn Sina in *Majma' al-Fusaha'* focuses on his role as a poet rather than as a scientist.[53] Shibli – positioned outside the Iranian nationalist discourse, as an Indian – does not mention Ibn Sina at all except as an occasional reference, whereas the Iranian Muhammad-Taqi Bahar deals with Ibn Sina because of the importance of his prose style.

Bahar (1886–1951), poet laureate, literary scholar, and politician, was another litterateur associated with the nascent University of Tehran. The university was established in 1935 as a successor to institutions like the Dar al-Funun and the Tehran Teachers' Training College, incorporating much of its predecessors' faculty and departments.[54] Bahar's *Sabkshinasi* (*Stylistics*, 1942) was commissioned by Iran's Ministry of Culture in 1937 as a textbook for the university's inaugural doctoral program in Persian literature. Its inclusion of Ibn Sina, along with other figures important to Iran who wrote in Arabic rather than Persian, belies the subtitle of the book: "or, the history of the evolution of Persian prose" (*ya tarikh-i tatavvur-i nasr-i farsi*).[55] Bahar's canon, like that of Browne, was a national one comprising Iranian literature, rather than a linguistic canon of Persian literature, as the subtitle implies.[56] This is why Wali Ahmadi suggests that "it is necessary ... to situate and examine *Sabk-shinasi* precisely within the context of a literary history bound to a national imaginary order *and* the institutional politics of literary studies."[57] It is literary modernity, especially its particular understanding of the nation and narrative time, that makes such a national canon possible and imaginable.

---

[53] Hidayat, *Majma' al-Fusaha'*, 1:259–60.

[54] Technically the university was established in 1934, but it was inaugurated in 1935. Banani, *Modernization of Iran*, 98–9.

[55] Other Iranian historians such as 'Abbas Iqbal Ashtiyani also made sure to include in their works those Iranians who had written in Arabic rather than Persian. See Vejdani, *Making History*, 89–90.

[56] Though "Persian" (the language) and "Persian" (the ethnicity, or the nationality, as it was referred to prior to 1935) may be confused in English, the original word used (*farsi*) refers explicitly to the language.

[57] Ahmadi, "The Institution of Persian Literature," 142, emphasis in original.

Ibn Sina was also taken up by Badiʿ al-Zaman Furuzanfar (1903–70), another Iranian literary scholar who taught at some of Iran's first modern institutions of higher learning, including the Dar al-Funun and later the University of Tehran.[58] His interest in Ibn Sina is primarily for his significance as a scientist and an important Iranian national figure rather than a poet; evidently the latter qualification is of secondary importance to his inclusion in Furuzanfar's work (which, like Bahar's, also covers Arabic works by Iranian writers in general). Furuzanfar merely notes that some have attributed Arabic and Persian poetry to Ibn Sina, and he quotes an Arabic *qasidah* (panegyric) attributed to him.[59] Browne claims that "of all the scientific writers of the time, none were greater than Avicenna (Abu ʿAli ibn Sina)."[60] He provides a biography of Ibn Sina[61] wherein Browne considers him a poet of Arabic as well as Persian and quotes (in translation) the same Arabic *qasidah* cited by Furuzanfar.[62] Browne later quotes a Persian quatrain "ascribed" to Ibn Sina.[63] Interestingly, Browne holds Ibn Sina up as a moral standard in his discussion of the poet Anvari, whom he describes as "longing to follow in the steps of Avicenna, yet living the life of [the famously debauched poet] Abu Nuwas."[64] Ibn Sina was not the only scientist to be featured in literary histories of Persian; perhaps even more important was ʿUmar Khayyam.

ʿUmar Khayyam's inclusion as a poet in literary histories may be slightly less of an innovation than the inclusion of Ibn Sina, as there is more precedence for Khayyam's poetry; although he is absent

---

[58] On Furuzanfar within the context of Iranian nationalism and education, see Vejdani, *Making History*, 164–5.

[59] Furuzanfar, *Tarikh-i Adabiyat-i Iran*, 257.   [60] Browne, *Literary History*, 2:96.

[61] Ibid., 2:106–11.

[62] Ibid. The scholarly consensus today is that Ibn Sina did write a small amount of poetry in Arabic; historically a few lines of Persian poetry were occasionally attributed to him, and beginning in the late nineteenth century, as his importance as an Iranian national figure grew, more and more Persian poetry was attributed to him.

[63] Ibid., 2:267.

[64] Ibid., 2:377. This is one of Browne's rare and completely indirect references to the salacious life and poetry of Abu Nuwas, a subject dealt with in greater depth in the next chapter, "Erotics."

from early *tazkirah*s like *Lubab al-Albab* and *Tazkirat al-Shu'ara'*,[65] he does appear in some later *tazkirah*s.[66] Khayyam (1048–131) was a polymath, scientist, and ostensibly a poet, hailing from Neyshabur, a city located within the confines of what is now the modern nation of Iran.[67] Shibli evidently took Khayyam seriously as a poet. He begins his extensive section on Khayyam with a detailed biography, followed by a deep analysis of his poetry.[68] As Khayyam is famous for the religious skepticism and hedonism expressed in the poetry attributed to him, it is perhaps surprising that he would be the subject of praise by Shibli, a Muslim religious scholar and cleric ('*alim*). Yet it is precisely Khayyam's criticism of the clerisy ('*ulama*') and pious ascetics (*zuhhad*) that Shibli appreciates. He provides detailed, precise information on translations of Khayyam's poetry into European languages and the broader impact of these translations in Europe, where he rightly notes that Khayyam has found greater popularity as a poet than in Asia.[69]

Shibli may have taken some of this information from Browne, who mentions that "'Umar Khayyam, who is not ranked by the Persians as a poet of even the third class, is now, probably, better known in Europe than any of his fellow-countrymen as a writer of verse."[70] Browne later reiterates his point, stating that Khayyam, "thanks to the genius of FitzGerald, enjoys a celebrity in Europe,

---

[65] Browne himself notes Khayyam's absence in these texts (ibid., 2:249).

[66] For Khayyam's twentieth-century transformation into Persian poet and Iranian national figure, see Marashi, *Nationalizing Iran*, 110–14, and Grigor, *Building Iran*, 144–73. It should be noted that in this case, like most or perhaps all other such modern transformations, there was local precedence that was built upon; figures like Ibn Sina or Khayyam and their popularity were not fashioned out of whole cloth but rather made anew from preexisting material. *Tazkirah*s that mention Khayyam only as a poet and ignore his significance as a scientist altogether include the *Atashkadah* (Azar, *Atashkadah*, 675–85); *Riyaz al-Shu'ara'* (Valih Daghistani, *Riyaz al-Shu'ara'*, 2:706–7); *Majma' al-Nafa'is* (Arzu, *Majma' al-Nafa'is*, 1:401–2); and *Majma' al-Fusaha'* (Hidayat, *Majma' al-Fusaha'*, 2:731).

[67] Contemporary scholars tend to agree that the majority of Persian poetry attributed to Khayyam is apocryphal and most likely attached to his name posthumously. See de Blois, *Persian Literature*, 299–318, and Morton, "Some 'Umarian Quatrains."

[68] Nu'mani, *Shi'r al-'Ajam*, 1:178.   [69] Ibid., 1:202–4.

[70] Browne, *Literary History*, 1:84.

especially in England and America, far greater than that which he has attained in his own country, where his fame rests rather on his mathematical and astronomical than on his poetic achievements."[71] Browne also notes that Khayyam appears in the *Chahar Maqala* (*Four Discourses*, a famous twelfth-century Persian prose work by Nizami ʿAruzi Samarqandi) "not in that section of the work which treats of Poets, but that which treats of Astrologers and Astronomers."[72]

Furuzanfar's treatment of Khayyam, like his treatment of Ibn Sina, primarily considers Khayyam's importance as a scientist and "great man" of Iranian history, whereas his poetry seems to be of secondary importance even in a work on Persian literary history.[73] In fact, Furuzanfar dismisses Khayyam's importance as a poet quite unsentimentally: "The quatrains that have been published in Khayyam's name, the number of some of which has reached up to 1200, are a collection of the philosophical thoughts of [various] different people and have been blindly attributed to Khayyam."[74] The inclusion of such national figures while dismissing their literary significance altogether would have been completely out of place in the earlier *tazkirah* tradition.

I.4   NEW READINGS OF OLD TEXTS

At the same time that the older genre of *tazkirah* is refashioned into the new genre of literary history (*tarikh-i adabiyat*), new ways of reading old texts also appear, emblematized by modernizing literary historians' increased attention to Firdawsi's *Shahnamah* and their reading of it as *tarikh*, or history in the modern sense.[75] Though labeling the *Shahnamah* as history is nothing new in the Persianate tradition, here what is meant by *history* is distinct from premodern

---

[71] Ibid., 2:246. The reference here is to the famous translation of Khayyam's quatrains by the English poet Edward FitzGerald (1809–83), beginning in 1859.

[72] Ibid.   [73] Furuzanfar, *Tarikh-i Adabiyat-i Iran*, 321.   [74] Ibid., 324.

[75] Literary historians were not alone in this; on the importance of Firdawsi's *Shahnamah* for Iranian nationalists of various stripes, see Marashi, "The Nation's Poet" and Adib-Moghaddam, *Psycho-nationalism*, 30–7.

uses of the word. The *Shahnamah* is an eleventh-century epic poem that narrates Iran's pre-Islamic history and mythology; the modernizers read it as a source for a modern approach to history, dedicating significant space to historical analysis of the text and praising it for its precision and historical accuracy. Premodern Persianate historians, however, were interested "less in recording the 'facts' of history than in the construction of a meaningful narrative."[76] Indeed, Julie Scott Meisami argues that, in the Persian historiography of Firdawsi's period, style and rhetoric came to take precedence over content or truth, and "message and style [were] inseparable."[77] She also suggests that premodern Persian historiography sought to represent the past "in terms of its meaningfulness for the [historiographers'] present," in contrast with the modern concern with recovering an image of the past as it was.[78] As Nasrin Askari shows, when medieval historians referenced the *Shahnamah*, they did so primarily for its poetic erudition, often citing verses containing maxims or eloquent turns of phrase, rather than as a means of retrieving information.[79]

Pasha M. Khan claims that the *Shahnamah* was indeed understood as history – in addition to romance – in nineteenth-century India, but what *kind* of history was meant must also be clarified. Khan proposes that a methodological split between *naqli* (transmission-based) and *'aqli* (intellect-based) approaches to historiography allowed for the former to accommodate a text with romantic and apparently supernatural elements such as the *Shahnamah*. *Naqli* historians judged the soundness of a history's chain of transmission (from the informants who witnessed the original event, to the transmitters to whom the information was relayed

---

[76] Meisami, *Persian Historiography*, 3.   [77] Ibid., 11–12.

[78] Ibid. See also Azimi, "Historiography in the Pahlavi Era," 368–9.

[79] Askari, *Medieval Reception*, 68–79. Mahmoud Omidsalar also stresses the point that while the *Shahnamah* contains a historical narrative, it was not written as a historical treatise and "strictly speaking, it is literature – *not* history" (Omidsalar, *Poetics and Politics*, 6, emphasis in original). He suggests that selective reading of parts of the poem, rather than reading it in its entirety, is the "reason for mistaking the poem for history" (Omidsalar, "Review," 238).

before their reports reached the historians), without necessarily considering the rationality of the historical narrative (which was the prerogative of 'aqli historians); thus they could treat the Shahnamah as a historical work on that basis. As Khan explains, "Once it has been established that the testimony [witnessing the original event] was sincerely given and properly transmitted, the report is not to be sifted by reason."[80] By focusing on naql (transmission of the story) rather than 'aql (intellect), an eleventh-century epic that includes tales of demons and dragons still can be seen by modernizers as recuperable for historiographical purposes.

While premodern historians may have read the Shahnamah as a kind of history, for modernizers it became the history, and in the early twentieth century it can be seen everywhere: in Shibli Nuʿmani's history of Persian literature (1918),[81] in a speech given by the German Orientalist Ernst Herzfeld to the Iranian Society for National Heritage (1926),[82] in the Iranian scholar Jalal al-Din Humaʾi's Tarikh-i Adabiyat-i Iran (History of the Literature of Iran, 1929),[83] and in the Iranian scholar Muhammad-Taqi Bahar's introduction to his critical edition of the Tarikh-i Sistan (History of Sistan, 1935),[84] to name only a few examples. Rather than reading the text as history per se, the Iranian historian Hasan Pirniya (1871–1935) took a different, albeit also innovative, approach to the Shahnamah in his Iran-i Qadim (Ancient Iran, 1928), treating the text as "an artifact ... rather than a source of knowledge."[85] In other words, for Pirniya the Shahnamah could be appreciated as a work of art and studied as a relic of particular historical circumstances rather than being read at face value as a source of accurate historical information.

---

[80] Khan, "Marvellous Histories," 542.   [81] Nuʿmani, Shiʾr al-ʿAjam, 1:110–23.

[82] Anjuman, Majmuʾah, 151–79.

[83] Humaʾi, Tarikh, 93. Humaʾi was a historian and educator who wrote one of the earliest Iranian literary history textbooks for pedagogical purposes, on which see Vejdani, Making History, 162–3.

[84] Bahar, Bahar va Adab, 1:316.   [85] Marashi, Nationalizing Iran, 102–3.

In the reading of the *Shahnamah* as history in the modern sense, it can be seen how the tropes of ancient modernity (locating Iranian modernity in the pre-Islamic past rather than the present) and *Shahnamah* as modern circulated not only textually, but also orally.[86] Textual influence was often more one-sided, as many more Iranian intellectuals were reading French texts than vice versa, and more Urdu speakers read Persian texts than the reverse. However, when examining how these ideas traveled verbally, a different dynamic – one of mutual exchange – can be observed.[87] Looking at interpersonal relationships between Iranians, Indians, and Europeans can give us a sense of that verbal exchange.

Shibli Nu'mani was one of the first modernizers to write at length about the importance of the *Shahnamah* as a historiographic source. In the first and fourth volumes of his *Shi'r al-'Ajam*, he dedicated several sections to reading the *Shahnamah* as a historiographic source and praising Firdawsi as a historian. Shibli was exposed to European thought and writing primarily through his friendship with the British Orientalist T. W. Arnold (1864–1930), his colleague at the Muhammadan Anglo-Oriental College. Their friendship was based on mutual exchange, as they taught each other Arabic and French, respectively. Muhammad-Taqi Bahar was unable to read Urdu, the language in which Shibli wrote about Firdawsi, but he learned about Shibli through conversation with Urdu-speaking friends like Da'i al-Islam Isfahani.[88] Bahar also may have discussed these ideas with his friend and Middle Persian tutor, Ernst Herzfeld (1879–1948), an archaeologist and philologist who delivered a speech in French before the Iranian Society for National Heritage titled "The *Shahnamah* and History." In his speech, Herzfeld groups Firdawsi together with premodern historians such as Tabari (839–923), Abu

---

[86] On this ancient modernity see Zia-Ebrahimi, "Self-Orientalization," 465–8.

[87] This type of mutual exchange is also addressed in Vejdani, *Making History*, 145–66.

[88] Bahar, *Bahar va Adab*, 2:139. Bahar was also familiar with Shibli via Browne's *Literary History*, which makes numerous references to Shibli's work; Browne read Urdu fluently, having studied it at Cambridge.

Hanifa Dinawari (828–96), and others and, like Shibli before him, considers the *Shahnamah* as an important source for Iranian pre-Islamic history.[89]

Bahar's model of Persian literary history and Herzfeld's model of Iranian art history also bear striking resemblance to one another. Bahar's division of Persian literature into periods follows the tripartite model (ancient, middle, and later) that had developed throughout the history of the *tazkirah* genre and was adopted by Shibli as well. However, one of Bahar's innovations was to add ethnogeographic and linguistic characteristics ("Khurasani style," "Iraqi style," and "Indian style") to what had been a vaguely defined and largely temporal periodization, as well as to identify a fourth period of literary renaissance (*bazgasht-i adabi* or literary return). Similarly, Herzfeld divides Iranian art into dynastic periods, beginning with the Achaemenid period, when "Iran was the center of the known world," followed by the Sasanian period, the "period of Iran's modernity," then the Seljuq period, when Iran was leading the Muslim nations and Europe had just begun to emerge from savagery, and finally the Safavid period, when Iranian art "was especially glorious."[90] While Herzfeld's model does not map directly onto Bahar's, the two still share many similarities: four periods, the issues of center and periphery,[91] and the decline model of history that locates Iranian modernity in the past rather than the present or future.[92] These similarities indicate that Bahar and Herzfeld were both contributing to and participating in the same discourse of modernization, a discourse that traveled as much verbally as textually.

In addition to sharing a modernizing approach to Firdawsi, there is significant overlap in Shibli and Bahar's respective Persian literary histories, and in Herzfeld's speech "The *Shahnamah* and History," in

---

[89] Anjuman, *Majmuʿah*, 151–79.   [90] Ibid., 42.

[91] On the question of center and periphery in Bahar's work, see Smith, "Literary Courage," 42–78, and Smith, "Literary Connections," 199.

[92] On the decline model in narratives of Iranian history, see Vejdani, "The Place of Islam" and Zia-Ebrahimi, "Arab Invasion."

terms of other figures they referenced as early (premodern) historians as well as contemporary Orientalists worthy of note. As can be expected, Shibli and Bahar both rely heavily on *tazkirah* sources (sharing most of their Iranian sources) and speak critically about the genre, particularly about its earliest and most prominent examples ('Awfi's *Lubab al-Albab* and Samarqandi's *Tazkirat al-Shu'ara'*). However, Shibli also cites a number of contemporary European Orientalists: his friend and French tutor T. W. Arnold, the French scholar James Darmesteter, the German Theodor Nöldeke, and the Russian Valentin Zhukovskii.

Similarly, Bahar cites Herzfeld, his Middle Persian tutor, as one of the masters of the "new science" of Iranian philology (calling to mind Foucault's description in *The Order of Things* of the modernizing trend toward the fragmentation of traditional knowledge production into distinct new sciences which organize knowledge into increasingly specific categories). Herzfeld also refers to the "new sciences" early in his speech to the Society for National Heritage.[93] Bahar and Herzfeld's shared use of this term reveals their common orientation as modernizers. They are also engaged with the same references, both premodern and contemporary. In addition to citing Herzfeld, Bahar also cites several premodern historians, including Tabari and Abu Hanifa Dinawari. Meanwhile, Herzfeld shares with Bahar his citation of Tabari and Dinawari, among others, and shares with Shibli his citation of the Orientalists Darmesteter and Nöldeke. This shared set of references further indicates that Shibli, Bahar, and Herzfeld, despite writing in different languages and in different contexts, drew on the same sources (and on each other). They were active participants in the same intertextual discourse that made use of premodern Iranian and Islamic sources as well as contemporary Orientalist sources in the writing of modern Persian literary history.

Bahar engaged critically with the work of his contemporaries and immediate predecessors. Just as the first generation of literary

---

[93] Anjuman, *Majmu'ah*, 151.

historians, like Shibli and Browne, had found in the deficiencies of the *tazkirah* genre an invitation to respond and produce literary history, so did Bahar a generation later, explaining that the history of Iranian literature is a story that has not yet been written, as what had been recorded in *tazkirah*s was incomplete and erroneous, not truly the history of Iranian literature. He identified the European and Indian literary historians who preceded him as similarly insufficient. "We don't have literary history" in the true meaning of the genre, Bahar proclaimed in a 1938 essay on the Persian translation of the fourth volume of Browne's *Literary History of Persia*. Browne's work had not done Persian literature justice, because in Bahar's view it lacked soul; nevertheless, he saw it as an "introduction" to his own project. Bahar also lauded Shibli as the first person outside Iran to manage to write a "critical history" of Persian literature, but faulted Shibli's *Shi'r al-'Ajam* for not addressing enough of the corpus of Persian poetry, especially the poets of India (indeed, it is true that Shibli neglected much of the Persian poetry of the subcontinent).[94] To do justice to Persian literary history, Bahar argued, one must research the rites, religion, customs, history, language, and politics of the Persianate world, and combine this knowledge with access to the great libraries of both Europe and Asia, as well as philological mastery of pre-Islamic Iranian languages like Avestan, Old Persian, and Middle Persian.[95] Bahar's manifesto in his review of Browne, laying out what he views as necessary for literary history, closely resembles the introduction to his later textbook *Sabkshinasi*.[96] In addition to these scholarly quali-fications, Bahar added one more: the scholar must be a Persian speaker (*ahl-i zaban*). He thereby positioned himself as uniquely qualified to complete the project begun by Shibli and Browne, to take advantage of

---

[94] Bahar, *Bahar va Adab*, 1:340–1.

[95] The relevance of pre-Islamic Iranian philology to the project of literary history is addressed in Chapter 3, "Origin Myths."

[96] In the introduction to *Sabkshinasi*, Bahar describes the science of stylistics as teaching students "ancient Iranian history, civilization, and customs" and familiarizing them with languages like Middle Persian (Bahar, *Sabkshinasi*, 1:*yad*.)

their accomplishments and surpass their shortcomings. Bahar would write the "unwritten history" of Persian literature, treating it as neither Islamic inheritance nor Orientalist curiosity, but rather as the *national* heritage of Iranians.

I.5   CONCLUSION

At the turn of the twentieth century, Iranians, Indians, and Europeans "converged in the writing of a comprehensive literary history without making a complete break with the *tazkira* tradition."[97] By viewing these texts as part of a larger genre of Persian literary history, a genre written not only in Persian, but in Urdu, English, German, Italian, and other languages, it can be seen that the genre of Persian literary history writing has developed through European Orientalists and Indian and Iranian litterateurs speaking in reply to one another, and has served as a vehicle for literary modernization, which was a verbal as well as textual discourse, sharing a particular set of boundaries and references. Literary modernization, while considered by its proponents to be novel, was more accurately a method of preserving tradition. This is best exemplified by a text like *Shi'r al-'Ajam*, which negotiates the encounter with colonial modernity by using European methodologies in order to preserve, reform, and promote the best of what Shibli viewed as Islamic civilization, including Persian literature. Likewise, while later Iranian textbooks appear fully modern, they are part of a trajectory that stretches back to the premodern *tazkirah* tradition, and they preserve some elements of that tradition even as they refashion them as a vehicle for nationalist modernization. Lefebvre's claim that modernity consists of endless repetition and refashioning of the old into the new rings true. Nevertheless, modernizers did not deem all of the premodern Persianate tradition salvageable. The next chapter will address their efforts to deal with Persian literature's homoerotic heritage.

---

[97] Sharma, "Redrawing the Boundaries," 60.

2   Erotics
From Bawdy to Bashful

The perspicacious ones turn in prayer towards the faces of
beautiful male youths / O Shaykh, whoever does not believe this is
not a Muslim

(Muhammad Fuzuli Baghdadi, d. 1556)[1]

Modernizing intellectuals who sought to write the history of Persian
literature faced a dilemma. For most of its millennium-long history,
Persian had abounded in frank, unabashed depictions of the erotic.
This had been the dominant literary convention for depicting love.
Moreover, much of the love and eros depicted in Persian poetry was
homoerotic. Poetry was a male-dominated profession, and the ideal
subject of beauty was a male youth on the cusp of puberty, with either
a hairless face or the earliest traces of hair (*khatt*) beginning to blos-
som on his cheeks and upper lip. Youths at this stage were referred to
as *amrad*s, among other names, and much poetry was dedicated to the
depiction of their beauty and to *amrad-parasti* or "*amrad*-worship":
older men gazing at them, desiring them, and engaging in sexual acts
with them.[2] A number of homoerotic themes are common in Persian
and Urdu poetry, whether merely contemplating the beauty of male
youths or describing physical acts like sodomy; these are called by a

---

[1] "*Rukh-i ziba-pisaran qiblah-yi ahl-i nazar ast / har kih bavar nakunad nist
musalman ay shaykh.*"

[2] As Joseph Allen Boone and Afsaneh Najmabadi have pointed out, the *amrad* is often
at an age that modern societies would term "adult." Translating *amrad* as "boy,"
which has conventionally been the case in the academic literature on Islamicate
sexualities, therefore inaccurately introduces pedophilic connotations (Boone,
Homoerotics of Orientalism, 64; Najmabadi, *Women with Mustaches*, 15). Here
I have opted to retain the word *amrad* or to translate it as "youth."

variety of names depending on the particular act described. At the risk of collapsing what were understood as separate practices into a single collective, for the sake of simplicity in this chapter I use *amrad-parasti* to refer to homoerotic practices in general. *Amrad-parasti* was frequently described or referenced in *tazkirah*s. *Tazkirah* writers were quite open – even gossipy – about sexuality, and often celebrated the homoerotic sexual exploits of the poets they discussed, and the wit and wordplay exercised in their bawdy poetry.

In the early modern period preceding the era of "Persianate modernity," many poets and authors of *tazkirah*s continued to revel in descriptions of carnal love and homoerotic practices. *Faqih*s, or Muslim jurists, condemned the latter as religiously illicit, but did not shy away from discussion of the details. Not everyone was so unreserved on sexual matters, of course. The poet and *tazkirah* writer Hazin Lahiji (1692–1766)'s account of his own love affair was quite chaste and restrained in its language.[3] However, in the nineteenth century these conventions began to shift, and the range of possibilities present in the early modern period narrowed significantly with the emergence of modern literary histories.[4] It is no coincidence that, from among these possible approaches to erotic matters, the approach that ultimately achieved hegemony was the one that aligned most closely with the puritanical conventions of a kind of ersatz Victorianism.

While homoeroticism had earlier been the dominant convention for discussing love in genres like the *ghazal*, by the end of the nineteenth century it ceded its influence to a new prudishness. The modern convention that emerged, especially in early literary

---

[3] Hazin Lahiji, *Tarikh-i Hazin*, 29–31; translated in Kia, "Muhammad 'Ali 'Hazin' Lahiji."

[4] On the shift in sexual conventions in Iran see Najmabadi, *Women with Mustaches*. These homoerotic conventions were also the norm in premodern Arabic, Urdu, and Turkic literary traditions, and were similarly erased by modernizers in the nineteenth and twentieth centuries. For the Arabic context see El-Rouayheb, *Before Homosexuality* and Massad, *Desiring Arabs*; for Urdu, Kugle, "Sultan Mahmud's Makeover" and Naim, *Urdu Texts and Contexts*, 19–41; for Turkish, Ze'evi, *Producing Desire*, and Andrews and Kalpaklı, *Age of Beloveds*.

histories, was a Victorian-influenced puritanism in matters of sexuality.[5] This approach, emphasizing bashfulness and silence about sexuality (particularly homoeroticism), ultimately narrowed the range of acceptable literary discourse on love and pleasure. The challenge for the first modern historians of Persian and Urdu literature was to reconcile themselves with the values they held as European-oriented modernizers, who disparaged homoerotic practices, and the homoeroticism and ribald, frank sexuality of the literature they discussed. Modernizers viewed their Victorian-influenced approach to sexuality as part of the conventions of modern writing, distancing themselves from the "unruly" sexuality of premodern genres.

Persianate writing cannot be accurately parsed without first understanding the relevant genre conventions. In the modern period, while some conventions may have shifted, others have endured, and the impact of these conventions has sometimes been underestimated in scholarship about modern Persianate writers. For example, historians of Persianate sexuality have argued that Iranians traveling to Europe encountered the heterosocial public space of European cities as a kind of paradise. Mohamad Tavakoli-Targhi describes Iranian travelers to Europe depicting it as heaven on earth, with "houri-like" women. "For them," he suggests, "the only cultural equivalent to the public display of male–female intimacy was the imaginary Muslim heaven."[6] Afsaneh Najmabadi concurs, noting that while travelers also portrayed Iran as a paradise, "what made Europe unique as a paradise ... was the sight of the hur [houri] and the ghilman," the maidens and male youths, respectively, found in Muslim depictions of heaven.[7]

---

[5] I use the term "Victorian-influenced puritanism" rather than simply "Victorianism" because actually existing Victorianism was much more complex than mere puritanism. See Steven Marcus, *The Other Victorians*. This complexity was largely lost on Iranians and Indians, who encountered an idealized form of puritanical Victorianism through their personal encounters with Europeans (many of whom were missionaries), as well as a sanitized English canon approved for export.

[6] Tavakoli-Targhi, *Refashioning Iran*, 54–5.

[7] Najmabadi, *Women with Mustaches*, 46.

These scholars are likely correct in their claims that Iranian travelers were dazzled by Europe and enchanted by the opportunities they encountered to socialize in mixed company, but what they overlook is the *conventionality* of these depictions. Describing various sites as paradise on earth and their inhabitants as houris and *ghilman* was a well-worn trope in Persianate writing, and this trope was often used to praise Asian locales as well. Seydi ʿAli Reis, the sixteenth-century Ottoman traveler, used the same language to describe Kabul in his Turkish-language travelogue *Mirʾat al-Mamalik* (*The Mirror of Countries*). Praising Kabul's beauty and its gardens, he compared the city to paradise and the city's gypsies (*luli*) to houris.[8] As Sunil Sharma has demonstrated, using the language of paradisiacal gardens, houris, and *ghilman* to depict Mughal courts and cities was a ubiquitous cliché.[9] Iranian travelers described Europe using the imagery of heaven not because they were at such a loss to describe what they saw, but because that was the standard imagery for describing wondrous new places in the tradition of Persianate travelogues. Clearly, there is much that can be missed (or misunderstood) without proper attention to conventions. This chapter examines the emerging sexual conventions of Persianate literary historiography, a set of thematic conventions developed and shared by those who set out to write the first literary histories of Persian, whether writing in Persian, Urdu, or European languages. The reader is duly warned that this chapter will contain several examples of vulgar, lascivious Persian poetry, replete with strong language and suggestive images.

2.1   PREMODERN CONVENTIONS

Before examining how modern literary historians dealt with the homoerotic heritage of Persian literature, we must first understand how *tazkirah* writers treated the same. Many *tazkirah*s displayed a

---

[8] Reis, *Mirʾâtüʾl-Memâlik*, 61. For an English translation, see Reis, "The Mirror of Countries," 369.

[9] Sharma, *Mughal Arcadia*. Examples include poets describing Akbar's court (24), Kashmir (86), and Agra (116) using this trope.

great deal of openness around sexual matters. Amir Kamal al-Din Husayn Gazurgahi's *tazkirah, Majalis al-'Ushshaq* (*Assemblies of the Lovers*, 1503–4), to take an example from relatively early on in the tradition, was specifically dedicated to the love lives of Sufi saints and other important figures. *Majalis al-'Ushshaq* featured many a tale of homoerotic love, and vividly illustrated manuscripts of this *tazkirah* circulated widely across the Persianate world.[10] By the later years of the Safavid–Mughal period, it had become conventional for *tazkirah* writers to include tales of certain poets' homoerotic exploits.

One of the places where homoerotic themes were frequently dealt with is in the story of the famously lewd satirist Suzani Samarqandi (d. 1166). Suzani was well-known for his *hazl* (or *hazliyat*), a genre of humorous, often obscene verse.[11] The story goes that the poet fell in love with a needlemaker's son (or his apprentice, in some versions) and took up an apprenticeship in the needlemaker's shop so that he could be close to the youth, thus earning him the *takhallus* or pen name of "Suzani" (needlemaker). Many *tazkirahs* also claim that Suzani repented at the end of his life and wrote a couple of pious *qasidahs* about the oneness of God (*tawhid*).

There are two interesting things to note here that illustrate how *tazkirah* writers were operating with a different set of assumptions, and a different set of conventions, than modern literary historians. Across a range of *tazkirahs* spanning different time periods and regions, the point the writers emphasize is that Suzani is a satirist (*hazil*), which is the most salient and even praiseworthy aspect of his poetry career. Take Amin Razi's *tazkirah, Haft Iqlim* (*The Seven Climes*, completed in 1593–4), as an example. Razi adds more texture to the story of Suzani falling in love with the needlemaker's son. His entry, in which he calls Suzani "Crown of the Poets" (*taj al-shu'ara*), is much longer than the entries on Suzani in earlier *tazkirahs*, yet

---

[10] On illustrated manuscripts of the *Majalis al-'Ushshaq* see Rizvi, "Between the Human and the Divine," and Uluç, "The *Majālis al-'Ushshāq*."

[11] On this genre see Meisami, "Genres of Court Literature," 265–8; on Suzani see Sprachman, *Suppressed Persian*, 18–25; Zipoli, *Irreverent Persia*, 31, 69–74.

while it still cites Suzani's *qasidah* on divine unity, it does not provide an account of his alleged repentance; the main thrust of the biography is the love story.[12] In Riza-Quli Khan Hidayat's *Majma' al-Fusaha'* (*Assembly of the Eloquent*), as in other *tazkirah*s, Suzani is praised as a master of mockery, famed for his coarse and satirical language that pierces his contemporaries like an arrow (*khadang-i haja*). Notably, Hidayat's entry on Suzani is five times the length of his entry on 'Umar Khayyam.[13] What is important about Suzani is his skilled invective, and if a *tazkirah* writer is going to erase aspects of his biography, it is Suzani's pious phase that can be ignored, not his homoerotic love affair.

In these *tazkirah*s Suzani's love of the needlemaker's son is not presented as a flaw that besmirches his reputation as a poet, nor is it a problem resolved by the solution of repentance. Instead, both are meaningful stages of his life. In the first stage of a young man's life, before his facial hair has filled in, he may become an *amrad*, the object of older men's desire. The next stage is adulthood, when a man grows a full beard and becomes a desiring subject himself. Suzani's repentance is not a denial of his earlier homoerotic dallying; as 'Ali Shir Nava'i states in his *tazkirah*, Suzani wrote devotional poetry to apologize for his vicious satires (*dar i'tizar-i hazl*), not to repent for his love life.[14] His atonement is an acceptance of the fact that he is an old man who has reached the final stage in a poet's life, when he turns to God and prepares for death. Though not every person would pass through all of these phases – for example, not every youth became an *amrad* – they were the conventional stages of a man's life, especially for poets. Sa'di was traditionally said to have spent thirty years studying, thirty years traveling (during which time he recorded much unorthodox behavior) and the final thirty years of his life in prayer. Traces of this life cycle linger on even in the modern period. The lack

---

[12] Razi, *Haft Iqlim*, 3:1571–4.

[13] Hidayat, *Majma' al-Fusaha'*, 2:920–31. See the previous chapter, "Histories," for Khayyam's position in *tazkirah*s and literary histories.

[14] Nava'i, *Majalis al-Nafa'is*, 351.

of contradiction between these life stages is illustrated convincingly by the character Yasin, a debauched young libertine in Naguib Mahfouz's *Cairo Trilogy* (1956–7), who explains: "Yes, we're dissolute inebriates [*sukriyyun fasiqun*], but we all plan to repent eventually."[15]

Throughout a wide range of *tazkirah*s, wherever issues of *amrad-parasti* ("worshipping handsome male youths") and *hazl* (bawdy verse) were addressed, it was with approbation rather than censure. In his seventeenth-century *tazkirah* titled *'Arafat al-'Ashiqin va 'Arasat al-'Arifin*, Taqi Awhadi praises Sa'di for his mastery in the genres of *ghazal* and *nasayih* (advice), but also *hazl*.[16] He similarly praises 'Ubayd-i Zakani (d. ca. 1370) for the same, and rather than castigating the notoriously bawdy fourteenth-century poet, he praises 'Ubayd for upright moral character.[17] Evidently, for Taqi Awhadi, writing vulgar poetry does not reflect poorly on a poet's morality. Nor did the *tazkirah* writers feel any need to comment negatively on Sa'di's homoerotic poetry. This is not out of any squeamishness on the matter – as demonstrated above, the *tazkirah*s are quite open in discussing lascivious anecdotes – but because there was no need to castigate or explain something they saw as quite normal and conventional.

Sa'di himself offers a facetious apology in Arabic prefacing his *khabisat* or obscene verses, in which he claims that some princes obliged him to write a book of nonsense (*laghw*) for them in the style of Suzani. Sa'di claims to have refused (and, in some variations of the preface, was duly threatened with death due to his refusal) before, having no other choice, yielding to the princes' demand. "I seek forgiveness from God the Almighty," he says, then notes that "people of virtue will not find fault in it [the poetry], for humor in speech is

---

[15] Mahfouz, *Cairo Trilogy*, 1274; the original Arabic is in Mahfuz, *al-Sukkariyyah*, 353. Yasin's father, al-Sayyid Ahmad 'Abd al-Jawad, is also depicted across the trilogy as living a life of licentious dissolution before piously repenting at the end of his life.

[16] Taqi Awhadi, *'Arafat al-'Ashiqin*, 3:1602.   [17] Ibid., 4:2470.

like salt in food."[18] Like my warning to the reader at the beginning of this chapter, Sa'di's apology is more tongue-in-cheek than serious. Premodern *tazkirah* writers sometimes apologized for citing obscene verses, but like Sa'di, they did so playfully rather than sincerely, much unlike the gravity with which modernizers would later treat the subject – that is, if they addressed it at all. Dawlatshah Samarqandi, whose *Tazkirat al-Shu'ara* (*Memorial of the Poets*) is one of the earliest extant *tazkirah*s, exemplifies this playfulness in his long and laudatory entry dedicated to 'Ubayd-i Zakani. Dawlatshah states that 'Ubayd's satirical and humorous works (*hazliyat, mutayyibat, ahaji*') are extremely famous but that "citing this kind of speech in this book is not appropriate." He then approvingly quotes a *qit'ah* (fragmentary poem) from 'Ubayd lampooning one of his contemporaries, the female poet Jahan Khatun:

> My lord, the world's [i.e., Jahan's] a faithless whore;
> Aren't you ashamed of this whore's fame?
> Go, seek some other cunt out, God
> Himself can't make Jahan feel shame.[19]

As can be seen, vulgar words like "whore" (*qahbah*) or "cunt" (*kus*) were hardly out of place in a *tazkirah*. Dawlatshah cites these obscene lines without censorship, as if to say with a wink, "this poetry is terribly inappropriate; here are some examples so you can see just how inappropriate it is."

Hidayat is just as frank and unabashed when mentioning various poets' homoerotic love affairs ('*ishq-bazi*), such as those between Muhtasham Kashani and the male minstrel Shatir Jalal,[20] Ahi Turshizi and Sultan Husayn Mirza,[21] and of course Suzani

---

[18] Sa'di, *Persian and Arabick Works*, 467. "People of virtue" (*ulu al-fadl*) is a Qur'anic phrase (24:22), while "humor in speech is like salt in food" is an Arabic adage.

[19] Dawlatshah, *Tazkirat al-Shu'ara*', 288–94. The translation is from Dick Davis, *Faces of Love*, lxi. *Jahan* means "world," hence the pun in the first line.

[20] Hidayat, *Majma' al-Fusaha*', 4:113. On this relationship between Kashani and Jalal, see Shamisa, *Shahidbazi*, 199–200.

[21] Hidayat, *Majma' al-Fusaha*', 4:5.

Samarqandi and the needlemaker's son.[22] Hidayat casually mentions that during the poet Shams al-Din Tabrizi's youth, his father forbade him from leaving the house until his beard began to grow, out of fear of accusations (presumably of Tabrizi being an object of interest to older men) and "because of [his] excessive beauty" [*az fart-i husn*].[23] He is similarly open when it comes to citing vulgar verse, such as that of the twelfth-century poet Mahsati Ganjavi. A rare female voice in classical Persian poetry, Mahsati is said to have composed bawdy, and sometimes even obscene, quatrains (*ruba'iyat*) in the court of the Seljuq ruler Ahmad Sanjar. Hidayat quotes quatrains by Mahsati which are so explicit that later editions of the *tazkirah* had to be censored when republished under the Islamic Republic of Iran. For example:

> The judge wept bitterly when his wife became pregnant / he asked spitefully, "what is all this?
>
> I'm old and my cock doesn't rise at all / and this whore is no Maryam, [so] whose child is this?"[24]

Expressing neither prudishness nor reproach about homoeroticism or *hazl*, Hidayat's reaction differed significantly from the Victorian-influenced modernizers whose early literary histories appeared soon after *Majma' al-Fusaha'*, as I detail later in this chapter.

2.2   TRANSITIONAL TEXTS

As the previous chapter "Histories" has demonstrated, Indians writing in Urdu played an especially salient role in refashioning the

---

[22] Ibid., 2:920.

[23] Ibid., 2:1043. The sixteenth-century Syrian mystic Muhammad ibn 'Iraq kept his pre-pubescent son veiled for the same reason; see El-Rouayheb, *Before Homosexuality*, 31.

[24] Hidayat, *Majma' al-Fusaha'*, [1961 CE] 1:3 1334. The censored edition ([2003] 1:3 2074) gives the first couplet and only the first two words of the second ("I'm old ..."), leaving the rest to the reader's imagination. There is doubt as to whether Mahsati was a real, historical figure, or merely a name to which various quatrains have been attributed, much in the vein of the similarly dubious 'Umar Khayyam; see Rypka, *History of Iranian Literature*, 199; Sharma, "Wandering Quatrains," 156–60.

tazkirah genre into modern literary history. In the late nineteenth-
and early twentieth-century texts that transitioned between the *tazkirah* and modern literary history, Persianate intellectuals strived to
negotiate between the conventions around sexuality discussed in the
previous section, and the emerging conventions of modern European-
style writing. Among these intellectuals was Muhammad Husayn
Azad, a "South Asian Victorian"[25] who sought to modernize Urdu
literature by calling for the abandonment of some of its classical
heritage, to be replaced with a new set of conventions rooted in
Indic and English traditions rather than in Persian.

Azad associated various languages with different sexual
conventions,[26] and his repudiation of "Persian" aesthetics lent itself
to a rejection of Persianate homoeroticism. In his history of Urdu
literature, *Ab-i Hayat* (*Water of Life*), he viewed the Indic language
Braj as possessing a natural and organic simplicity compatible with
the romanticism he favored, as opposed to the baroque and decadent
Persian tradition.[27] Reading these views against Azad's comments on
sexuality reveals how the poetics he favors is consonant with a
Victorian-influenced discomfort with homoeroticism. He claims that
the "love of boys instead of women" (*baja-e 'aurat ke larkon ka 'ishq*)
is "specific to the land of Persia [*mulk-i fars*]" in its origin.[28] This is to
be contrasted with the convention, found in numerous Indic literary
traditions, of females addressing a male beloved, which Azad says is
"a peculiar feature of the poetry of India."[29] Thus, while Azad
frames the issue as one of Indic simplicity versus Persian complexity,

---

[25] Pritchett, *Nets of Awareness*, xvii.

[26] This association had a good deal of precedence and was not a novel feature of Azad's
thought; see Sharma, "Translating Gender" for an eighteenth-century example.

[27] Ibid., 34. Braj, or Braj Bhasha, is a Hindi literary dialect that takes vocabulary,
poetics, and literary models from Sanskrit rather than Persian and Arabic.
Elsewhere, Azad describes it as a "purely [*khass*] Indian language" (Azad, *Ab-i
Hayat*, 6; Azad, *Shaping the Canon*, 57). He differed from many of his
contemporaries writing in Hindi, who considered Braj backwards and decadent; see
Busch, *Poetry of Kings*, 202–39.

[28] Azad, *Ab-i Hayat*, 53; Azad, *Shaping the Canon*, 85.

[29] Azad, *Ab-i Hayat*, 73; Azad, *Shaping the Canon*, 101.

it can also be read as Indic heteroeroticism versus Persian homoeroticism, tying together modernizing affinities for simplicity and heteroeroticism.

Azad's other remarks on Urdu poetic conventions were also congruent with a distaste for homoeroticism, for example in his call for novelty in poetic language. Writing about the need to reform Urdu, he declares:

> You have seen that whatever store of literature Urdu has, is thanks to Persian. The ancient poets of Persia extracted pleasure from every type of theme. ... The Urdu poets ... adopted the themes of beauty and love ... The wretched themes of beauty and love, the beloved's downy cheek [khatt] and beauty spot, and the words about the springtime in the garden – these have soaked deep into [our] mouths and tongues. If we want to say something, first we must forget these things, then after that we can bring forth, in their proper places, similarly novel metaphors, new similes, innovative constructions, and sophisticated verbal forms.[30]

Azad's primary concern is with eliminating tired clichés to make room for fresh and innovative modes of expression, yet it is worth focusing more closely on Azad's use of the word *khatt*. *Khatt* refers to the faint traces of facial hair that appear on a pubescent youth's upper lip and cheeks, an indicator of specifically male beauty and a common subject of praise in premodern Persian and Urdu poetry. Praise of a young man's *khatt* does not appear in the corpus of Urdu and Indo-Persian poetry in which a female addresses a male beloved; it belongs exclusively to the homoerotic tradition.[31] Azad's call for a new poetics free of the old clichés, therefore, is a call for a poetics that is also free of the conventions of homoeroticism. While Azad was himself hardly prudish, perhaps his text found such purchase – quickly

---

[30] Azad, *Ab-i Hayat*, 79; Azad, *Shaping the Canon*, 105–6. I have slightly modified Pritchett and Faruqi's translation.

[31] Shamisa, *Shahidbazi*, 51–3, 84.

becoming the "most widely read Urdu book of the past century"[32] – because it was so compatible with a larger cultural realignment. Replacing aestheticized Persianate erotics with "natural" (heteroerotic) poetics squared neatly with the coming of sexuality and the emergence of a heteronormative society.

A few decades later, one of Shibli Nu'mani's disciples, 'Abd al-Salam Nadvi (1883–1956) would reiterate Azad's point in similar language in his *Shi'r al-Hind* (*Poetry of India*, 1926): "Although moral philosophy [*falsafah-i akhlaq*], asceticism, and Sufism are all present in Urdu poetry, amorous topics [*'ashiqanah mazamin*] comprise the greatest share of it, and in passion and love as well, leaving aside emotions and events our poets have mostly become entangled in the snares of tresses and ringlets [*zulf u gesu*]." As Nadvi describes, this amorous tradition appeared "limited, outmoded, and inappropriate" in the eyes of a new, English-educated group of poets who sought to bring about a revolution in Urdu verse. They made the following "reformist demands":

(1) In the *ghazal*s of the Urdu language, amorous topics are always composed, which are mostly depraved [*mukhrib-i akhlaq*]. Therefore, moral and civilized [*tamadduni*] topics should be composed in their place and scenes of nature, for example mountains and steppes, deserts and wilderness, lightning and rain, and so on, should be depicted, just as these things are depicted in English poetry.

(2) Sometimes the beloved [*ma'shuq*] of the Urdu ghazal-composers is a man, and men loving men is unnatural [*mard se mard ka ta'ashshuq khilaf-i fitrat hai*]. Although expressing love and desire for women is not unnatural, it is uncivilized. Therefore, in order to express love and desire, the general, open form of beauty and elegance should be kept in mind, so that it can be applied to every beautiful person, or rather every beautiful thing.[33]

---

[32] Azad, *Shaping the Canon*, 1; on the text's ubiquitous influence see also Pritchett, *Nets of Awareness*, 40.

[33] Nadvi, *Shi'r al-Hind*, 376–7. Numbering is in the original.

Like Azad, Nadvi called for reforming the aesthetics and poetics of Urdu, but here he made the sexual dimension of that call to reform more salient and more explicit. He clearly juxtaposes "depraved" homoerotic Urdu *ghazal*s with "civilized" English landscape poetry.[34]

Azad returns to the subject of facial hair later in *Ab-i Hayat*. He notes with squeamishness that "because of their extreme obscenity [*fuhsh*], I have refrained from recording" some of Sayyid Insha's satiric verses [*hajv*],[35] and he mentions disapprovingly that Insha shaved his beard completely, making similarly moralistic observations about other male poets who shaved their beards.[36] Prior to the popularization of European beauty standards, for an adult Muslim man to shave his beard was to imitate the *amrad*, or beardless youth, and seek to be the object of an adult man's sexual desire. This practice was stigmatized as deviant behavior; for men to gaze at pubescent male youths with desire was celebrated, but for a grown man to seek to be gazed at was condemned.[37] Azad's distaste for adult male beardlessness indicates how, despite his enthusiastic embrace of Western culture and Victorian-influenced sexual mores, his views on masculinity and sexuality still retained elements of propriety that predate British colonialism. Rather than replacing one set of views with another, he may have found it easier to combine the two, resulting in the ideal of a man who does not shave (according to Indo-Muslim values) and does not engage in homoeroticism (according to European values, which were steadfastly becoming Indian values as well).[38]

Following *Ab-i Hayat*, and, as discussed in Chapter 1, most likely under its influence, came Shibli Nuʿmani's literary history of

---

[34] On the kind of "natural" English aesthetics Nadvi calls for, see Pritchett, *Nets of Awareness*, chapter 11; Burney, "Locating the World."

[35] Azad, *Ab-i Hayat*, 260; Azad, *Shaping the Canon*, 233.

[36] Azad, *Ab-i Hayat*, 242, 270; Azad, *Shaping the Canon*, 218, 238.

[37] For a mid-nineteenth-century example of Indian Muslims' distaste for beard trimming, see Sen, "Contested Sites"; for contemporaneous Iranian views on the subject see Najmabadi, *Women with Mustaches*, 15–25.

[38] For another contemporary example of this combination of values see Kia, "Indian Friends," 411.

Persian, *Shi'r al-'Ajam* (*Poetry of the Persians*). Shibli addresses the issue of homoeroticism in Persian literature several times in this work. After describing how, in his view, human nature dictates that men desire women, and that Hindustani literature is *unusual* though not *unnatural* in depicting women desiring men, he states that Persian literature, which is the "highest and most subtle in the world," is "laid to waste" through the "absurdity" of the depiction of male–male desire, in particular *amrad-parasti* or "worshipping handsome male youths."[39] Shibli expresses bashfulness and reluctance to even mention the subject, but continues, after stating that it is the author's religious duty (*farz*) to explain the causes of this practice. This warning to the reader is of a fundamentally different nature than Sa'di's facetious apology for his crude verses. Shibli then goes on to cite the Arab scholar Abu Hilal al-'Askari (d. 1005) as saying that the Bedouins were originally unfamiliar with *amrad-parasti*, but after spending so much time away from their wives, alone with beautiful young Turkish male slaves, Arab soldiers developed a taste for male youths, and by the third or fourth Islamic century, Arab poets extolled the virtues of *amrad-parasti*, and similar conditions led to its prevalence among Iranians as well.

C. M. Naim argues that premodern Indo-Muslim society was "mostly indifferent . . . in matters related to sexual tastes and habits," including the matter of *amrad-parasti*,[40] but for Shibli sexuality is a source of anxiety; he feels a "duty" to locate the origins of homoerotic practices. This is something he shares not only with Azad, but also with early modern Arab literary critics, as Joseph Massad describes in detail in *Desiring Arabs*. Massad cites various Arab literary critics under European influence who claim that Bedouin men had no sexual interest in male youths and who locate the origins of *amrad-parasti* among the Arabs either with the Persians or with the mixture of Arab soldiers with Turkish male slaves as Shibli contends. These critics

---

[39] Nu'mani, *Shi'r al-'Ajam*, 4:190.
[40] Naim, *Urdu Texts and Contexts*, 31, 33, 39–40.

included numerous literary historians of Arabic like Jurji Zaydan (1861–1914), Ahmad Amin (1878–1954), and others.[41] Muhammad-Taqi Bahar also deploys a strikingly similar argument, claiming that Arab commanders were "forced" (*majbur*) to indulge in *amrad-parasti* because of the lack of opportunity to socialize with women.[42]

The concern with origins is part of the pathologization of divergent sexual practices; locating the cause of a disease is the first step toward finding a cure, and it is precisely this kind of medical language Shibli deploys when discussing *amrad-parasti*, referring to it as a disease (*bimari* or *maraz*). Shibli addresses *amrad-parasti* elsewhere when talking about the great classical Persian poets Hafiz (1326–90) and Shaykh Saʿdi (ca. 1210–92). He explains away Hafiz's *amrad-parasti* as simply following the thematic conventions of Sufi poetry; when it comes to Saʿdi, he excuses this "blemish" (*dagh*) by pointing to Saʿdi's piety and showing how Saʿdi's indulgence in *amrad-parasti* allows him to later condemn it convincingly: "The Shaykh, having become sick and then recovered, was better able than others to be aware of the reality, nature, signs, and cure for those moral diseases."[43] One might think similarly of a recovering alcoholic who can make a far more compelling case against alcoholism than a life-long teetotaler. In these discussions, Shibli reiterates his discomfort with discussing the topic, saying that the details of Saʿdi's *amrad-parasti* "cannot even be mentioned." Such reticence is noteworthy. Saʿdi himself notes in his *Gulistan* that some would consider it a weakness (ʿajz) were he to avoid the subject.[44] Saʿdi, of course, belonged to the tradition discussed at the beginning of this chapter, one that spoke openly and without embarrassment about homoeroticism. Shibli sees himself as preserving tradition, but here he breaks

---

[41] Massad, *Desiring Arabs*, 54–63, 72–6, 83–6.

[42] Bahar, *Bahar va Adab*, 1:146. This argument was widespread among Iranian reformers of the era; see Najmabadi, *Women with Mustaches*, 55–7. Many European Orientalists also believed that homoerotic practices in the Islamicate world stemmed from men lacking access to women due to gender segregation.

[43] Nuʿmani, *Shiʾr al-ʿAjam*, 2:51–2.   [44] Saʿdi, *Gulistan-i Saʿdi*, 113.

with that earlier Persianate convention of unabashed openness;
instead, Shibli is "inciting discourse" on sexuality.[45]

Shibli's primary concerns were the preservation and modernization of Islam and Arabic education and, more broadly, the welfare of
the Indian subcontinent's Muslim communities. Shibli's mindset was
similar to that of other reformers across the Muslim world whose
religious identities and outlooks became influenced by European scientific rationalism as well as a kind of Victorianism. Thus, while he
gives a particularly Islamic framework to *Shi'r al-'Ajam*, his uneasi-
ness in discussing homoerotic practices seems more Victorian than
strictly Islamic. While injunctions against same-sex sexual activity
can be found in Islamic religious texts, no such injunctions against
open discussion of sexual matters existed in the Islamic tradition.
Again, a parallel can be drawn to the Arabic context; the precolonial
Arabs, including Muslim religious scholars, tended to be frank and
rather unhesitant in openly discussing sexual practices, including
homoerotic ones, whereas modernizing intellectuals under Western
influence inherited not only the Victorian distaste for homoerotic
practices, but the prudishness about sexuality altogether as well.[46]

All the books of Hanafi *fiqh* (jurisprudence) which formed the
tradition Shibli engaged with were straightforward and unapologetic
on sexual matters, including sodomy. The Hanafi jurist al-Sarakhsi

---

[45] "Incitement to discourse" is how Foucault describes the modern compulsion to
transform sex into discourse, to speak of sex not only as something to be morally
judged but as something to be managed and administered. Foucault sees as essential
the "recognized necessity of overcoming this hesitation" to speak about the topic.
He writes, as if describing Shibli, that "one had to speak of sex; one had to speak
publicly and in a manner that was not determined by the division between licit and
illicit, even if the speaker maintained the distinction for himself (which is what
these solemn and preliminary declarations were intended to show)" (Foucault,
History of Sexuality, 1:24).

[46] For the views of precolonial Arab Muslim religious scholars, see El-Rouayheb,
Before Homosexuality, 111–51; on Arab modernizing intellectuals see Massad,
Desiring Arabs, 51–98. Writing only a few decades earlier than Shibli, the Lebanese
intellectual Ahmad Faris al-Shidyaq laments the prudery of his era but notes that
the *'ulama* discussed sexual issues openly, without embarrassment (Al-Shidyaq,
Leg over Leg, 2:186–9).

(d. 1090), much admired by Shibli, was frank and unembarrassed when discussing these subjects.[47] A later scholar, ibn 'Abidin (1784–1842), author of the authoritative Hanafi commentary *Radd al-Muhtar 'ala al-Durr al-Mukhtar*, displayed no reticence in addressing the subject. As is typical of *fiqh* literature, he was straight to the point and did not mince words. In *Radd al-Muhtar* under the heading "[On the] Issue of Anal Intercourse [*wat' al-dubr*]," he stated that Abu Hanifa's position was that there is no *hadd* punishment for anal intercourse with a male youth (*sabiyy*), wife, or female slave (*amah*).[48] The canonical *al-Fatawa al-'Alamgiriyyah* (also known as *al-Fatawa al-Hindiyyah*, completed in 1672), a source of Anglo-Muhammadan law in British India during Shibli's time, was just as blunt: "according to Abu Hanifa, if [a man] has sexual intercourse with a woman in her anus or sodomizes a male youth [*wati'a imra'ata fi dubriha aw lata bi-ghulamin*]" there is no *hadd* punishment.[49] No apologies, no hand-wringing. The precolonial Islamic tradition had little of Shibli's scruples about discussing sexuality.

2.3 THE CONVENTIONS OF LITERARY HISTORY

A far more pronounced example of the modern reluctance about sexuality can be found in E. G. Browne's massive *Literary History of Persia*. His work spans four volumes and over 2,200 pages, covering an even more expansive time period than Shibli's *Shi'r al-'Ajam* – from the Sasanian period, beginning in the year 226, to the contemporary poets of his time in 1924 – and yet, it is totally silent on the subject of sexuality. None of the words relevant to this topic – *sexuality, homoerotic, homosexual, pederasty,* or *sodomy* – appear at all in any of his four volumes; nor do any of their derived forms

---

[47] For al-Sarakhsi's treatment of sodomy see Yacoob, "Hermeneutics of Desire," 97–108.

[48] Ibn 'Abidin, *Radd al-Muhtar*, 6:38. *Hadd* (plural *hudud*) refers to fixed punishment for severe crimes. Abu Hanifa considered sodomy to be illicit, but its punishment fell under the category of *ta'zir* or discretionary punishment.

[49] Nizam, *Al-Fatawa al-Hindiyyah* 2:166.

(for example, *homosexuality* instead of *homosexual*), nor any relevant Persian terms (*amrad, ghulam, bi-rish, shahid, nazar-bazi, bachchah-bazi*, and so on). Browne omits discussion of sexuality even where warranted by the subject matter. For example, in his discussion of the *tazkirah Majalis al-'Ushshaq*, on the (often homoerotic) love lives of notable figures, Browne neglects the erotic character of the work and merely refers euphemistically to the "Platonic love-affair[s]" of the personages mentioned, after dismissing the text with the claim that it "hardly deserves to be mentioned as a serious biographical work."[50] Only on occasion does Browne even hint at the subject, for example in his biography of the poet Fakhr al-Din 'Iraqi (d. 1289), where he suggests that 'Iraqi's ghazals have an "erotic character," leading to them being harshly criticized by Europeans like the Austrian Orientalist Aloys Sprenger (1813–93), who "find scandalous in a Persian sentiments which in Plato they either admire or ignore." Browne also obliquely refers to the story of how 'Iraqi became enamored of a beautiful young man and, "attracted by the beauty of the young dervish," joined his party of Sufis and followed them from Hamadan to India.[51]

Another scabrous poet Browne discusses is 'Ubayd-i Zakani. He says of the "unscrupulous" 'Ubayd that "his language is frequently so coarse as to render a large part of his writings unfit for translation."[52] Browne treads carefully in translation, rendering profanities like *guh* (shit) as "dirt" and homoerotic terms like *shahid* (beautiful male youth) in gender-neutral language ("beauties"). When the word *amrad* is quoted, he leaves it untranslated and even untransliterated, written in the Persian script so as to be unintelligible to the

---

[50] Browne, *Literary History*, 3:439–40.

[51] Ibid., 3:124–5. Sprenger himself says of 'Iraqi that "he was given, even more than other Persian poets, to the *disgusting crimes* of which they boast" (*Catalogue*, 440–1, emphasis added). On 'Iraqi and the homoerotic tradition see Miller, "Embodying the Beloved."

[52] Browne, *Literary History*, 3:230–57. Despite Browne's warning, Paul Sprachman has translated some of 'Ubayd-i Zakani's most obscene poetry. See Sprachman, *Suppressed Persian*, 44–75.

Anglophone reader. Elsewhere, he follows the practice of other European Orientalists of translating racy words or phrases into Latin rather than English. This protects the innocent reader, as anyone educated enough to read Latin will likely have already encountered the homoerotic poetry of Catullus. Browne even censors some "unsuitable passages" when translating biographical details about the poet. In fact, one of the passages he removes from his translation is ʿUbayd's satirical verses about Jahan Khatun, discussed earlier in this chapter. As usual, he does *not* clarify the nature of ʿUbayd-i Zakani's ribaldry. His laconic single-sentence description of ʿUbayd's *Rishnamah* (*Book of the Beard*) is particularly telling: "a fantastic dialogue between ʿUbayd-i Zákání and the beard considered as the destroyer of youthful beauty." Nowhere does Browne mention the homoerotic focus of the *Rishnamah*, yet his praise for the text reveals that Browne is no prude; instead, he is bound to follow the Victorian-influenced conventions of literary history.

The Iranian literary historian Badiʿ al-Zaman Furuzanfar is just as reticent as Browne on the subject. Furuzanfar describes Abu Nuwas as being of Iranian origin, a "sweet-tongued" poet with a special talent for describing and celebrating hunting and wine. However, missing from Furuzanfar's depiction is the other subject Abu Nuwas was famed for describing: beautiful male youths. There is no mention of Abu Nuwas's homoerotic poetry, though he does note that the poet was best known for *hijaʾ*, a genre of satiric, invective verse which frequently made use of crude sexual references and obscenity.[53] When another Iranian literary scholar, Muhammad-Taqi Bahar, discusses *hijaʾ*, he is similarly silent about its sexual aspects, describing the composition of *hajv* (another word for *hijaʾ*) as a wretched profession, one without an iota of respect. Of note, he references Saʿdi's humor (*shukhi-ha*), found at the end of Saʿdi's *kulliyat* (collected works), without any mention of its crudeness or sexuality.[54]

[53] Furuzanfar, *Tarikh-i Adabiyat-i Iran*, 62–3. [54] Bahar, *Bahar va Adab*, 1:285–6.

The fact that Furuzanfar makes absolutely no mention of anything related to homoeroticism in his *Sukhan va Sukhanvaran* (*Poetry and Poets*, 1933) is understandable given that the book (which retains the traditional biographical anthology format of the *tazkirah*) was ordered by Iran's Education Commission, which outlined his task in no uncertain terms. In addition to specifying the book's structure and its contents, including the need for footnotes to clarify unfamiliar vocabulary, they instructed him to "avoid citing poems which have unpleasant [*napasand*] words or meanings and everything which is opposed to morality [*akhlaq*] and that which refers to unnatural love [*'ishq-i ghayr-i tabi'i*] and that which is incompatible with civilization [*munafi-yi tamaddun*]."[55] Furuzanfar is equally silent in *Tarikh-i Adabiyat-i Iran* (*History of Iranian Literature*, 1938); the only time he comes close to mentioning anything homoerotic is a brief mention of the "friendship" (*dusti*) between Sultan Mahmud of Ghazni and his male slave Ayaz, an oblique reference to their storied love.[56]

The *Encyclopædia Iranica* notes in its entry on "Homosexuality in Persian Literature" that:

> it is surprising that among historians of Persian literature, from Hermann Ethé (q.v.), E. G. Browne (q.v.), A. J. Arberry (q.v.), and Jan Rypka, to Badi'-al-Zamān Foruzānfar (q.v.), Moḥammad-Taqi Bahār (q.v.), Ḏabiḥ-Allāh Ṣafā (q.v.), and 'Abd-al-Ḥosayn Zarrinkub, none has broached the issue as such and discussed the implications of homosexual love in the development of the motifs, images, and metaphors in Persian poetry.[57]

Some silences, like Furuzanfar's, may be explained by their institutional restraints, while other silences are more complex. The convention of silence developed in relation to legal conditions; Browne in England and Shibli in India had British obscenity laws to

---

[55] Furuzanfar, *Sukhan va Sukhanvaran*, 9. On the Education Commission in Iran see Vejdani, *Making History*, 61–2.

[56] Furuzanfar, *Tarikh-i Adabiyat-i Iran*, 185.

[57] "HOMOSEXUALITY iii. IN PERSIAN LITERATURE."

contend with, and Iranians faced censorship as well. In the 1940s, publishing "material subversive to public morality" in Iran was punishable with a year in prison.[58] "Public morality" was not necessarily synonymous with "popular sentiment"; the official censor of cinema and theater in Tehran at that time, for example, was an American woman, Nilla Cram Cook.[59] Yet silence across the board – from British, German, and Czech Orientalists to Iranians and Indians alike – indicates that this is more than the product of legal or institutional repercussions in one setting, but a nearly universal convention of the genre of modern literary history. The networks of citation and circulation outlined in the introduction and Chapter 1 ensured that even as settings shifted and censorship laws changed, the puritan conventions remained. By examining epistolary correspondence, private diaries, and other unpublished sources, new insight is gained which helps us go beyond the legal context to make sense of some of the silences in literary histories.

2.4 THE LIVES OF LITTERATEURS

In their influential study of early modern Ottoman love poetry, Turkish literature scholars Walter G. Andrews and Mehmet Kalpaklı analyze what they call "scripted behavior." Borrowing the concept from the sociology of sexuality, they explore how social constructs both reflect and are constitutive of social behavior.[60] Literature and behavior, for them, interact mutually. Although their argument is compelling, I suggest something different here: that the genre of Persian literary history was, like literature itself, highly conventional, and therefore can sometimes be completely detached from life experiences.

If the idea that in the premodern Persianate tradition homoeroticism was a genre convention is taken seriously, then

---

[58] McFarland, "The Crises in Iran," 162.
[59] Cook, "The Theater and Ballet Arts of Iran," 409.
[60] Andrews and Kalpaklı, *Age of Beloveds*, 37–8.

whether or to what degree it corresponded to lived experience is beyond the point; this was a generic ideal for depicting beauty and love. This point has long been accepted in the scholarship on premodern Persianate literature, but I suggest we apply it to modern literature as well. The puritanism of the modern genre of literary history is, like the homoeroticism of premodern genres, conventional, and not necessarily grounded in the reality of the lives of the literary historians themselves. Shibli Nu'mani, for example, harshly criticized homoerotic literature, yet he may have shared a homoerotic relationship with his student Abu'l Kalam Azad (1888–1958).[61] Although E. G. Browne seemed to faithfully adhere to Victorian sexual mores in his *Literary History of Persia*, his personal diaries reveal quite another story.

As discussed above, Shibli waxes Victorian in his *Shi'r al-'Ajam*, adopting a tone of discomfort when discussing homoeroticism, which he treats as if clinically diagnosing a patient with an unpleasant condition whose origins must be sought out. Yet consider Shibli's relationship with Abu'l Kalam Azad. The two met in Bombay in early 1905, when Azad was sixteen – still a "beardless, mustacheless youth" in the words of Shibli's biographer Muhammad Amin Zubairi – and they soon grew close.[62] Azad became Shibli's protégé and worked with him as editor of the journal *al-Nadwa*, published from the Nadwat al-'Ulama Islamic seminary in Lucknow. Azad recalls in his memoirs how he fell under Shibli's spell. He describes his childhood (*'ahd-i tifli*) as a "dream of pleasure" (*khvab-i 'aysh*) and continues to refer to a period of his youth, lasting a year and five months, in entirely abstract, ambiguous language. Therein he alludes to earthly love (*'ishq-i majaz*), using a term that evokes the homoerotic subtext of *amrad-parasti*, along with allusions to his

---

[61] Not to be confused with Muhammad Husayn Azad. I thank Gregory Maxwell Bruce for suggesting this possibility to me and sharing relevant sources.

[62] Zubairi, *Shibli ki Rangin Zindagi*, 88. In other words, he was an *amrad*.

own licentiousness (*rindi*).[63] "The profligacy of pleasure-seekers brought me to the highway of passion and love," Azad writes, before he eventually overcame this state: "the pain first became a wound, then a scar, and now, having become an ulcer, is kept safe in a hidden chamber of my heart."[64] Shibli himself writes in a letter that among his "crimes" (referring to the events that led to his expulsion from the Nadwat al-'Ulama seminary), one crime was "loving Abu'l Kalam."[65] His wording, like Azad's, is too ambiguous to allow us to draw conclusions, but all their recollections suggest the possibility of Shibli and Azad trekking along the well-traveled path of earthly love between the older male guide and his younger male initiate. Such a possibility may allow us to interpret Shibli's remarks on the homoeroticism of Sa'di ("the Shaykh, having become sick and then recovered, was better able than others to be aware of the reality, nature, signs, and cure for those moral diseases") as autobiographical.

Silence can be understood, as Foucault argues in his *History of Sexuality*, not as a limit to discourse, but as another element of discourse alongside the things one does say.[66] Browne's silence on sexuality and homoeroticism, topics about which he was no doubt well aware, speaks volumes both about his anxieties regarding these subjects and about his relationship to his object of study.[67] His private diaries hint at a similar homoerotic affair at odds with his properly Victorian *Literary History of Persia*. While the diaries of his travels in Iran in 1887–8 have received scholarly attention and were ultimately published as *A Year Amongst the Persians* (1893), Browne's earlier personal diaries dating to his late teens and early twenties have never before been studied. Today, these diaries sit neglected in the archives

---

[63] The expression used here comes from Sufi terminology, differentiating between *'ishq-i haqiqi* "real love" – that is, love of God – and *'ishq-i majazi*, "earthly love," more literally translated as "metaphorical love" because it is understood to be a metaphor for divine love. The latter typically refers to homoerotic practices between adult men and male youths.

[64] Quoted in Zubairi, *Shibli ki Rangin Zindagi*, 83–5.   [65] Ibid., 89.

[66] Foucault, *History of Sexuality*, 1:27.

[67] Here I am influenced by the approach taken by Anjali Arondekar in *For the Record*.

of Pembroke College at the University of Cambridge. By reading across multiple diaries from 1879–89, a story about Browne's private life unfolds.

In a diary branded T. J. & J. SMITH'S SMALL SCRIBBLING DIARY WITH AN ALMANAC FOR 1879, Browne doodled and wrote notes to himself in various languages, above all English.[68] He also developed a secret code for writing private notes that would be unintelligible to prying eyes: English idiosyncratically transliterated into Perso-Arabic or Ottoman Turkish orthography. Anyone sneaking a look at Browne's diary would have to know multiple languages to even begin attempting to crack his code.[69] The code was sometimes used for seemingly banal points such as recording whether he was late for breakfast (a point he noted on many days); most likely, he was simply livening up this mundane task by writing in code.[70] However, Browne also noted more personal affairs in his private code. He wrote (in code) of visitors that they had a lady he "thought rather pretty but I didn't ..."[71] Browne left the sentence unfinished.

By the mid-1880s, Browne had advanced significantly in his language studies and progressed to writing private notes to himself in Persian about love prospects.[72] He titles an entry on February 15, 1884 "*asrarnamah-yi man*" ("my book of secrets") and proceeds to write in Persian about a letter he received. Browne enigmatically

---

[68] Cambridge University Library Browne Papers, Box 1– Diaries 1879–83. Atop one page early in the journal, he wrote "this book is my diary" in both Turkish and Persian, with slight mistakes in each language.

[69] Some letters made use of Arabic pronunciation, such as the three-dotted *tha'* to spell "th" as in "thing" (this letter would have been pronounced as [s] in Persian and Turkish); others were strictly transliterated based on English spelling such as نوز for "now" or داوغتر for "daughter."

[70] Given that he often noted his progress in studying Turkish, the code may have been a form of practice more than anything else. For example, Tuesday, January 21, 1879. Browne writes in code: "I think I make [*sic*] progress with my Turkish and got to know more words but it is rather difficult."

[71] Thursday, January 9, 1879. Ellipsis in original. Browne's practice was not unique. Half a century earlier, David Ochterlony Dyce Sombre, an Anglo-Indian, kept an English diary in which he switched to Persian to record intimate thoughts of erotic nature. See Fisher, "Conflicting Meanings," 232–5.

[72] For example, the entries dated February 13, 1885 or March 2, 1885.

mentions male companions such as *Ebdun*, writing in Persian that "last night I did not sleep well and constantly imagined Ebdun."[73] Another male companion who appears frequently in the diary is referred to as the "Ferishta" ("angel" in Persian). One entry reads "the FERISHTA came to dinner with me, & we sat & smoked & talked all the evening. I then walked back with him (bázú dar bázú) [arm in arm]."[74] Browne writes these men's names in Persian in the middle of otherwise English sentences. He does this as well when referring to illicit activities. For example, in a later entry he mentions the arrival of a box of items imported from Persia; two days later, he says he "awoke very late after my *tiryak*," using the Persian word for opium.[75]

Elsewhere, Browne says the Ferishta "was so nice and looked so jolly" (again in code).[76] Two days later, he mentions that he met with the Ferishta. In a different diary, the entry for the corresponding day says, underlined in blue ink, "Fox & I went for a walk &" – and the rest of the sentence is erased. About a week later, he writes "I was very blue & depressed on account of ... not having seen the Ferishta to say goodbye."[77] Browne writes in the "Brief Diary" that the "Ferishta came for a few minutes" – corresponding to an entry with the same date in the large diary, which reads in Ottoman Turkish "the Ferishta visited me for one or two minutes."[78]

Most likely the "Ferishta" was someone named Willie Latham – though unfortunately nothing more is known about him.[79] He hints at their relationship in another entry in the Brief Diary: "Ferishta

---

[73] March 13, 1884. This could be how he transliterated the "Ebden" he refers to (in English) elsewhere in his diaries.

[74] April 24, 1884. Browne's transliteration. Here Browne has written "arm in arm" in transliterated Persian rather than English.

[75] January 22, 1889. Browne had become addicted to opium during his travels in Iran over the previous year (Browne, *A Year Amongst the Persians*, 476–7).

[76] May 28, 1881, in "Brief Diary of My Life History December 1882."

[77] June 8, 1881 (Brief Diary).

[78] "*Firishtah beni ziyaret ... bir iki dakika.*" July 11, 1881 (Brief Diary); July 11, 1881 (large diary).

[79] On July 14, 1881, Browne writes in the Brief Diary that "the Ferishta came in for a minute," and on the same date he writes in the large diary that "Willie Latham came at 9.20, but went away directly [when] he saw Johnson was there." The next

came, & woke me up ... he was cheeky" (July 21, 1881); on the same day he writes in the large diary "was woke up by Willie Latham coming. He was very cheeky." While certainly more colorful than his *Literary History*, Browne nevertheless censors even his own diaries at times. Many entries on the "Ferishta" have parts which have been erased or blacked out. On January 11, 1883, in the large diary Browne writes that he showed a friend the Ferishta's photograph. The rest of the entry is erased with such vigor that the eraser tore a small hole in the page. The following day, an entry in the same diary contains a note, written in all capitals and underlined, which says "EVIL THOUGHTS NECESSARILY PRODUCE UNHAPPINESS, & PAIN."

On April 26, 1883, Browne was visited by the "younger Lathams" Arthur and Percy. Arthur "looked charming." Much of the rest is erased, but *husn-i u ta'ajjub kardam* "I was surprised [by] his beauty" is legible. On June 22, 1883, Browne mentions seeing the Ferishta again after a long time: he describes him as "charming as ever," adding: "O the delight of seeing him again, even for 5 minutes." On the following day Browne "was allowed again to enter the sanctum of the FERISHTA, & spent an hour in his delightful society."

Browne often summarized personal correspondence in Persian. On April 3, 1884, he mentioned "letters from Fox & Gibb [regarding] bacha-parasts," that is, pederasts (literally "boy-worshippers") – a term that does not appear anywhere in his *Literary History of Persia*. He frequently recalls discussing *'ishq-i majazi* ("allegorical love," often referring to the homoerotic practice of *amrad-parasti*) with his tutor Chatterjee and others. These topics are never directly broached in his *Literary History* – neither the words he uses in his diary, nor the concepts they refer to, are ever mentioned.

Like Shibli, Browne is more allusive than explicit, writing in code to avoid being discovered. Given the context of late nineteenth-

---

day, he writes in the Brief Diary "Ferishta came for 20 minutes" and confirms in the large diary that "Willie Latham came, but only stayed about 20 min. or so."

century England, Browne's need for secrecy is understandable. Sodomy was illegal, and in 1885 – in the midst of his relationship with the Ferishta, as recorded in his diary – the Labouchere Amendment was passed in the United Kingdom, making "gross indecency" between men illegal. The author of the bill, Henry Labouchere, apparently could not bear to be more specific; the euphemism "gross indecency" here referred not only to sodomy but to any homosexual act. Oscar Wilde was famously convicted under the Labouchere Amendment in 1895.

Browne's diaries suggest a significant disconnect between his personal life and the conventional silence on homoeroticism he adopts in his *Literary History of Persia*. It is not that he or Shibli were overcompensating, but that they deemed their personal romantic lives as separate from the genre conventions of modern literary history. In other words, they were not hypocrites, covering up or publicly denouncing their own hidden desires; rather, their personal lives were not bound to the Victorian-influenced genre conventions of modern literary history. Their prudishness in print did not contradict the reality of their lives any more than premodern erotic poetry had necessarily reflected real-life experiences. Whether depicting love in a premodern Persian ghazal or a modern literary history, one had to conform to the dominant genre conventions of the day.[80] Premodern Persian literature celebrated sexuality and found the homoerotic relationship of a man gazing at a male youth's beauty to be the ideal expression of love; an individual poet's own life circumstances or personal romantic inclinations were less relevant, and he might even choose to depict his female beloved as an *amrad* in order to protect her honor and uphold the genre's conventions. In the same way, modern literary history was circumspect about sexuality and disparaged homoeroticism; the actual life circumstances of a literary

---

[80] Selim Kuru has argued the same of another Persianate tradition, that of Ottoman poetry. Kuru, "Generic Desires."

historian like Browne or Shibli notwithstanding, one had to adhere to and write according to the conventions.

2.5   CONCLUSION

While Hidayat and other *tazkirah* writers showed no signs of discomfort with homoeroticism as a subject, for literary historians like Shibli and Bahar, discussing homoerotic acts was an uncomfortable but nevertheless unavoidable and scholarly responsibility, which they handled by apologizing to their readers, pathologizing *amrad-parasti* as a practice that owes its origin to a particular context of sexual scarcity, and providing a rationale for some of its most esteemed practitioners. Browne often engaged with Hidayat's *Majma' al-Fusaha'* and cited Shibli's *Shi'r al-'Ajam* numerous times in his *Literary History of Persia*, expressing his admiration and respect for Shibli's work. Yet in contrast with both *tazkirah* writers like Hidayat and modernizers like Shibli, Browne addressed this uncomfortable topic in what may be an even more properly puritan manner: ignoring it altogether. Browne's studied silence on erotic matters may have also been motivated by his desire to defend Iran against imperialism and British depictions of Iranians as moral degenerates, but other European Orientalists, contemporaries of Browne who did not share his politics, also censored homoeroticism from their scholarship; others, like the Iranian Furuzanfar, were constrained into silence on this matter by institutional patrons.[81] Browne was able to avoid addressing *amrad-parasti* while writing for an anglophone audience likely unfamiliar with the subject, whereas Shibli and Azad, writing in Urdu, and Bahar, writing in Persian, had to anticipate a readership already acquainted with the homoerotic conventions of Persian literature and could therefore not afford to remain silent on the matter, unless forced to do so like Furuzanfar.

Literary history and sexual pathologization share a concern with origins, a concern maintained by the modernizing Iranian and

---

[81] DeSouza, "The Love That Dare Not Be Translated," 67.

Indian litterateurs. For them, when the origins of *amrad-parasti* are discussed, they are always claimed to be foreign; the practice is often described as being imported from another nation or resulting from socializing with another ethnic group. The varied strategies and approaches to homoeroticism used by these reformist litterateurs, from pathologizing homoerotic practices and drawing national or ethnic borders around them, to total silence on the matter, share a set of modern sexual conventions that deem sexuality in general, and homoeroticism in particular, distasteful. These conventions differ notably with the homoerotic conventions and frank sexuality of the classical literary past, and they significantly restrict the range of possibilities for discussing love and sex from what was available in the early modern period. The shared discourse of literary modernization, with its inherent nationalism and Victorian-influenced puritanism, led modernizers to work together to remake their shared Persianate heritage and create chaste, heteronormative, nationally bounded literary histories. Taken together, the modernizing historians in Iran and India resemble their contemporaries in the Arab world, something that speaks to broader continuities not only in the conventions of sexuality in Islamicate literatures, but in the intellectual responses to the Islamicate literary heritage, whether from Persianate litterateurs or European Orientalists.

However, not all genres of writing were subject in the same way to these conventions. The strictures of the Victorian-influenced sexual conventions, which became nearly hegemonic in modern literary histories, were not so sclerotic in poetry, at least not early on. For example, the Iranian poet Iraj Mirza (1873–1926), himself a modernizer and reformist, wrote and publicly performed bawdy, even vulgar poetry with explicit sexual and homoerotic themes.[82] It was not until later that the once-homoerotic conventions of Persianate literature disappeared from poetry. But when they did, not even classical poetry was spared. Saʿdi's jocular apology was not enough to save his

---

[82] See Sprachman, *Suppressed Persian*, 76–96.

salacious verses from censorship. In 1941, the Iranian scholar and politician Muhammad-ʿAli Furughi produced a semi-critical edition of the collected works (kulliyat) of Saʿdi. Furughi's edition, which remains popular even today, and completely omitted Saʿdi's bawdy poetry.[83] The genres effaced include Saʿdi's khabisat, hazliyat (satire), and muzhikat (humorous verses), present in some of the earliest extant manuscripts of Saʿdi's kulliyat which date to the late thirteenth and early fourteenth centuries.[84] Manuscript catalogues record that while those genres were often grouped together in earlier editions of the kulliyat – sometimes appearing at the end of the manuscript – they had consistently been included from at least the early fifteenth century on.[85] Furughi excised sections that readers had enjoyed for half a millennium, without spilling so much as a drop of ink in explanation.

Literary histories, produced as they most often were for modernizing educational institutions, likely not only reflected changing conventions but also played a pedagogical role in spreading them. The generations who began to receive a modern education grew up writing poetry differently under these influences. In this way, the modernizing conventions that were first developed or deployed by literary historians impacted other genres of Persianate literature. The conventions of modern literary historiography were not limited to sexuality; a concern with origins, extending far beyond the question of sexual pathology discussed above, also characterizes the genre. The following chapter examines how the adoption of Orientalist philology and evolutionary theories shaped the origin stories told in Persianate literary histories.

---

[83] Saʿdi, Kulliyat. In addition to his role as a literary scholar, Furughi served as prime minister of Iran. He was the son of Muhammad-Husayn Furughi, author of a literary history discussed in Chapter 4, "Print." Nineteenth-century collections lithographed in British India had also censored Saʿdi's salacious verses. I thank Mana Kia for pointing this out.

[84] Ingenito, Beholding Beauty, 33–4. Domenico Ingenito notes that Furughi sought to "protect the moral integrity of younger readers" (ibid., 26).

[85] Arberry, Minovi, and Blochet, Catalogue, 1:42–4; Hukk, Ethé, and Robertson, Descriptive Catalogue, 253–6; Sachau and Ethé, Catalogue, 526–39.

3 **Origin Myths**
Indigeneity and Hybridity in National Narratives

O Saʿdi, although "love of the homeland" is a sound hadith / You can't die in deprivation just because you were born there

(Saʿdi)[1]

Modernity is as obsessed with the past as it is with the future; questions of identifying beginnings, or origins, preoccupied the minds of modernizers. As we have seen in the preceding chapters, Persianate modernizers sought to develop a new genre with modern conventions in order to consolidate their literary heritage. Beyond refashioning the archive of Persian letters, however, these literary historians were also concerned with new questions of origins: where does the language begin? As Chapter 1 demonstrated, the nascent genre of literary history offered a linear, progressive narrative of development for Persian literature, tied to the Iranian nation. This model was made possible by changing understandings of time, history, and literature. As literature was transformed from *adab*, or belles-lettres into *adabiyat*, the modern institution of literature, it was no longer approached as a timeless tradition of cultivation but rather became a corporate entity whose historical development could be traced.[2] Literature, however, is a product of language, and languages come to be conceived of as independent entities with their own developmental histories. This chapter examines how evolutionary theories and Orientalist philology shaped new narratives of the origins and nature of discrete languages, impacting the project of literary history.

---

[1] *"Saʿdiya hubb-i vatan garchih hadisist sahih / natavan murd bah sakhti kih man inja zadam.* Saʿdi, *Kulliyat,"* 762.
[2] Fani, "Becoming Literature," chapter 1.

The linguist Ross King notes that "the average speaker of any language usually holds a number of beliefs about supposedly unique or characteristic features of that language – about its writing system; about its history, prehistory, or both; about what constitutes 'good language'; and so on."[3] These comprise what he calls the "vernacular belief system" of a language. Persian and Urdu were both shaped by contact with other linguistic traditions, yet, in the nineteenth and early twentieth centuries, they developed opposing narratives about such contact and their respective origins. Iranian nationalists articulated a vision of linear, progressive linguistic history, emphasizing continuity with pre-Islamic precursors to modern Persian, such as Middle Persian, the court language of the Sasanian empire (r. 225–650). The very term "Middle Persian" reflects this notion of continuity, suggesting that Middle Persian is a different stage in the life of the same Persian language – a view that Iranian nationalists shared with Orientalist philologists. Despite the significant impact of Arabic on Persian and its profound role in giving the Persian language a new identity, many Iranian nationalists defined themselves and their language in opposition to the Arabs, offering a narrative of continuous Iranian civilization that even the Arab-Islamic conquest could not interrupt. In short, they rejected a hybrid identity in favor of one imagined to be pure and homogenous.[4] Some even disavowed the Arabicized name for their language (*farsi*), and instead insisted on calling it by a pseudo-archaic name, *parsi*.

In contrast, many Urdu-speaking South Asian Muslims considered hybridity and mixing to be constitutive elements of their nascent Indo-Muslim identity. Rather than continuity, they emphasized rupture with pre-Islamic South Asia, tracing their origins to the introduction of Islam to the subcontinent with travelers from the

---

[3] King, "Nationalism and Language Reform in Korea," 33.
[4] On imagined purity in Iranian nationalist thought see Zia-Ebrahimi, *The Emergence of Iranian Nationalism*; Marashi, *Nationalizing Iran*, 49–85; Marashi, *Exile and the Nation*, 45–7; Vejdani, *Making History in Iran*, 82–5; Vaziri, *Iran as Imagined Nation*, 100–13.

Middle East and Central Asia.[5] They also highlighted the role of Arabic and other supposedly non-local languages in forming Urdu. When writing histories of Persian literature, Indians approached the question of origins differently than Iranians, conceiving of the Persian language and literature as beginning with Islam, in a way reminiscent of their accounts of Urdu's history.

We therefore encounter a narrative for Persian that asserts that the language has always been Persian regardless of language contact, and a narrative for Urdu that declares that Urdu begins with language contact. Why did Iranians and South Asians develop such different narratives about their languages? These two highly divergent narratives have much to do with the different character of Indian and Iranian nationalisms, and of the relationships that Iranian and Indian Muslim intellectuals had to Orientalism. Juxtaposing Persian and Urdu reveals the two opposing narratives about language and literary history to be historically contingent. Rather than seeking to adjudicate how scientifically accurate each narrative is, this chapter instead examines how particular historical circumstances led to Iranians' and Indians' different relationships to Orientalist philology.

3.1 LANGUAGE AND NATIONAL LITERATURE

Where should a literary history begin? The modern genre typically starts with an account of the origins of the language itself. Nations, languages, and literatures – abstract entities which nevertheless have a relationship to reality – are treated as historical agents, as subjects about whom it was possible to construct a biography.[6] The aim of literary history, in the view of its proponents, is to narrate the story of a people, the history of a nation, through the history of its literature, which is the recorded history of the language. Literary history is understood to be the history of a language; consequently, Persianate

---

[5] Zaman, "Definition of Muslim Identity"; Wasif Khan, *Who Is a Muslim?* 92. For the colonial genealogy of this idea, see also Asif, *A Book of Conquest*, 162–71.

[6] Perkins, *Is Literary History Possible?* 1–3.

litterateurs integrated philological narratives inspired by Orientalist scholarship into the nationalist 'origin stories' they told about the history of Persian.

This concern with national origins is a key difference between literary histories and *tazkirah*s. The author of a *tazkirah* felt no need to explain the nature or origins of the Persian language. Instead, some *tazkirah*s began with a narrative of the origins of poetry itself (regardless of language), and often sought to defend poetry against those who saw it as Islamically suspect. The earliest extant *tazkirah*, Muhammad ʿAwfi's *Lubab al-Albab* (*The Piths of Intellects*), begins with discussions of the excellence of poetry, the meaning of poetry, and the first poets. Like the historian Tabari (839–923) before him, ʿAwfi sees the Edenic Adam as the "Father of Poetry" and believes he composed poetry in Arabic: an elegy (*marsiyah*) on Cain's slaying of Abel.[7]

Writing half a millennium later, in the introduction to his eighteenth-century *Majmaʿ al-Nafaʾis* (*Assembly of Subtleties*), the Indian litterateur Siraj al-Din ʿAli Khan-i Arzu also begins with a discussion of the origins of poetry, and offers an overview of the various approaches to the question taken by other *tazkirah* writers since ʿAwfi's time. Several historians, according to Arzu, have claimed that the first person to compose poetry was Adam, but when it comes to the question of Persian poets (*shuʿaraʾ-yi farsi*), there are differing and divergent opinions. Some begin with the Sasanian king Bahram Gur (r. 420–38) – that is, in late antiquity prior to Islam – while others begin with the Saffarid dynasty in the tenth century. The anonymous seventeenth-century *Dabistan-i Mazahib* (*School of Doctrines*), as Arzu goes on to explain, locates the origins of Persian poetry in the mythical Abadiyan era, predating even Adam. Arzu concludes with a justification of poetry, citing well-known prophetic sayings in Arabic: "verily there is wisdom in poetry" and "the poets

---

[7] ʿAwfi, *Lubab al-Albab*, 1:67. ʿAwfi's preface is analyzed in Keshavmurthy, "Finitude and the Authorship of Fiction."

are princes of speech."[8] Such a justification was typical, nearly stand-ard; many *tazkirah* writers defended poetry by noting how prophets and saints composed and listened to poetry, citing these and other sayings like "God has a treasure under the throne, the keys to which are the tongues of poets."[9] In addition to his Islamic citations in Arabic, Arzu also quotes lines of verse from the luminaries of Persian literature, among them Rumi, Amir Khusraw, ʿAttar, and others, attesting to the importance of poetry. Nowhere in this intro-duction does Arzu mention language – and not because Arzu lacked interest in or knowledge of Persian philology. In fact, he dedicates an influential treatise (*Musmir*) to linguistic issues. The question of the origins of Persian was simply not germane to the writing of a *tazkirah*. Arzu was not alone; none of his peers in the *tazkirah* tradition addressed this issue. Conversely, modern literary histories – whether written by Iranians, Indians, or Europeans – conventionally begin with an account of the origins of the language itself rather than with apologetics for poetry.

Many of the new literary histories portrayed Persian literary history as bound to the Iranian people and continuous across various Iranian languages rather than specific to New Persian. Italo Pizzi's *Manuale di letteratura persiana* (1887) is one of the earliest literary histories of Persian in a European language. Pizzi suggests that his work shows the continuity of Iranian thought "from the earliest times" beginning with Old Persian and the Achaemenids (r. ca. 700–330 BCE), through Middle Persian (*pehlevico*) and then "modern Persian" (*persiano moderno*) all the way until his time of writing. He views Iranian "thought" (*pensiero*, used here in the Herderian sense of a national spirit) as an unbroken chain, occasionally modified or led astray but never interrupted. "Rather than Persian literature, this

---

[8] Arzu, *Majmaʿ al-Nafaʾis*, 1:44–8. Some of this is repeated in Arzu's *Musmir*, 14–18, and discussed in Dudney, *India in the Persian World*, 70–2. On the *Dabistan-i Mazahib* see Sheffield, "Exercises in Peace"; Tavakoli-Targhi, *Refashioning Iran*, chapter 5; Mojtabāʾī, "DABESTĀN-E MAḎĀHEB."

[9] Valih Daghistani, *Riyaz al-Shuʿara*, 1:3.

little manual should be called [a manual] of Iranian literature, for it intends to deal with all the literature of Iran in ancient times, in the Middle Ages, and in the modern age, albeit quite summarily," admits Pizzi at the onset. E. G. Browne would later make a similar caveat while introducing the first volume of his *Literary History of Persia* (1902), confessing that his work is "not, however, precisely a history of Persian Literature," but rather a literary history of the Iranian people, including texts written by them in other languages, and excluding the Persian literature of India, Turkey, and other countries.[10] Browne only begins to address post-Islamic "New Persian" literature toward the end of the first volume of his literary history, after more than three hundred pages discussing writing in earlier languages. Bahar similarly devotes the first third of the first volume of his *Sabkshinasi (Stylistics)* to pre-Islamic languages and writing.

Browne's *Literary History of Persia* emphasized continuity between pre-Islamic languages and the modern Persian language, claiming that contemporary Persian is the offspring of the language recorded in Achaemenid inscriptions, which show us "what the Persian language was more than 2,400 years ago."[11] Browne's work was modeled after John Richard Green's *Short History of the English People* (1874, which begins with the Angles, Saxons, and Jutes) and Jean Jules Jusserand's *Literary History of the English People* (1893, which similarly offers not the history of English literature, but rather a literary history of the English people, and begins with the Celts, long before the Germanic invasions of the British Isles). Browne explicitly draws analogies between the histories of English and Persian, with the "kindred dialects" of the peoples of Parthia, Media, and Persis blending together to form Persian, just as the Angles, Saxons, and Jutes had merged along with the dialects of various parts of England to form the English language. Browne's model of nations and

---

[10] Pizzi, *Manuale di letteratura persiana*, vii–1; Browne, *Literary History*, 1:3–4.
[11] Browne, *Literary History*, 1:5.

languages is composite (comprising Angles, Saxons, and Jutes), but only of elements deemed "national"; supposedly non-national elements, like French in the case of English, or Arabic for Persian, are not part of the equation. Browne's project, after all, was a literary history of the Persian *nation* – as opposed to the history of Persian literature, which historically spanned many nations and lands. The four volumes of Browne's *Literary History of Persia* were quickly translated into Persian as *Tarikh-i Adabi-yi Iran* (*Literary History of Iran*) or *Tarikh-i Adabiyat-i Iran* (*History of Iranian Literature*) and inspired many imitators. As I have discussed in Chapter 1, works like this preponderated in the first half of the twentieth century, and almost all of them titled their works *Tarikh-i Adabiyat-i Iran* – history of Iranian literature, not Persian literature.[12] Even the German Orientalist Hermann Ethé's chapter "Neupersische Literatur" ("New-Persian Literature"), from the encyclopedic *Grundriss der iranischen Philologie* (1895–1904), was translated into Persian as *Tarikh-i Adabiyat-i Iran* (*History of the Literature of Iran*, 1958) by the Iranian historian Rizazadah Shafaq.

Despite its ambiguous title, Shibli Nuʿmani's Urdu-language *Shiʿr al-ʿAjam* (*Poetry of the Persians*) also favors Iranian poets, following Browne's Iran-centrism.[13] However, Browne's nationalist framework of continuity across Iran's pre-Islamic and Islamic history is absent from Shibli's work, which proclaims in its opening that "Islam was a cloud of munificence which rained on the surface of every land."[14] For Shibli, Persian poetry begins with Islam. He

---

[12] Furughi, 1917; Humaʾi, 1929; Shafaq, 1933; Furuzanfar, 1938; Husayn Farivar, 1945–6.

[13] Though historically *ʾajam* connoted "barbarians" and referred to non-Arabs in general, from the ninth century onwards it was used primarily to refer to Persians. See Gabrieli, "ʿAdjam."

[14] In the preface to his *Gulistan*, often memorized by children across the Persianate world, Saʾdi declares that "the rain of [God']s countless mercy has reached everyone, and the tablecloth of His unsparing bounty has been laid everywhere." Here, Shibli evokes a line from Saʾdi sure to be familiar to his readers and gives an Islamic framework to his history of Persian poetry.

contests Browne's narrative directly, arguing that Browne does not prove his claim that poetry predates Islam in Iran. "European researchers have found a great many Middle Persian [*pahlavi*] books, but did not turn up even four lines of poetry," contends Shibli, who goes on to argue that what Orientalists identified as pre-Islamic Persian "poetry" was in fact rhythmical [*mawzun*] prose.[15] In fact, according to Shibli, not only poetry but the New Persian language itself begins with Persian's encounter with Arabic. "Gradually, as Persian and Arabic mixed, *like Urdu* a new language was born, and one would say it was a particularly Islamic language," he writes.[16] The historical trajectories of Persian and Urdu, in his view, are similar: both born out of mixture with Arabic, both vehicles for Islam. Like Shibli, Muhammad Husayn Azad begins his Urdu-language literary history of Persian, *Nigaristan-i Fars* (*Picture-Gallery of Persia*, published posthumously in 1922), in the Islamic period, with the New Persian poet Rudaki (860–940). Azad had the philological knowledge to address pre-Islamic languages, as he did at great length in another work, *Sukhandan-i Fars* ([*On the*] *Poets of Persia*, 1907), so just like Arzu before him, his choice to begin where he did was significant and not simply out of ignorance about Iran prior to Islam.

It is striking that these two Urdu-language histories of Persian literature begin from a different starting point than their Iranian (and European) counterparts. For Shibli and Azad, Persian starts with the encounter with Islam rather than in pre-Islamic times. This is the result of a different position vis-à-vis Iranian nationalism in which they were not invested, but also that while Persian literature was being made into national heritage for Iranians, Indians perceived of it as Islamic heritage. This concept also shaped different vernacular beliefs about Persian and Urdu.

---

[15] Shibli, *Shi'r al-'Ajam*, 4:114–16.

[16] Ibid., 16, emphasis added. Fakhr-i Da'i Gilani, who translated *Shi'r al-'Ajam* from Urdu into Persian, omitted the words "like Urdu" (*urdu ki tarh*) in his translation (1:18).

3.2 ORIGIN MYTHS

The first to suggest a model of linguistic continuity may have been Arzu. In his philological treatise *Musmir*, Arzu identified a single trajectory for the Persian language that includes the pre-Islamic languages known today as Old Persian and Middle Persian, though, as Arthur Dudney explains, Arzu was unable to distinguish between them, viewing the two as a single entity, "Ancient Persian" (*parsi-yi qadim*). Arzu also discusses how the word *parsi* became *farsi*.[17] Crucially, however, the undergirding concerns and logic guiding Arzu's mid-eighteenth-century treatise *Musmir* differ from the nationalist literary historians a century and a half later. Arzu did not consider Persian to be inherently linked to Iran; instead, he argued that Indians had just as much authority in the language as Iranians. Moreover, as Dudney aptly puts it, "for Arzu, the boundary between languages was a productive zone and not a cause for anxiety as it was for some later critics."[18]

The British Orientalist and philologist Sir William Jones (1746–94) may have learned from Arzu's discovery of affinities between Persian and Sanskrit, providing the basis for the later development of Indo-European linguistics.[19] These new philological discoveries offered greater insight into the history of Iranian languages. In the wake of Jones, Aryanist philology – or what Aamir Mufti terms "Orientalist-nationalist philology" – identified a number of related but nevertheless distinct languages and grouped them together as the evolutionary stages of a single Persian language.[20] The earliest stage included royal inscriptions at Achaemenid-era sites such as Behistun and Pasargadae, identified by modern philologists as "Old Persian."

---

[17] Arzu, *Musmir*, 1–4; Dudney, *India in the Persian World*, 64–73.

[18] Dudney, "Urdu as Persian," 48.

[19] Tavakoli-Targhi, *Refashioning Iran*, 18–34. Like Arzu, Jones did not consistently differentiate between pre-Islamic languages, referring to both "Pehlevian" (Middle Persian) and "Zend" (Avestan) as "old Persian" (Jones, *The Works of Sir William Jones*, 1:182; 2:186).

[20] Mufti, *Forget English!* 121.

The later descendants of this language are known today collectively as "Middle Persian," but the singular name belies the variegated nature of the multiple linguistic varieties it identifies. These varieties include *dari*, the language of the Sasanian court (*dar*), and *parsig*, referring to the Pars region of southern Iran (from which the English terms "Persia" and "Persian" are derived).[21] The modern Persian language (*farsi*) is a descendant of these Middle Persian languages. Iranian nationalist literary historians were deeply influenced by both European Orientalists and Indian philologists.[22] While philology provides a narrative of continuity between different "stages" of Persian, the literary histories paper over this messy multiplicity, collapsing all of these languages – along with others like Avestan and Parthian – into a single package.

The tripartite model of "Old," "Middle," and "New Persian" was borrowed from Germanic philology. The German philologist Jacob Grimm (1785–1863), one of the Brothers Grimm, had coined the term "Middle English" (*Mittelenglisch*) in his 1819 *Deutsche Grammatik*. This was soon taken up by Anglophone philologists, and within a few decades his framework had become widely accepted. What had been known earlier as the Anglo-Saxon language was now described as Old English, the earliest stage of development of the English language. Similarly, the language of the Achaemenid-era inscriptions at Behistun was dubbed "Old Persian" and attached to a single trajectory including *dari* and *parsig*, now "Middle Persian," and *farsi* or "New Persian."[23]

In fact, Persian as we know it today was born out of interaction with Arabic, though dominant narratives about the language, the "vernacular belief system" of average speakers, argue precisely the

---

[21] Maggi and Orsatti, "From Old to New Persian," 26, 31.

[22] As Afshin Marashi has convincingly demonstrated, Europeans were not alone in promulgating Aryanism in Iran. Indian Zoroastrians, or Parsis, also played a significant role in popularizing knowledge about pre-Islamic Iran. See Marashi, *Exile and the Nation*, 86, 107–10, and *passim*.

[23] "Middle Persian" is in use at least as early as 1844; see Ellis, "Phonetic Literature," 135n2.

opposite. The Middle Persian language (*parsig*) was the court language of the Sasanians, and following their defeat in the seventh century Arab-Islamic conquest of Iran, Arabic became the primary language of letters, rather than Middle Persian. Within a couple of centuries, however, what linguists call "Early New Persian" began to be written down using Arabic orthography, rather than with the cumbersome Aramaic-derived script it had previously used, and New Persian in the Arabic script developed its own identity. Developments which had been taking place in spoken Middle Persian were now captured for the first time in writing. Just as the written tradition in the nascent Romance languages reflected regional colloquial developments that had emerged out of Vulgar Latin but had not been reflected in standard written Latin, "New Persian" was a new written standard using the Arabic script, which captured grammatical and morphological changes that had taken place in spoken Middle Persian, but had not been reflected and codified in the written language. For example, the consonant at the end of adjectives like *parsig* was lost, transforming the word into *parsi*. As classical Arabic (unlike Persian) lacked the phoneme [p], the language became widely known by the Arabicized name *farsi*, and this usage eventually prevailed among Persian speakers as well.

Persian remained in productive engagement with Arabic for the following millennium. Because Arabic learning endured as part of education, literacy in Persian was almost inseparable from literacy in Arabic, and a well-educated person could be expected to know both.[24] Persian-Arabic bilingualism, and the use of the Arabic script for Persian, facilitated the introduction of large amounts of Arabic vocabulary into Persian. In later periods, Persian took loanwords from Turkic languages, and from the nineteenth century on from French, Russian, and eventually English. However, Persian did not borrow from these languages to an extent at all comparable with its extensive

---

[24] Spooner and Hanaway, *Literacy in the Persianate World*, 14–21.

level of borrowings from Arabic, which fundamentally changed the nature of the Persian language.[25]

With this new, Arabic-influenced idiom, Persian-speakers also began to produce literature using Arabic literary forms. Persian took the majority of its most important literary forms from Arabic, in both poetry and prose. Persian borrowed from – and contributed to – the metrics, stylistics, standard imagery, and topoi of these forms, some of which eventually flourished far more in Persian than in Arabic. In sum, it was the encounter with Arabic that bestowed on this language an identity, with a writing system, vocabulary, grammatical forms, literary models, and a name (*farsi*) that are all different from Middle Persian, its pre-Islamic precursor. New Persian emerged as a language patronized by various Muslim courts, and it spread to the Indian subcontinent as a vehicle for Islam. Despite Persian's profound and enduring relationship to Arabic, modern Iranian nationalists defined Iranian identity in opposition to the Arabs and emphasized continuities between the present and pre-Islamic (thus pre-Arabic influence) culture.

In some ways the relationship between Persian and Urdu came to mirror the earlier relationship between Arabic and Persian. Persian became the language of Islam, and more broadly the language of learning and high culture, in much of South Asia not only for Muslims, but for many non-Muslims as well. As such, Persian began to influence local languages. One of those local languages is what would eventually be referred to as Urdu: a South Asian language written in the Perso-Arabic script, with large amounts of Persian vocabulary (including all those Arabic loanwords which had made their way into Persian), literature in Perso-Arabic forms, and

---

[25] On French loanwords, see Kłagisz, "Hints on French Loanwords in Modern New Persian." On Turkic loans see Perry, "The Historical Role of Turkish in Relation to Persian of Iran," and Perry, "Persian during the Safavid Period: Sketch for an Etat de Langue." On Arabic loans see Perry, "ARABIC LANGUAGE v. Arabic Elements in Persian."

ultimately a new name (*urdu*, which is derived from a Turkic word meaning "camp") and a new identity as a language.

Both Persian and Urdu borrowed their endonyms from other languages, but modern speakers make very different meanings of this fact. Modern nationalists sought to distance Iranian identity from the Arabs and to purge the language of its Arabic elements; some rejected *farsi*, taking up the archaic form *parsi* as a more authentic and proper name for the language.[26] Iranian nationalists disavowed the Arabicized name and rejected a hybrid identity in favor of one imagined to be pure and archaic, emphasizing Iranian indigeneity and the continuity of Iranian civilization and culture before and after the Arab-Islamic conquest of Iran. In contrast to the Iranian nationalist quest for purity, some Indian nationalists embraced hybridity and accepted loanwords as constitutive of their nascent identity. Proponents of Indian Muslim nationalism often emphasized the foreign origins of their identity and rupture with pre-Islamic South Asia. Their language was historically known by a number of names, including Hindi, Hindvi, Hindustani, Rekhta, and Urdu.[27] The last two such names are particularly relevant for the present discussion. *Urdu* is originally a Turkic word for "army" or "camp" and, according to a popular narrative about the language's origins, refers to the military camps where Persian, Turkish, and Arab soldiers mingled with Indians, producing Urdu, a creole language that facilitated communication among them. While this narrative's veracity is discredited, it is nevertheless worth exploring the work that it did for South Asians and British Orientalists alike in producing an Indo-Muslim identity predicated upon foreign origins.

Rekhta is a loan from Persian meaning "poured," "scattered," or "mixed," referring to the mixture of Indic elements with Persian and other languages. John Shakespear (1774–1858), celebrated British

---

[26] On the Pahlavi state-led project to replace Arabic loanwords in Persian with "native" equivalents, see Ludwig, "Iranian Language Reform in the Twentieth Century."

[27] Rahman, *From Hindi to Urdu*, 16–44.

grammarian and lexicographer of Hindustani, remarks that Urdu is used "especially among the Muhammadan inhabitants" of India, but "it is also termed *Rekhtah* (scattered) on account of the variety of languages interspersed in it."[28] Thomas Grahame Bailey (1872–1942), a Scottish philologist born in British India to a missionary family, similarly states in his 1932 *History of Urdu Literature* that Urdu "was called rekhta because it consisted of Hindi into which Arabic and Persian words had been *poured.*"[29] Bailey subscribed to the hypothesis that Urdu arose out of encounters between the Khari Boli (Hindustani)-speaking population of North India and Persian-speaking soldiers. Already in 1932, he noted that "much has been written on the origin of Urdū."[30] Many South Asian Muslims also enthusiastic-ally upheld this narrative. Muhammad Husayn Azad explains that Urdu is also called *Rekhta*, as "different languages have made it 'mixed' [*rekhtah*]," including Arabic, Persian, and Turkish.[31] This idea first appears in Urdu writing in Mir Amman's celebrated and influen-tial *Bagh u Bahar* (*Garden and Spring*, 1803), commissioned by the British at Fort William College.[32]

The still ubiquitously popular idea that Urdu is a mélange of languages, viz. Indic (Sanskritic or Prakritic) vocabulary, Persian, Arabic, and Turkish, relies on the peculiar nationalist idea that Persian, Arabic, and Turkish have all separately contributed to Urdu. In fact, there is no reason to treat the Arabic element of Urdu vocabulary as separate from the Persian, as the vast majority of Arabic loanwords entered Urdu via Persian and according to Persian orthography and phonology.[33] Identifying these words as coming from

---

[28] Shakespear, *A Grammar of the Hindustani Language*, 1.

[29] Bailey, *A History of Urdu Literature*, 4 (emphasis in original). Bailey acknowledges that "it is difficult to distinguish precisely between Kharī [Bolī] and Urdu," making the distinction in "the fact that Kharī [Bolī] uses very few, and Urdu very many, Persian and Arabic words" (ibid., 9).

[30] Ibid., 5.   [31] Azad, *Ab-i Hayat*, 20; Azad, *Shaping the Canon*, 67.

[32] Amman, *Bagh u Bahar*, 5; see also Faruqi, *Early Urdu Literary Culture*, 36–8.

[33] For example, many Arabic words ending with a *ta' marbuta* had this ending changed to a *ta'* in Persian, and this is the form in which they were borrowed into Urdu. See Perry, *Form and Meaning in Persian Vocabulary*.

Arabic illustrates how the logic of nationalism ensures that words remain wedded to their "origin": words ultimately derived from Arabic, which entered Urdu via Persian, become "Arabic loanwords" rather than Persian loans, even as they carry with them Persian rather than Arabic phonology. A comparable argument for English would be to claim that the transparently French phrase "Art Nouveau" used in English is actually to be counted as a Latin borrowing rather than French, as the word *art* ultimately derives from the Latin *ars*, and *nouveau* from the Latin *novus*. The nationalist logic that links language to nation makes a question of etymology into a question of origins and gives Urdu an Arabic (and thus more explicitly Islamic) pedigree.

Aside from the name *Urdu*, the Turkish element, much of which also entered Urdu through Persian, is negligible. One study found a total of 118 Urdu words of Turkish origin, including several words which are also similarly used in Persian.[34] The Indian scholar Vahid al-Din Salim (1869–1927) concluded that there are 105 Turkish words out of 54,009 total words included in the comprehensive Urdu monolingual dictionary *Farhang-i Asafiyyah*. English has borrowed a comparable number of words from Japanese (*rickshaw, karaoke, tycoon, soy,* and *tsunami,* to name only a few), and while popular narratives about the origins of the English language may include Germanic, French, Latin, and Greek vocabulary, they would not likely include Japanese in the mix. Alongside the 105 words he alleges to be of Turkish origin, Salim gives the total number of Urdu words derived from Arabic as 7,584 and from Persian as 6,041.[35] Taken together, this would amount to 13,625 words, or a little over 25 percent of the 54,009 words included in the monolingual dictionary. The proportion of Perso-Arabic words used in Urdu writing is often even higher, amounting to as much as 50 percent of the basic vocabulary,[36] and

---

[34] Türkmen, "The Turkish Elements in Urdu," 28.
[35] Salim, *Vaz'-i Istalahat*, 156–7.
[36] Maldonado Garcia, "Persian and Arabic Elements."

even more in some texts. While Perso-Arabic vocabulary may be overrepresented, however, the Turkish words included in Urdu lexicons are largely obscure. For example, Erkan Türkmen's list of Turkish words in Urdu consists mostly of Turco-Persian vocabulary; arcane equestrian terms like *boz* (white horse), *yabu* (small horse), *yargha* (trotting horse), and *yal* (horse's mane); and obscure military terminology. Thus, an even smaller proportion of these 105 Turkish loanwords are actually used to any degree of frequency in Urdu.

The reasons for identifying Urdu with Turkish (likewise Arabic and Persian) are more identitarian than linguistic. Arabic, Persian, and Turkish were upheld as "Muslim languages" spoken by "Muslim nations" and thus Urdu, which in the nineteenth century was being refashioned into a communal language of Muslims in opposition to the Hindi of Hindus, emphasizes its own "Islamic character" through association. Ironically, at the same time Arabic, Persian, and Turkish were being transformed into vehicles for *secular*, discrete nationalisms elsewhere. Furthermore, while Iranians could lay claim to a Persian literary tradition with a millennium of history behind it – or 2,500 years, according to the nationalists who traced their origins back to the Achaemenids – Urdu literature was a relatively recent phenomenon. Written Urdu poetry only began to flourish in the eighteenth century, and it was not until the nineteenth century that it developed a prose tradition.[37] Denied the opportunity to locate their linguistic origins in Sanskrit (a privilege colonial discourse reserved for Hindi), Urdu-speakers turned instead to Arabic and Persian in order to anchor their identity in antiquity.

The two narratives outlined above – Persian discreteness, Urdu hybridity – are revealing of the two national movements' differing relationships with Orientalist forms of knowledge about language. Iranian nationalism aligned itself with Indo-Aryan philology, so national and literary history was read through the lens of linguistics: linear, progressive developments from Old Persian to Middle Persian

---

[37] Ahmad, "The Emergence of Urdu Literary Culture."

to New Persian, thus emphasizing continuity with the pre-Islamic. However, this narrative was unavailable to Indian Muslims. As the British emphasized a narrative of enduring Aryan civilization in the subcontinent, they positioned Indian Muslims as outsiders to India, aligning Indology, the Indian branch of Indo-European linguistics, with Hindu nationalism.

The British understood Indian religious groups through "classical" languages and sacred texts.[38] For them, the Hindus were indigenous to the subcontinent; their sacred texts, like the Vedas, were composed in India and written in Sanskrit, deemed the classical language of the Hindus. British philologists identified a linear linguistic development leading from Sanskrit to Hindi, the language they most associated with North Indian Hindus. However, this arrangement construed Indian Muslims as the descendants of foreigners. Their sacred texts, like the Qur'an or works of Sufi literature, were composed in Arabic and Persian, and often came to the subcontinent from the Middle East or Central Asia. While no one at the time would have contested that Sanskrit was local to India, Arabic and Persian were associated with other regions. In this way, Aryanism or Indo-European philology allowed Hindus to envision themselves as the heirs to a long tradition in India, but it situated Muslims as outsiders identified with the Arab, Persian, and Turkish traders and invaders who had brought Islam to the subcontinent. This British narrative of foreign origins was enthusiastically embraced by Indians – Hindu and Muslim alike – in the nineteenth century.[39]

These divergent and contingent accounts of Persian and Urdu's origins invite us to imagine alternative ways of constituting a language. Could the history of Persian be told as a story of rupture and hybridization? Could the story of Urdu be told as one of continuity and indigeneity? Such alternate possibilities are not only

---

[38] Cohn, *Colonialism and Its Forms of Knowledge*, 61.

[39] King, *One Language, Two Scripts*; Asif, *A Book of Conquest*. As Asif points out, in the twentieth century some Indian historians also challenged this narrative.

hypothetical, but were quite real: Muhammad-Husayn Furughi took a composite view of Persian quite similar to the way Urdu speakers viewed their language in his untitled literary history (lithographed in 1917). Furughi describes Persian as a mixture or combination of "Parsi" (perhaps meaning Middle Persian) and Arabic words, saying that "in the end, we got a new language which was neither pure Arabic ('arabi-yi khalis) nor pure Persian (farsi-yi yakdast)," using the Arabic-origin khalis to describe Arabic and the transparently Iranic yakdast for Persian. Later, he seemingly makes a distinction between Arabic lexical items (lughat-i 'arab) and "Persian language" (zaban-i 'ajam); by "language," he likely means grammar. This distinction is not systematic, and furthermore, Furughi is not above boasting that Firdawsi's Shahnamah is superior to any divan of Arabic poetry. Yet the narrative he offers, of Persian as a mixed language which is greater than the sum of its parts, is unique.[40] His position is completely contrary to that of most of the later Iranian literary historians, such as Muhammad-Taqi Bahar, who argued for the separate greatness of Persian and Arabic.[41]

Furughi's composite view of Persian did not become hegemonic; instead, the purist view of scholars like Bahar came to dominate Iranian thinking about language. This was overdetermined by several factors, including the role of European Orientalists and the Pahlavi state's adoption of Aryanism as ideology. Additionally, Furughi's literary history never made it to print, and the 1917 lithograph was not widely reproduced.[42] Could it be that this text did not endure *because*

---

[40] Furughi, *Tarikh-i Adabiyat*, 5–9. His son Muhammad-'Ali Furughi also ridiculed the idea of linguistic purity; see Ansari, "Nationalism and the Question of Race," 108–9.

[41] For an example see Bahar, *Divan*, 2:467, analyzed in Jabbari, "The Sound of Persianate Modernity."

[42] I thank Shahla Farghadani for helping me gain access to the manuscript. The text was lithographed together with Furughi's *'Ilm-i Badi'* (*Rhetorical Embellishment*, 1335 AH/1916–17 CE, Matba'ah Mirza 'Ali Asghar) but remained in extremely limited circulation. A short extract from this work, in revised form, was later published as "*Asar va Fa'idah-yi Adabiyat*" ("The Effect and Benefit of Literature") in the Iranian journal *Akhgar*, Mihr 1328 HS/September–October 1949, issue 43,

of its approach, which contradicted the narrative of Persian continuity that would become hegemonic under Riza Shah? Or did the hegemony of that narrative remain unchallenged because works like Furughi's were unincorporated into more influential projects like Browne's *Literary History of Persia*, and confined to gather dust in the archives of the National Library? These questions might be unanswerable, but examining the manuscript of Furughi's literary history (which, until now, has scarcely been dealt with in Persian scholarship and remains completely absent from scholarship in English) does shed light on the historical contingency of the narrative that now dominates histories of Persian literature. The example of Urdu, with its self-conception as a mixed language, shows that the myth of purity of origins is not a *sine qua non* for the creation of modern communal and linguistic identities, and Persian could have narrated itself similarly.[43]

3.3 EVOLUTION AND LANGUAGE

What both the narratives of continuity and hybridity share is a view of language as a distinct historical entity, developing over time and encountering other discretely bounded languages. This historical approach was shaped by the growing influence of evolutionary theory and its conceptual language. Darwin himself had compared the evolution of species to the evolution of languages in *On the Origin of Species* and other works, contending that "the formation of different languages and of distinct species, and the proofs that both have been developed through a gradual process, are curiously parallel."[44] As many nineteenth-century philologists began to conceive of language as a living organism, the impact of natural history works like Charles Darwin's *On the Origin of Species* on historical linguistics led to

---

5–11. This section of the text did not concern issues of language. For an in-depth study of this text see Fani, "Iran's Literary Becoming."

[43] The Maltese linguist Joseph Aquilina (1911–97) similarly praised the Maltese language for the richness it takes from its mixed lexical sources (vernacular Arabic, Sicilian, Italian, and others). See Versteegh, "The Myth of the Mixed Languages," 217–18.

[44] Darwin, *The Origin of Species*, 465. See also ibid., 324–5.

discussion of "mixed" or "hybrid" languages, as if they were organisms of mixed parentage. The lifespan of an organism, with its periods of growth followed by eventual decay, maps neatly onto the narrative of literary flourishing and then decline which is a ubiquitous staple of Persian literary histories. In the late nineteenth and early twentieth centuries, first Indians and then Iranians introduced evolutionary language and metaphors into their literary histories. Reading across languages and borders is crucial in order to grasp how this conceptual framework spread, as itinerant intellectuals and transnational translators engaged directly with each other, passing Darwinist ideas between Arabic, Persian, Urdu, Turkish, and other languages.

The Urdu poet Shad ʿAzimabadi (1846–1927) wrote in 1891 that "these days the debate on evolution [irtiqa] is roaring / wise men discuss how it all began."[45] As we have seen, a concern with origins – "how it all began," as the poet put it – was one of the essential questions raised in literary histories. The adoption of evolutionary theory significantly informed that quest for origins. Sir Sayyid Ahmad Khan (1817–98), perhaps the most prominent popularizer of science in the subcontinent at the time, advocated naturalist ("naichari," from English "nature") beliefs in the 1880s and 1890s in Urdu. He held Darwinism and Islam to be compatible and advocated a view of human evolution as teleological and guided by God. Despite Ahmad Khan's efforts to defend the Islamic tradition by reconciling it with the "new sciences," his ideas were met with derision and harsh criticism, at least initially.[46] Naichari became a pejorative term for materialists and persisted well into the twentieth century with that meaning. Jamal al-Din al-Afghani attacked the naicharis in his polemical Persian-language The Truth about the Naichari Sect and an Explanation of the Naicharis, published in Hyderabad, 1881. Within two years it was translated into Urdu and published in Calcutta, and in 1886 it was translated into Arabic by the Egyptian Islamic

---

[45] ʿAzimabadi, Furugh-i Hasti, 66.
[46] Lelyveld, "Naichari Nature"; Qidwai, "Darwin or Design?"

modernist Muhammad 'Abduh (with the help of 'Arif Abu Turab) and subsequently published in Beirut. Yet, as David Lelyveld points out, al-Afghani took issue more with Ahmad Khan's politics than with his scientific views; the two men's belief in the compatibility of Islam and European science was, in fact, remarkably similar. Despite such repudiation of the "*naichari*s," the language and metaphors of bio-logical evolution spread throughout the Islamicate world, and soon found their way into works on literature.

Rather than refute evolution, many Muslims in South Asia and elsewhere instead argued that the concept had been articulated in Persian poetry centuries before Darwin. The Indian Muslim jurist Syed Ameer Ali (1849–1928) wrote in his English-language *The Spirit of Islam* (1891) that the thirteenth-century Persian poet Jalal al-Din Rumi expressed "the doctrine of evolution and progressive development" in his *Masnavi*, citing the following lines first in Persian and then in Ali's English translation: "Dying from the inor-ganic we developed into the vegetable kingdom. Dying from the vegetable we rose to the animal. And leaving the animal we became men."[47] The idea that Rumi had espoused a theory of evolution more than half a millennium earlier quickly became popular among South Asian Muslims.[48] Shibli Nu'mani was the first to write a full-length biography of Rumi in any language, and dedicated the final section of his book, *Savanih-i Mawlana Rum* (*The Life of Mawlana Rumi*, 1906), to "the issue of evolution" (*mas'alah-i irtiqa*). Shibli credited Darwin with developing the theory of evolution, noting that "in truth, Darwin proved this issue with such detail and precision that he can be called the originator of this issue," but concluded with the same lines from

---

[47] Ameer Ali, *The Spirit of Islam*, 392–3. In fact, Rumi simply reproduces Aristotle's "great chain of being." See Foltz, "Islam," 209.

[48] This idea was also quoted or expressed in Sarwar, *Philosophy of the Qur-an* [*sic*], 119–21, and in Rahman, "Sufism and Islam," 643. For additional discussion see Schimmel, *Mystical Dimensions of Islam*, 322; Schimmel, *The Triumphal Sun*, 329–32; and Lewis, *Rumi: Past and Present*, 482–5.

Rumi, which he claimed expressed the idea clearly.[49] Like Ameer Ali and Shibli, intellectuals across the Persianate world identified various literary figures as proto-evolutionists. In 1914, the Ottoman intellectual 'Abdullah Cevdet described the poetry of the Arab skeptic al-Ma'arri (973–1057) as verse anticipating Darwinism.[50] A decade later in 1924, the Bukharan reformer 'Abd al-Ra'uf Fitrat would similarly argue that the Persian poet 'Abd al-Qadir Bidil of Delhi (1644–1721) had discovered Darwinian evolution.[51]

Shibli was exposed to evolutionary thought from multiple sources, which demonstrate the period's expansive, multilingual circulation of ideas. He was close friends with Sayyid Ahmad Khan, who had done much to introduce Darwinism in South Asia, and the two worked together at the Mohammedan Anglo-Oriental College (later renamed Aligarh Muslim University) from 1883 until Ahmad Khan's death in 1898. Though Shibli and Ahmad Khan had their disagreements, it is likely that their long period of association left a lasting mark on Shibli's thinking. Shibli was also an avid reader of Arabic newspapers and would have been familiar with the debates over Darwinism in the pages of *al-Muqtataf* and *al-Hilal*.[52] Arabic

---

[49] Shibli, *Savanih-i Mawlana Rum*, 199–200. Translated into Persian by Muhammad-Taqi Fakhr-i Da'i Gilani as *Savanih-i Mawlavi Rumi* (1953).

[50] Cevdet had translated the French scientist Gustave Le Bon's *Les lois psychologiques de l'évolution des peuples* (1894) as *Ruh al Aqvam* (*The Soul of Peoples*, 1907), using the word *tekâmül* to translate "evolution." On the introduction of Darwinism to Ottoman Turkish contexts see Hanioğlu, "Blueprints for a Future Society" and Doğan, *Osmanlı aydınları ve sosyal Darwinizm*. Le Bon's book was later translated into Arabic by the Egyptian nationalist Ahmad Fathi Zaghlul as *Sirr Tatawwur al-Umam* (*Secret of the Evolution of Nations*, 1913), using the word *tatawwur* for "evolution."

[51] Hodgkin, "Classical Persian Canons," 191–3. Like Bahar, Cevdet and Fitrat were both political and literary reformers. As Hodgkin demonstrates, these Turkic reformers belonged to literary circles that overlapped and interacted with those of the Iranian Constitutionalists like Bahar or Abu al-Qasim Lahuti.

[52] Shibli read and praised both papers specifically. See Shibli, *Safarnamah*, 180; translated in Shibli, *Turkey, Egypt, and Syria*, 178–9. He also lauded *al-Safa*, which published Arabic translations of Darwin; see ibid., 134. Elsewhere, Shibli spoke favorably of Cornelius Van Dyck (1818–95), an American professor of medicine in Beirut known as a defender of Darwinism and a contributor to *al-Muqtataf*. See ibid., 126; on Van Dyck, see Elshakry, *Reading Darwin*, chapter 1.

newspapers played a significant role in spreading evolutionary and Darwinist ideas across the Middle East and South Asia.[53] Two of the most popular and widely-read such journals, *al-Muqtataf* (published in Beirut and Cairo) and *al-Hilal* (based in Cairo), were key venues for engagement with Darwin through translations, analysis, and polemics both for and against his theory of evolution. These papers helped evolutionary debates circulate among Iranian intellectuals. They were popular among Iranians in Cairo because of their active and sympathetic coverage of the Iranian Constitutional Revolution (1905–11).[54] They were also available in Iran.[55] The religious scholar Muhammad-Riza Najafi Isfahani (d. 1943) responded to the Darwinist ideas he encountered in the Arabic press in his Arabic-language *Naqd falsafat Darwin* (*Critique of the Philosophy of Darwin*, 1913–14), arguing for a vision of evolution that was compatible with Islam. Isfahani taught his book in the Qom seminary.[56] Muhammad-Taqi Bahar read periodicals from Egypt in order to strengthen his knowledge of Arabic, but they also provided him with exposure to the latest scientific developments. Bahar was particularly interested in learning about "the natural philosophy of Darwin" and Shibli Shumayyil (1853–1917), the influential popularizer of Darwinism in Arabic.[57]

By the turn of the century, evolution was fervently discussed throughout the Islamicate world in a variety of contexts.[58] The Baha'i

[53] See Marwa Elshakry's excellent book on the subject, *Reading Darwin in Arabic.*

[54] Rastegar, *"Mashruteh* and *al-Nahda."*

[55] The Iranian historian and literary critic Ahmad Kasravi (1890–1946) was reading both newspapers in 1911. Kasravi, *Pindar-ha,* 40.

[56] Al-Najafi al-Isfahani, *Naqd falsafat Darwin, panjah,* and see Seidel, "The Reception of European Philosophy in Qajar Iran," 347–8. Ruhollah Khomeini was one of Isfahani's students.

[57] 'Irfani, *Sharh-i Ahval,* 43.

[58] Majid Daneshgar discusses the reception of Darwinism in two parts of the Islamicate world, Iran and the Malay peninsula, in "Uninterrupted Censored Darwin." However, he significantly overstates the degree to which Darwin was censored or otherwise rejected in Iran, distorting what was in fact a largely positive reception of Darwinism. As I demonstrate here, Darwinism and other evolutionary theories were far better received than in Daneshgar's account. Today they are part of the compulsory science curriculum in Iranian schools (Burton, "Evolution and Creationism," 301–2).

religious leader 'Abd al-Baha' 'Abbas (1844–1921) addressed evolution in talks he gave in 'Akka between 1904 and 1906.[59] Beginning in the late 1910s, Persian-language scientific journals and magazines proliferated.[60] In 1921, Darwin's ideas were discussed in the Berlin-based Persian newspaper *Kavah*, though apparently they were still unfamiliar enough to need to be introduced to Iranian readers. Darwin's discoveries, referred to in the article as "Darwinism" (*darvinism*), are described as "the growth and promotion [*nashv va irtiqa*] of species [*anva'*]" and "the principle of solving and discovering the secret of creation/nature [*khilqat*]."[61] The collocation *nashv va irtiqa* "growth and promotion" was borrowed from the Arabic press, where these terms had already been established as the standard translation of "evolution" in Arabic.[62]

Did the various species of plants and animals to be found across the lands, seas, and skies of the earth always exist in the form we observe today? Or did they have a different shape at first and slowly evolve over time? So asks Muhammad-'Ali Furughi in his influential introduction to European thought, *Sayr-i Hikmat dar Urupa* (*The Development of Philosophy in Europe*, 1931–41).[63] He dedicates part of his chapter on "German philosophers: the philosophies of materialism and spiritualism" to evolution (*tahavvul-i takamuli*, which he indicates is his translation of the French *evolutionisme* and

---

[59] Published in 1908 as *Mufavazat*, with the English title *Some Answered Questions*. The Persian terms he used for evolution include *taghyir-i anva'* ("transformation of species") and *nashv va taraqqi* ("development and progress"). He addressed evolution again in his talks in Paris, the United States, and Canada, 1911–12.

[60] For a list of the early periodicals popularizing science in Iran, see Schayegh, *Who Is Knowledgeable*, 220–1, fn. 53.

[61] "Mashahir-i Marduman-i Maghrib va Mashriq," *Kavah* No. 7, Berlin, 27 Bahman 1290 / July 7, 1921, 4–7. Though the author is unnamed, the article was most likely written by Sayyid Hasan Taqizadah.

[62] See for example Hurani, *Manahij al-Hukama'*; Shumayyil, *Al-Haqiqah*; and Shumayyil, *Falsafat al-Nushu' wa al-Irtiqa'*. The terms used in the *Kavah* article, *nashv va irtiqa*, are simply the Persian pronunciations of the Arabic *al-nushu' wa al-irtiqa'*.

[63] Seyyed Hossein Nasr, a creationist himself, credits this work with being "the single most influential text in introducing European philosophy to Persians" (Nasr, *Islamic Philosophy*, 253).

transformisme). Furughi describes Darwinism as one of the most important theories in the history of science (*'ilm*), stating that despite Darwin not being a philosopher per se – and thus outside of the scope of Furughi's work on philosophy – Darwinism is so foundational that contemporary philosophy (*falsafah-yi imruzi*) cannot be understood without it.[64] He notes that, by his time of writing in the late 1930s, Iranians had heard of Darwinism and begun to debate it, but that researchers needed to become more familiar with Darwin's ideas. What follows is a biography of Darwin and a detailed description of his discoveries, including situating Darwin in a lineage beginning with the French naturalist Jean-Baptiste Lamarck (1744–1829). Furughi is similarly superlative regarding Herbert Spencer (who coined the phrase "survival of the fittest"), discussing his ideas in detail and naming him the "greatest English philosopher" of his time.[65]

Furughi is a central figure in the process of Persianate modernity narrated in this book, belonging to the same intellectual circles described in Chapter 1 as a founding member of the *Anjuman-i Asar-i Milli* (Society for National Heritage) and the *Farhangistan-i Zaban-i Iran* (Academy of Persian Language). While Furughi did not connect naturalism and evolution to literature, we can see in his work how evolutionary ideas shaped new modes of historical narration, evident when we compare his own writing to that of his father. The discrete biographical sections of Muhammad-Husayn Furughi's untitled literary history lacked the positivist sense of chronology and causality that typically marks the modern genre. In contrast, the younger Furughi's *Development of Philosophy in Europe* views philosophy as a discrete body developing and changing over time, showing how individual philosophers built on their predecessors' work and were directly influenced by their milieus. His discussion of Spencer, for instance, notes how he built on the work of Darwin, and Darwin on Lamarck. Alongside the volumes of Furughi's *Development of*

---

[64] Furughi, *Sayr-i Hikmat*, 3:145–59.   [65] Ibid., 159–80.

Philosophy in Europe came other works introducing Darwinism, and in 1939, a Persian translation of Darwin's *On the Origin of Species* was published in Tehran.[66]

Social Darwinism was promulgated by modern institutions such as the Boy Scouts. Established in Iran in 1925, the scouting movement (*pishahangi*) soon received state support from Riza Shah's Ministry of Education and spread across the country. By the end of the 1930s, participation in scouting was made mandatory for schoolchildren, boys and girls alike.[67] The international scouting movement in the first half of the twentieth century was characterized by a strong sense of Spencerian social Darwinism, as Bahar himself alludes to in a *qasidah* (ode) dedicated to the Scouts. He cautions against social Darwinism, warning that "the philosophy and principles of Darwin are science, not the rites of government."[68]

From the beginning, discussions of evolution were not limited to biology, and Arab writers such as Shibli Shumayyil applied the evolutionary model to the rise and fall of nations and advocated social Darwinism. Litterateurs soon applied this model to literary history as well. As nations were viewed in evolutionary terms, so was literary history – the story of a nation through its literature. Roxane Haag-Higuchi notes that the germ of Bahar's magnum opus *Sabkshinasi, ya Tarikh-i Tatavvur-i Nasr-i Farsi* (*Stylistics, or the History of the Evolution of Persian Prose*, 1942) can be found in a 1918 essay where he uses the term *takamul* (perfection).[69] By the time of writing *Sabkshinasi* he replaces *takamul* with the more neutral *tatavvur* (development, evolution). Unlike *takamul* which implies constant

---

[66] See Zarrinkub, "Evolution." Darwin's original text was published in 1859.

[67] On the scouting movement in Iran, see Pazargad, *Pishahangi-yi Iran*; Koyagi, "Moulding Future Soldiers"; Balslev, *Iranian Masculinities*, 260–8; Kashani-Sabet, "Cultures of Iranianness," 172–3; Matthee, "Transforming Dangerous Nomads," 139–40.

[68] See the poem "*nisar bah pishahangan*" in Bahar, *Divan*, 1:658–61. On the Scouts and Social Darwinism, see Warren, "The Scout Movement."

[69] Haag-Higuchi, "Modernization in Literary History." On Bahar's evolutionary language see also Karimi-Hakkak, *Recasting Persian Poetry*, 113–16.

improvement toward ultimate perfection, *tatavvur* merely connotes change, without value judgment. The change in terminology suggests a shift from the earlier conception of biological evolution as progressive to the later understanding of non-teleological natural selection. Bahar's shift from using *takamul* to *tatavvur* was reflected in the language more broadly. Sulayman Hayyim's 1934 Persian-English dictionary only records *takamul-i tadriji* "gradual *takamul*" as a translation of the English "evolution." Muhammad-ʿAli Daʿi al-Islam's monolingual Persian dictionary *Farhang-i Nizam* (1927–39), produced in Hyderabad in the Deccan, captures the neologism *tatavvur*: "this word does not exist in the reputable Arabic dictionaries, but it has been used in modern Arabic [*ʿarabi-yi jadid*] and [so] it has become used in Persian as well."[70]

In *Sabkshinasi*, Bahar discusses Darwin, providing a brief biography and summary of *On the Origin of Species*, along with an explanation of the evolutionary theories of German materialist Ludwig Büchner (1824–99). He quotes the following from Büchner, translating into Persian:

> Different languages have developed like different species (*anvaʿ*); they stem from each other and also struggle with one other. The difference between languages and species is that languages become subject to transformation and change more quickly than species, and in this respect the transformation and change of languages is more obvious and can be understood sooner. For species sometimes endure for a hundred thousand years, but among words and languages we have no such language that has endured for more than ten centuries without observable changes.[71]

---

[70] Daʿi al-Islam, *Farhang-i Nizam*, 2:265. This explanation was quoted verbatim in the entry on *tatavvur* in ʿAli Akbar Dihkhuda's Persian monolingual dictionary, first published in Tehran in 1931. The Arabic term *tatawwur* was indeed used for "evolution"; see Elshakry, *Reading Darwin*, 17. In contrast, the terms *takamul* and *tatavvur* never gained currency in Urdu.

[71] Bahar, *Sabkshinasi*, 1:174–6.

Bahar goes on to argue that factors in language change are the same as those at work in biological evolution, like natural selection (*intikhab-i tabi'i*) and survival of the fittest (*baqa-yi ansab*). Haag-Higuchi claims that Bahar's application of the concept of evolution to literary history in *Sabkshinasi* is novel, but in fact it had precedents in other Persianate and Islamicate literatures. Bahar's application of Darwinism to literature was only the latest in a series of earlier developments in the writing of literary histories, preceded by works like Jurji Zaydan's *al-Lughah al-'Arabiyyah Ka'in Hayy* (*The Arabic Language: A Living Being*, 1904) and Jalal al-Din Huma'i's *Tarikh-i Adabiyat-i Iran* (*History of the Literature of Iran*, 1929).

Like Bahar, the Iranian literary historian Huma'i also states that language is subject to evolution in his *Tarikh-i Adabiyat-i Iran*. Though the term he uses for evolution is neutral (*nashv va irtiqa'*, "growth and promotion"), his language in the passage reveals that he understands evolution as gradual perfection, noting that language "traverses the path of perfection" and travels a course that is both "natural" (*tabi'i*) and "evolutionary" (*takamuli*, literally "perfect-ive"). At the same time, Huma'i continues, language represents a nation (*millat*) and race (*nizhad*).[72] This Herderian understanding of language and nation was a fundamental assumption of the genre of literary history.

3.4 FROM "BIRTHPLACE" TO "HOMELAND"

The divergences in Iranians' and Indians' relationships to Aryanist philology are apparent in their understandings of the Persian and Urdu word *vatan*. While both came to use this word to refer to a national "homeland," it developed different valences in Persian and in Urdu. The term *vatan* originally referred to one's birthplace or primary residence, at the scale of town or city, or sometimes province. Premodern poetry in Persianate and Islamicate languages often

---

[72] Huma'i, *Tarikh-i Adabiyat-i Iran*, 40–1.

described attachment to the *vatan*, and *vatan* was a religious concept as well: after voyaging a certain distance from one's *vatan*, a Muslim traveler would shorten his or her obligatory prayers and be exempt from fasting during Ramadan. Travelers who stayed for a longer period in a new locale would have to consider it their temporary *vatan* and perform their prayers and fasting just as if they were at home. In the nineteenth and twentieth centuries, *vatan*'s semantic range expanded to accommodate burgeoning nationalist sentiments, with the term coming to align itself with the French *patrie*.[73] For Iranians, the national meaning eventually superseded the older concept, whereas for Urdu-speakers, *vatan* has retained both senses.

Aryanist philology played a role in enabling this transformation. It allowed Iranians to see themselves as heirs to a glorious pre-Islamic Aryan past rooted in the land where Old Persian and Middle Persian had been spoken, rather than primarily identifying as Muslims with attachments to locales outside the national borders of Iran.[74] In contrast, the Urdu *vatan* never abandoned its original Islamic jurisprudential meaning. Urdu-speaking Muslims instead envisioned themselves as belonging to multiple polities, as both citizens of a national homeland *vatan* (eventually India or Pakistan), and members of a transnational Islamic *ummah*.

British Orientalists understood *vatan* in a national sense, as reflected in their Hindustani dictionaries. John Fergusson's dictionary (1773) defines *vatan* as country, and links it to the Latin *patria* – though the Hindustani word carried no such gendered connotation. John Gilchrist's dictionary (1787, 1790) captures both senses – *vatan* is recorded as both "birthplace" and "country," with *vatan-dost* (literally "*vatan*-friend") for patriot.[75] John Shakespear's dictionary from 1834 defines *vatan* as "native country" and lists the related terms

---

[73] Browne, *The Press and Poetry of Modern Persia*, xxxvi–xxxvii; Najmabadi, *Women with Mustaches*, 100; on a similar transformation in Turkish, see Özkan, *From the Abode of Islam*; for Arabic, which followed Ottoman usage, see Lewis, "Watan."

[74] Marashi, *Exile and the Nation*, chapter 4.

[75] Gilchrist, *Hindoostanee Philology*, 55, 133, 463.

vatan-dost (patriot) and *vatan-dushman* (traitor, "*vatan*-enemy").[76] S. W. Fallon's 1879 dictionary records the same.[77] The monolingual Urdu dictionary *Farhang-i Asafiyyah* (compiled by Sayyid Ahmad Dihlavi and published in installments from 1888–1901) defines *vatan* as place of residence or birthplace, but links it to the more expansive concept of *mulk* (kingdom, country).[78] These dictionaries do not merely capture various meanings of the word as it evolves over time, but play a role in shaping the meaning as well. The process of lexicography thus involves a kind of reflexivity akin to the observer effect in physics, where scientists cannot accurately measure an object without altering it in the process of measuring.[79] In this case, British lexicographers were forced to pair Urdu words like *vatan* with English equivalents that were laden with nationalist baggage, such as "country." Indians made use of the Urdu-English dictionaries produced by British Orientalists and shifts in meaning crept into native usage as well, thus reifying connections between land and nation that may not have originally existed.

Though in Persian *vatan* had been reconceived as national homeland as early as 1877, and its use as such had increased during the Iranian Constitutional Revolution (1905–11),[80] it took decades for the newly national sense of the word to replace the older, more local connotation. In the meantime, the two meanings overlapped in usage.[81] The *Farhang-i Nizam* dictionary recorded no national meaning for *vatan*, defining it simply as "a place where one remains for a long time, whether they were born there or not."[82] It similarly lacked compounds such as *vatan-parast* (patriot). This is especially

---

[76] Shakespear, *A Dictionary, Hindustani and English*, 1834.
[77] Fallon, *A New Hindustani-English Dictionary*, 1186.
[78] Dihlavi, *Farhang-i Asafiyyah*, 4:651.
[79] See Hakala's discussion of Urdu dictionaries as simultaneously descriptive and prescriptive in *Negotiating Languages*, 77.
[80] Kashani-Sabet, *Frontier Fictions*, 50.
[81] Najmabadi, *Women with Mustaches*, 98–9, 101.
[82] Da'i al-Islam, *Farhang-i Nizam*, 5:458.

noteworthy as *Farhang-i Nizam* documented new developments in Persian vocabulary, including neologisms from Iran.[83]

While the semantic shift eventually became complete in Iran, to the extent that the modern Iranian reader may anachronistically understand *vatan* in premodern Persian poetry to connote the national "homeland" rather than the narrower "birthplace,"[84] the two meanings have simultaneously persisted in Urdu. Much patriotic Urdu poetry exalts the *vatan*, as in Muhammad Iqbal's 1904 *Taranah-i Hindi* ("Indian Anthem"): *hindi hain ham, vatan hai hindustan hamara* ("we are Indians, our *vatan* is Hindustan.")[85] Iqbal's long Persian-language *masnavi* poem *Javidnamah* (*The Book of Eternity*, 1932) clearly understands *vatan* as *country* and links it to *millat* (nation) in a couplet:

> This handful of earth to which you give the name "country" [*vatan*] / this so-called Egypt, and Iran, and Yemen there is a relationship between a country [*vatan*] and its people [*ahl-i vatan*] / in that it is out of its soil that a nation [*millati*] rises.[86]

Meanwhile the narrow sense can be found throughout contemporary Urdu poetry in which the poet refers to his or her own birthplace, as in this line from Jan-Nisar Akhtar (1914–76) describing the city of Lucknow: *lakhna'u mere vatan mere chaman-zar vatan* ("Lucknow, my *vatan*, my verdant, meadowy *vatan*!")[87]

Both the premodern and modern senses of the term *vatan* coexist in Urdu. In his travelogue *Sayr-i Iran* (*Travels in Iran*, 1886), Muhammad Husayn Azad refers to Iran as the *vatan* of his ancestors, but India as his country (*mulk*). Yet he feels a sense of patriotism (*hubb al-vatan*, literally "love of the *vatan*") in Iran as well. At the

---

[83] Akhtar, "DĀ'Ī-AL-ESLĀM."   [84] Shafi'i-Kadkani, "Talaqqi-yi Qudama az Vatan."
[85] Iqbal, *Bang-i Dara*, 82.
[86] "*An kaf-i khaki kih namidi vatan / inkih gu'i misr u iran u yaman / ba vatan ahl-i vatan ra nisbati ast / zankih az khakash tulu'-i millati ast* (Iqbal, *Javid-namah*,"68). The translation is from Arberry in Iqbal, *Javid-Nama*, 56.
[87] Akhtar, *Khak-i Dil*, 158.

same time, he describes the city of Shiraz as the beloved *vatan* of the poets Saʿdi and Hafiz, a usage reflecting the original meaning of the word.[88] Mana Kia describes the polysemous nature of *vatan* as late as the eighteenth century in Persian, but the nineteenth century witnessed Iranians beginning to abandon this premodern, pre-national meaning of *vatan* in favor of a sense of national belonging.[89] Today, many Iranians are not even aware that the word *vatan* connoted something much more circumscribed in earlier times. *Vatan* expanded to accommodate a territorial nationalism in Iran as Iranians developed a shared national identity.

3.5   CONCLUSION

The idea of Aryan rootedness in India did not go unquestioned. The German Orientalist Max Müller, one of the great pioneers in Indology and comparative philology, popularized the term "Aryan" but also challenged the view of Sanskrit as originating in the subcontinent.[90] The Aryan migration theory – the idea that the ancestors of the first Sanskrit-speakers had originally migrated to northern India from elsewhere – eventually found scholarly acceptance, but the notion of Hindu natives and Muslim invaders proved to be deeply entrenched.[91] In August 1947, British India would be partitioned into the independent nations of India and Pakistan, on the basis of this belief that Hindu and Muslim pasts and futures were irreconcilably different. This resulted in the greatest mass migration in human history, with a million killed and fifteen million displaced in the upheaval that ensued.

---

[88] Azad, *Sayr-i Iran*, 11–13.

[89] Kia, *Persianate Selves*, 36–9; Kashani-Sabet, *Frontier Fictions*; Najmabadi, *Women with Mustaches*, 97–131; Tavakoli-Targhi, *Refashioning Iran*, 114–16. Compare with an interesting development in the opposite direction in 1870s Russian nationalism, from identifying with the state to identifying with a smaller locality, in Tolz, *Russia's Own Orient*, 37.

[90] On Müller see Olender, *The Languages of Paradise*, 82–92.

[91] On the Aryan migration theory see Witzel, "Indocentrism."

While the Iranian approach to national origins, emphasizing continuity, rootedness in place, and attachment to ancient traditions, is common to nationalisms throughout the world, Urdu's myth of exotic origins is not a unique anomaly. Many Swahili-speakers in East Africa similarly set themselves apart from indigenous peoples of the continent, seeing themselves not as Africans but as the descendants of Arabs and Persians, and their language as a mélange of Arabic and Bantu languages.[92] Other languages of the Middle East and South Asia (and elsewhere) can offer frameworks useful for making critical sense of Persian. By the nineteenth century, not only Persian and Urdu, but other languages throughout the world began to be portrayed as biological organisms with births and lifespans, illustrated beautifully in Lisa Mitchell's study of Telugu in South India.[93] The linguist Ghil'ad Zuckermann refuses the nationalist narrative of Modern Hebrew which posits the language as the revival – and continuation – of Biblical Hebrew. He instead offers a model of hybrid language in which the contemporary language (which he terms "Israeli Hebrew") can be seen as a hybrid of Hebrew and Yiddish (along with other "secondary contributors"). Rather than looking at languages through the *Stammbaum* or "family tree" model, he suggests the idea of congruence, with multiple, overlapping contributions from more than one language.[94] Zuckermann's model of Israeli Hebrew as a Semitic and Indo-European hybrid could be applied to Persian as well.

This chapter has sketched out the role of linguistic origin narratives in Persian and Urdu nationalisms, arguing that whereas both languages have been profoundly defined through their interaction with other languages, Iranians have emphasized indigeneity and continuity between the modern language and its pre-Islamic predecessors

---

[92] Spear, "Early Swahili History Reconsidered." For similar narratives of Malay identity, see Alatas, *The Myth of the Lazy Native*, 41; Henley, "Hybridity and Indigeneity," 184–7.

[93] Mitchell, *Language, Emotion, and Politics*, 68–99.

[94] Zuckermann, "A New Vision for Israeli Hebrew."

while Urdu-speakers have emphasized their own foreignness and dis-
continuity with their pre-Islamic past. While Chapters 1 and 2 focused
on the similar ways in which Persian and Urdu literary histories
adapted and refashioned the premodern Persianate heritage, this chapter has identified how differences in nationalist ideology between Iran
and India produced diverging origin narratives. The next chapter turns
to the materiality of printed books, tracing how these ideological
distinctions led to divergences in the transition from manuscript to
print culture.

4 Print

Typography, Orthography, Punctuation

It was a civilizing urge –
to bring closure, to come full circle,
to worship time by divvying it out
into portions, increments, sentences.

(Maurya Simon, "The Era of the Period")[1]

Urdu speakers – lovers of poetry, as they tend to be – often quote a well-known, anonymous couplet about miscommunication: "We kept writing 'prayers' (*du'a*) and they kept reading 'treachery' (*dagha*) / a single dot changed us from an intimate friend (*mahram*) to a criminal (*mujrim*)."[2] The poem relies on a pair of puns, two sets of words (*du'a/dagha; mahram/mujrim*) differentiated in the Perso-Arabic script by just a single dot. Debates on various dots and marks on the page – and the potential hazards of their misuse – were a crucial, though often overlooked, aspect of the transition from *tazkirah* to literary history, and more broadly from manuscript to print culture. Attention to the materiality of this transition affords us insight into the diverging ways the Persianate tradition found modern homes in Iranian and South Asian contexts.

As Walter Hakala has argued, Urdu literary culture developed over the past few centuries in tandem with lexicography, as dictionaries consolidated literary registers and decisively influenced literary

---

[1] Simon, "A Brief History of Punctuation," 519.
[2] *Ham du'a likhte rahe vuh dagha paṛhte rahe / ek nuqte ne hamen mahram se mujrim kar diya.* A famous line in Persian by Iraj Mirza expresses the same idea: *ba yak nuqtah zaban ziyan ast* ("with one dot, 'language' [*zaban*] is 'damage' [*ziyan*]"). Iraj Mirza, *Tahqiq dar Ahval*, 138.

production.[3] The dictionary – the subject of Hakala's study – forms part of the scaffolding which supports the institution of modern literary culture, other beams of which include literary canonization and the formation of literature as an academic discipline.[4] Hakala connects the dictionary to other processes of linguistic standardization, noting that "as a language comes increasingly to be written down and the orthography becomes increasingly stable, new possibilities emerge in the formal structure and contents of lexicographic works."[5] This is true of literary histories as well; changes in print, orthography, and punctuation afforded the modern literary history new possibilities, which differed from those available to the premodern *tazkirah* in the manuscript tradition. While literary histories plundered the *tazkirah*s for materials, the new textual conventions made the histories essentially new objects. Print was not only a matter of increased distribution; it significantly impacted how the literary heritage would be read.

The period of Persianate modernity was marked by extensive social changes and political upheavals in response to colonialism and despotism, such as the 1857 revolt in India and the Constitutional Revolution of 1905–11 in Iran. Established intellectual networks and centers of scholarship were disrupted, and new models of pedagogy emerged. The traditional mode of reading – together with an authoritative teacher – was increasingly unsustainable, and concern with the accessibility of texts for independent study grew alongside the emergence of private reading practices.[6] This shift in reading practices also coincided with new conventions of scientific veracity. The increasingly scientific understanding of history discussed in Chapter 1, the scientific rationalist approach to sexuality presented in Chapter 2, and

---

[3] Hakala, *Negotiating Languages*.

[4] On Persianate canonization, see Schwartz, *Remapping Persian Literary History*, especially chapters 1 and 4, and Hodgkin, "Lāhūtī," chapters 2 and 3; on Persian literature as an academic discipline, see Fani, "Becoming Literature."

[5] Hakala, *Negotiating Languages*, 197.

[6] On the emergence of leisure time and private reading in Iran see Gheissari, *Iranian Intellectuals*, 50–60.

the adoption of evolutionary models surveyed in Chapter 3 all stemmed from new conventions of what made for a systematic and accurate record of reality. Mass print reproduction of texts, standardized orthography, and systematized punctuation were harnessed to a project of modernization dedicated to scientific classification and standardization. The complexity and ambiguity once celebrated in literature were superseded by simple, straightforward styles of poetry and prose, and the idiosyncrasy and spontaneity inherent to the manuscript tradition were displaced by the uniformity and consistency of print.

Many of these changes were, and still often are, presented as purely functional and pragmatic, guided by a rational modernizing spirit. In fact, the story of how Persian and Urdu came to be written and printed in the formats they take today is anything but straightforward, and these changes were certainly not inevitable. Just as literary history conformed to sexual conventions, as outlined in Chapter 2, it also presented the Persianate literary heritage in accordance with new formal conventions, consisting of standardized type, reformed orthography, and a new system of punctuation. Moving from the *tazkirah* tradition to the genre of literary history was also a shift from manuscript to print culture. Tellingly, the shift to print culture was not uniform in Iran and India; the differing nationalist narratives held by Persian- and Urdu-speakers, explored in Chapter 3, led Iranians and Indians to develop different relationships to script and print.

The historiography of Persian printing has often been bifurcated by the borders of Area Studies, with Iranian or Middle Eastern Studies scholars addressing print in Iran, while South Asianists tackle print in India. Connected histories of print can overcome such arbitrary boundaries and are far more useful for understanding the texts, technologies, and thinkers which circulated rather freely between Iran and India.[7] In addition to connected history, comparison remains a

---

[7] Examples of such connected history include Gelvin and Green, *Global Muslims*; Green, "Journeymen, Middlemen."

valuable tool. As we have seen in Chapter 3, juxtaposing differences between developments in Persian and Urdu reveals how each is historically contingent, making it easier to question narratives produced about either language. If the classic *nasta'liq* hand is incompatible with modernity, as some modernizers alleged, then what of Pakistan today, where everything from science to statecraft is carried out in *nasta'liq*?[8] By the same token, traditionalists in contemporary Iran who read and publish their texts in *naskh*, the style of writing that became the standard for print in Iran, would find the suggestion that they are breaking with Islamicate tradition absurd.

While several studies have addressed the utilitarian and ideological reasons for the proliferation of proposals for language and script reform,[9] this chapter also traces *affective* attachments to scripts, shapes of letters, and punctuation marks. Print and its conventions were technologies of modernization as well as sites of affective investments, and the physical appearance of the text was as significant to its readers as its content. In this chapter I initially zoom out from the analysis of literary history to examine the modernizing debates that proliferated around print and book culture more broadly. These debates were nevertheless shaped by the same underlying tensions that animated literary histories, namely the search for new forms, in Persian and in Urdu, for the Persianate literary heritage. After considering some of the central processes of transition from manuscript to print culture, I will return to a 1917 manuscript of Furughi's Persian literary history, and examine how its innovative use of punctuation marks it as a transitional text, encompassing some of the key conventions of modern writing while featuring possibilities that went unrealized in later texts.

---

[8] On Urdu as a language of science, see Amstutz, "Finding a Home for Urdu."

[9] Kia, "Persian Nationalism and the Campaign for Language Purification"; Perry, "Language Reform in Turkey and Iran"; Zia-Ebrahimi, *The Emergence of Iranian Nationalism*, 45–6.

4.1 STANDARDIZING TYPE

Print arrived comparatively late to the Arabic-script languages, including Persian and Urdu. In India, the British upended the scribes' monopoly over Persian writing through the introduction of print, creating a new market for books with the first lithographed works appearing in 1824.[10] Persian print technology quickly found its way to Iran as well.[11] For the first time, books could be produced cheaply and made readily available to a wider audience. These technological developments impacted typographic considerations, as not all calligraphic styles lent themselves to type.

Prior to print, Persian writing could be challenging to read for many reasons. Simplicity and clarity in language were not always virtues, and readers did not expect to be able to glance at a page and instantly understand everything written there. Literary texts were often read together with a teacher who could clarify the meaning. Moreover, Persian was penned in intricate, beautiful calligraphic styles that did not always lend themselves to easy comprehension, hand-copied by scribes whose varying levels of proficiency could further complicate legibility. Wealthy patrons commissioning texts tended to prefer works that were both beautiful objects and engrossing reads that would keep them engaged for a long time, justifying the high cost of having a book produced. As Finn Thiesen observes:

Classical Persian books were never meant for armchair reading. The very word *book* had quite different connotations in those days. It was not a cheap mass-produced commodity, but a rarity and a luxury. Few could read one, still fewer could afford to possess one. In order to acquire a book one had to copy it oneself or pay someone

---

[10] On the history of Persian printing in India before the period under discussion here, see the very fine PhD dissertation "Persian Print Culture in India, 1780–1880" by Mehrdad Ramezannia. For more on Persian and Urdu print culture in colonial India see Stark, *An Empire of Books.*

[11] Green, "Persian Print and the Stanhope Revolution"; Marashi, "Print Culture and Its Publics."

a month's wage to copy it. … Certainly the reader who paid so
dearly for his book would not have been satisfied with a few hours'
light entertainment, and might prefer a work which could not be
understood without effort. Ideally, a literary Classical Persian work
should be so beautiful in form and so rich in content that the reader
would return to it again and again.[12]

With the high level of expertise needed to parse Persian texts and in
the absence of mass education, Persian literacy remained limited to a
minority of the overall population until late in the twentieth century.
In fact, the literati had a vested class interest in keeping Persian
writing inaccessible.[13]

Historically, a number of calligraphic handwriting styles had been
developed in Persian and adopted by Urdu as well. *Nasta 'liq* developed
in fourteenth-century Shiraz and became the dominant hand for poetry
manuscripts, as opposed to other hands used for more bureaucratic and
administrative purposes. Its ascendancy coincided with the rise of the
tazkirah genre, and it soon took over as the most popular style for
writing Persian (and, later, Urdu).[14] *Nasta 'liq* could be written quickly
and compactly, saving scribes time and allowing them to fit more text
on a single page, a valuable feature when paper was expensive.[15]
However, its sloping, cursive, nonlinear elegance later proved difficult
to reproduce with typesetting technology. *Naskh*, a more linear, orderly,
and consistent script was also used, especially for copies of the Qur'an
(where unambiguous intelligibility was especially important), and this
script lent itself much more easily to the development of type.

*Tazkirah*s and other texts written in manuscript could take
advantage of the differences between *nasta 'liq* and *naskh*. A copy of
Vajid 'Ali Shah's *Mubahasah bayn al-Nafs va al-'Aql* (*Debate between
the Ego and the Intellect*; see Figure 4.1) illustrates this point.

---

[12] Thiesen, *A Manual of Classical Persian Prosody*, xi.

[13] Spooner and Hanaway, *Literacy in the Persianate World*, 55–8; Robinson, "Islam
and the Impact of Print," 233.

[14] Wright, *The Look of the Book*, 234. Wright connects developments in calligraphy
and the rise of the *tazkirah* to "a growing fascination with the individual" (253).

[15] Yūsofī, "Calligraphy."

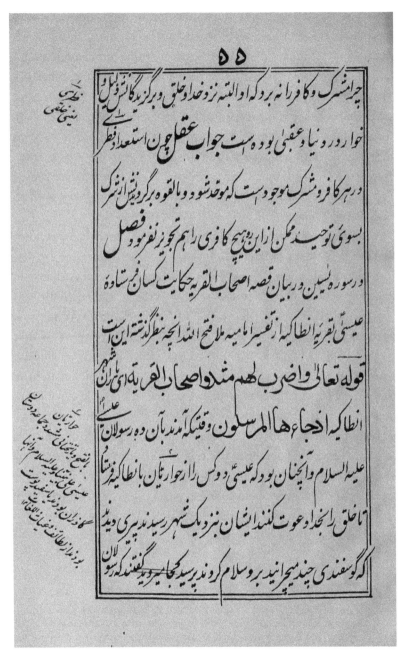

FIGURE 4.1 Folio from Vajid ʿAli Shah's *Mubahasah bayn al-Nafs va al-ʿAql*. Lithograph, 1874.

The Persian text is written in a fine *nasta'liq* hand, while a verse from the Qur'an (36:13) stands out from the text in *naskh*, preceded by the Arabic phrase "His exalted word" (*qawluhu ta'ala*).[16] The effect produced by giving a quotation in *naskh* in a text otherwise written in *nasta'liq* is similar to the use of italics in English. This manuscript convention has survived and been modernized. In modern printed Urdu, the body of a text is usually in *nasta'liq*, while *naskh* is primarily used for quotations from the Qur'an or other Arabic texts. Even when Urdu books are printed in *naskh*, an Urdu typeface is used for the main text whereas Arabic quotations are reproduced with an Arabic-style typeface.[17]

Naskh was easy to reproduce with movable type, but *nasta'liq*, with its greater number of context-dependent shapes, proved more difficult. Fort William College in Calcutta attempted to develop movable type in *nasta'liq*, but the technical challenges proved too great (see Figure 4.2).[18] In Iran the first printing press (using movable type) was established in Tabriz, publishing its first printed Persian book in 1817, but lithography initially proved far more popular. Lithography was less expensive to produce, and the equipment required less expertise than that of movable type. More importantly, it could reproduce aesthetically pleasing *nasta'liq*, while typesetting had to be done in *naskh*. With lithography, a calligrapher could handwrite the text in *nasta'liq* on a plate which would be duplicated entirely; it is therefore a form of handwritten print, unlike the entirely mechanical nature of type. As the scholar of Iranian lithography Ulrich Marzolph describes, "when set against the highly esteemed and aesthetically prestigious *nasta'liq*,

---

[16] Vajid 'Ali Shah, *Mubahasah bayn al-Nafs va al-'Aql*, 55.

[17] For an example see Shibli, *Shi'r al-'Ajam*, 1:1. The text opens with quoted lines of Persian poetry from 'Urfi Shirazi in *nasta'liq*, followed by an Arabic supplication in *naskh*, printed with an Arabic-style typeface. The Urdu which makes up the body of the text is in *nasta'liq*.

[18] On the earliest European experiments with *nasta'liq* typefounding see Izadpanah, "Early Persian Printing," 98–111.

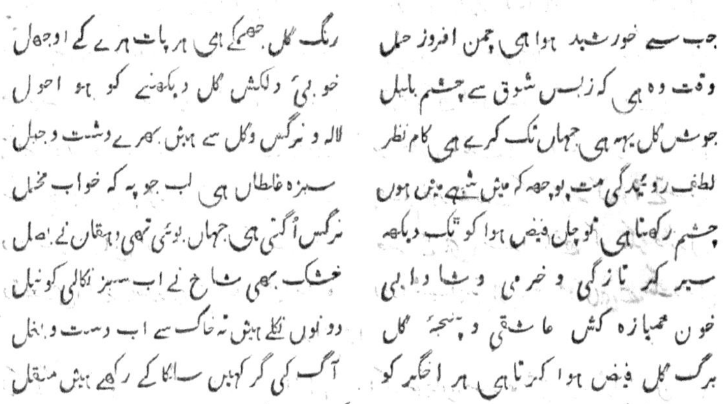

FIGURE 4.2 The Urdu poetry of Mir Taqi "Mir," in the clumsy typeset *nasta'liq* of Fort Williams College.

the *naskh* characters produced from movable type were bound to be regarded with disfavor by an Iranian audience and to be seen as unappealingly crude and unrefined." Lithography continued the Persian manuscript tradition in a way that type could not.[19]

As lithography allowed for the inexpensive reproduction of handwritten *nasta'liq* script, it helped popularize printed books among Iranians, who preferred *nasta'liq* over *naskh*.[20] Initially lithography and type coexisted in Iran, with lithography the favored method. Yet while lithographed *nasta'liq* helped make printed Persian ubiquitous, it was ultimately *naskh* in movable type that won out in Iran. By the middle of the twentieth century, lithography had disappeared, and eventually nearly all works printed in Iran would come to be set in *naskh*, with *nasta'liq* reserved for ornamental purposes. Afshin Marashi sees the triumph of *naskh* over *nasta'liq* as part of the larger language reform movement, enabled by Iranian state investment in typesetting technology and modern

[19] Marzolph, *Narrative Illustration*, 12–15. [20] Vejdani, *Making History*, 10.

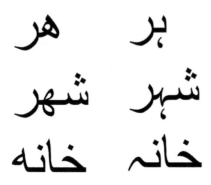

FIGURE 4.3 Compare the contemporary Persian (left) and Urdu (right) print forms of the initial, medial, and final *ha*.

schooling. Movable type was a vehicle for the expansion of Iranian literacy.[21]

This was not so in South Asia, where *nasta'liq* has retained its primacy until the present day, and where state efforts to promote *naskh* – by colonial and postcolonial regimes alike – were met with popular rebuke. While typeset *naskh* became dominant by the turn of the twentieth century in Iran, most printed works in Urdu were hand-written in *nasta'liq* and then reproduced with lithography until the 1990s, following the advent of digital *nasta'liq* fonts in the early 1980s. Urdu works have also been printed in typeset *naskh* (albeit more rarely), but standardized *naskh* in Urdu differs subtly from Persian *naskh* typefaces. In particular, it captures and retains elements of the handwritten *nasta'liq* tradition, such as in the shape of the initial, medial, or word-final connected *ha'* (Figure 4.3). In each of the examples of typed *naskh*, the letter *ha'* (initial, medial, and final, respectively) in the Urdu typeface more closely resembles its shape in *nasta'liq*.

For many contemporary Urdu speakers, *nasta'liq* is an integral part of the language. The linguist Mirza Khalil A. Beg, writing in 1995, considered it to be one of the characteristics inherent to the Urdu script: "Urdu script is characterized by the following features ... it has *nastaliq* [sic] (a fine round hand) style of writing."[22] Today, Urdu

[21] Marashi, "Print Culture and Its Publics," 100–1.
[22] Beg, "The Standardization of Script for Urdu," 232.

speakers colloquially use the term *"nasta'liq"* to refer to the Perso-Arabic script in general, including *naskh*, when differentiating between this script and another writing system such as the Latin alphabet or the Devanagari script used by Hindi.[23] This kind of synecdoche is never deployed by Iranians, for whom *naskh* and *nasta'liq* do not have the same identitarian valences. In other words, *nasta'liq* is merely one option among others for contemporary Iranians, but symbolizes an entire writing system and set of aesthetic values for South Asians.

Urdu printing continued to depend on lithography until the digital age, driven by a strong attachment on the part of Urdu readers to the *nasta'liq* style of writing. While elites sometimes sought to challenge this attachment, their efforts were ultimately unsuccessful. In a 1964 speech given at the foundation stone-laying ceremony for the Urdu College campus in Karachi, Pakistani president Ayub Khan called for Urdu to adopt the *naskh* script. Ayub Khan viewed *nasta'liq* as antiquated, arguing that

> the *Nastaliq* [*sic*] script, pretty though it looks, was in vogue during the days when calligraphists could afford to take their own time in writing out the text. … In view of these difficulties it is imperative to consider why we should not adopt Arabic *Naskh* script in place of the Persian *Nastaliq* [*sic*].[24]

Like many Urdu speakers, Ayub Khan associated *naskh* with Arabic because it was the style typically used for writing the Qur'an in South Asia, whereas *nasta'liq* had traditionally been the dominant script of the Persianate tradition. Switching to *naskh* would allow Pakistanis to use typewriting and typesetting technology which existed in *naskh*.

---

[23] Given the assumption that Urdu will be written in *nasta'liq*, a distinction in script choices is made not between *nasta'liq* and *naskh* but between the Perso-Arabic script and romanized Urdu in the Latin script, the latter of which now proliferates across Urdu-language social media, web forums, and SMS messages. In contemporary India, Urdu is also sometimes written in the Devanagari script. See Ahmad, "Urdu in Devanagari."

[24] Ayub Khan, *Speeches and statements*, 6:216–17.

"Experiments so far carried out on printing Urdu in *Naskh* were not pursued as a result of the bravura of the conservatives against it," Ayub Khan explained, as he urged a dispassionate, scientific approach to language.[25] He concluded his speech with a call for both Urdu and Bengali – the co-official languages of Pakistan at the time – to be written in *naskh*. Bengali had its own writing system, an Indic cousin of the Devanagari script used to write Hindi. In fact, efforts to impose the Perso-Arabic script on Bengali contributed to inflaming identitarian tensions in the buildup to the 1971 war which culminated in the secession of East Pakistan, now the independent nation of Bangladesh.[26] Attempts to impose *naskh* on Urdu did not fare much better, and *nasta 'liq* remains the style of choice for Urdu writing today.

Comparing the divergent trajectories of print in the two regions allows us to ask directly why *naskh* in movable type succeeded in Iran but failed in South Asia. Part of the answer lies in different forms of national and linguistic identity, shaped by different relationships to Orientalist knowledge, as explored in Chapter 3. Iranian nationalists articulated an identity that was not bound to a particular script, considering "Old Persian," "Middle Persian," and "New Persian" as varied stages in the long trajectory of a single language, written in multiple scripts. If the language could endure radical changes in script between these stages, surely the relatively minor change from *nasta 'liq* to *naskh* posed no essential issue. In contrast, the identity of Urdu speakers was far more fixated on the script itself, as it was the one feature that definitively demarcated their language from Hindi. For them, *nasta 'liq* was more than a style of writing; it was a synecdoche for the Perso-Arabic script altogether, which was a constitutive element of their identity.

The history of the early printing presses in India and Iran was another important difference. In India, the first printing presses were

---

[25] On Urdu typography and scientific modernity see Amstutz, "Finding a Home for Urdu," 74–124.

[26] Rahman, *Language and Politics in Pakistan*, 79–102.

operated by British colonial officials, often printing Christian missionary works. Some of the earliest Urdu publications were missionary literature, often romanized or in typeset *naskh*, and many Muslim intellectuals perceived them as an attack on Indo-Muslim tradition.[27] The impact of these colonial institutions on print in India left a lasting impression, despite the founding of numerous Indian-owned printing presses like Nawal Kishore by the mid-nineteenth century, and despite the fact that early printed works in India also included Persianate classics like the *divan* of Hafiz and Firdawsi's *Shahnamah*. In contrast, in Iran the first printing presses were owned by the Qajar state, and as Marzolph has argued, they played a significant role in disseminating popular religious texts. The first book to be typographically printed in Iran was the *Risalah-yi Jihadiyyah* (*Treatise on Jihad*, 1818), a collection of fatwas on jihad, and other early publications were of similar materials.[28] The different conditions of early print in Iran and India, and the distinct characteristics of nationalist narratives around Persian and Urdu, led to divergent outcomes for typography in the two countries. Modernizers were not only concerned with determining which hand the Perso-Arabic script should be written with; many challenged the orthography altogether, questioning whether to use the Perso-Arabic script at all or to replace it with another.

4.2 ORTHOGRAPHIES

Orthography – the conventions of writing, from script choice to spelling – can be a surprisingly contentious issue. In the Balkans, as the Slavist Robert D. Greenberg notes, orthographic manuals delineating different spellings for Bosnian, Croatian, and Serbian "were so politically explosive that they were destroyed upon printing" in the

---

[27] Lelyveld, "Sir Sayyid's Public Sphere," 101. Print itself was initially taken as an attack on Islamic authority in India. See Robinson, "Islam and the Impact of Print."

[28] Marzolph, *The Printing Press as an Agent of Tradition*.

1960s and 1970s.[29] Orthographic issues have been no less controversial in the Persianate world. Mustafa Kemal "Atatürk" famously engineered a switch from the Perso-Arabic script to a Latin-based one for Turkish, in what came to be known as the *harf devrimi* or "letter revolution."[30] In Persian-speaking Tajikistan, use of the Latin script over Perso-Arabic in the 1920s and 1930s "symbolized ... scientific and technical progress" and helped forge a Tajik identity separate from the other Persian-speaking countries.[31] Latin (and subsequently Cyrillic) eventually replaced Perso-Arabic across much of the rest of Central Asia and the Caucasus.[32] The Latin alphabet also replaced Arabic in places like Somalia and the Malay archipelago, and similar proposals were made across the Arab world, though none were ultimately successful. Script reform energized modernizers in China, Korea, and elsewhere as well.[33] While modernizers proposed several new scripts in Iran and India for Persian and Urdu, respectively, these efforts ultimately failed to gain traction.

Proposals for script reform were often entangled with identitarian concerns. One of the motivations for the Turkish state to adopt the Latin script for Turkish was to align Turkey with the "progressive" West rather than the "backwards," Muslim East. However, there were practical concerns as well. The Arabic script is uniquely well-suited to writing classical Arabic. There is a nearly one-to-one correspondence

---

[29] Greenberg, *Language and Identity in the Balkans*, 5. Bosnian, Croatian, and Serbian are largely mutually intelligible but are officially treated as separate languages, with some differences in orthography and formal vocabulary – similar to the relationship between Hindi and Urdu. On orthographies in Bosnian, Croatian, and Serbian see ibid., 41–7.

[30] Lewis, *The Turkish Language Reform*, 27–39.

[31] Bergne, *The Birth of Tajikistan*, 96. The Latin script would soon after be replaced with use of the Cyrillic script.

[32] In many of these locales, romanization was a colonial imposition, though in Turkey and Somalia it was organized under the auspices of independent republics.

[33] On romanization as a global phenomenon see Aytürk, "Romanisation in Comparative Perspective"; on romanization in the Middle East, see Shraybom Shivtiel, "The Question of Romanisation" and Aytürk, "Attempts at Romanizing the Hebrew Script"; on script reform in China, including romanization proposals, see Zhong, *Chinese Grammatology*; on script reform in Korea, see King, "Nationalism and Language Reform in Korea."

between spoken and written consonants, and while three of classical Arabic's six vowels are left unwritten, Arabic morphology is structured around highly regular, predictable patterns, so that educated readers can assume the missing vowels with a high degree of accuracy, even when encountering an unfamiliar word. However, this elegantly concise system becomes much less effective, and much more ambiguous, when applied to languages whose structure differs from Arabic. Words in Turkish – as well as Persian, Urdu, and other non-Semitic languages – are not built according to predictable patterns, making it more difficult for the reader to deduce the unwritten short vowels. Guessing is made all the more complicated when languages have larger vowel inventories that are left unwritten; Turkish, for example, has eight vowels, and Urdu has ten. For these reasons, confusion abounds between words that differ only in their unwritten vowels, such as Persian *gul* ("flower") and *gil* ("mud"), both written as *gl* in the Perso-Arabic script.

Modernizers across the Persianate world sought to eliminate ambiguity and imprecision in all aspects of language. Proposals to replace the Perso-Arabic script with a script deemed more precise and scientific – typically Latin – would present themselves as purely pragmatic.[34] Proponents of the Latin script insisted that its simplicity and accuracy would increase literacy rates. Even Geoffrey Lewis, author of the magisterial study *The Turkish Language Reform: A Catastrophic Success*, believes that Latinization "has played a large part in the rise of literacy [in Turkish] ... from 9 per cent in 1924 ... to 82.3 per cent in 1995."[35] But many other countries witnessed similarly dramatic increases in literacy without changing their script. Iran raised its general literacy rate from about 30 percent in 1968[36] to 85 percent in 2008, without abandoning or altering the same Perso-Arabic script once used to write Turkish.[37] Just as with the other conventions of Persianate

---

[34] Beg notes that script reform is often referred to as "script modernization" ("The Standardization of Script for Urdu," 227).

[35] Lewis, *The Turkish Language Reform*, 37.

[36] Iran Almanac, cited in Loeb, *Outcaste*, 132.

[37] UNESCO, "Adult and Youth Literacy," 35. In the final analysis, literacy rates depend on education and development, not script. This is why today Japan and Taiwan boast some of the highest literacy rates anywhere in the world, despite their

modernity examined in previous chapters – be they historiographical, erotic, or narrative – reform had more to do with image and identity than practical considerations, though the two are intimately intertwined. For westernizers, a convention like use of the Latin script is ultimately seen as modern and pragmatic because it is Western. Even those who advocated modifying, rather than abandoning, the Perso-Arabic script similarly fetishized orthography as a kind of technology through which modernization could be achieved.

As discussed in Chapter 3, just as Iranian nationalists were seeking to distance themselves from Arabic and Islam, in India Urdu began to assume an identity as an "Islamic" language. For Urdu-speakers, use of the Perso-Arabic script was an important – even constitutive – element of the language's identity, and proposals to change the script were seen by some as sacrilegious, threatening to undermine the language's Muslim identity.[38] The British in particular promoted Urdu transliterated into the Latin script (called "Roman Urdu" or "Roman Hindustani" in their terminology) for a number of reasons. It was used in the military to deliver unified instructions to Indian soldiers from various provinces who might not have a shared literacy in a single script (or been literate at all). Some Christian missionaries favored the Latin script not only for cultural reasons, but because evangelical material could be translated into local dialects and transcribed in the Latin script for easy use by proselytizers. Ease of use also motivated the British to employ the Latin script in preparing much of their educational materials for training officers in local languages. Already by 1803, the Scottish Orientalist John Gilchrist presented materials in a number of languages (Hindustani, Persian, Arabic, Braj, Bengali, and Sanskrit), all written in the Latin

notoriously difficult writing systems, while Somalia, which replaced the Arabic script with a simple, largely phonetic version of the Latin alphabet, has one of the lowest literacy rates. John R. Perry similarly inveighs against what he terms the "alphabetical fallacy" behind the "pseudo-scientific" assumption that the complexity of a writing system is directly tied to literacy. See Perry, "Comparative Perspectives on Language Planning," 158.

[38] The Turkish script change was initially met with hostility on the same grounds; see Lewis, *The Turkish Language Reform*, 32.

alphabet, and defended his transliteration methods as more pedagogic-ally sound than using the original scripts.[39]

In addition to the British, some Indian secular nationalists, like Subhas Chandra Bose (1897–1945), were in favor of writing Urdu and other local languages in the Latin script in order to promote national unity in face of the great diversity of scripts found on the Indian subcontinent.[40] Abu'l Kalam Azad conceded that the army's use of "Roman Hindustani" made it possible to quickly grant literacy to millions of previously unlettered Indian soldiers.[41] Among the Indian languages which did not use a variation of the Perso-Arabic script, the majority of the larger languages had their own unique scripts, tied to the identity of their speakers. While there was a greater degree of flexibility and fluidity in the past, with languages often written in multiple scripts, as the languages took on independent ethnic (and, in some cases, national) identities in the modern period, associations between language, script, and people calcified.

In Iran, proponents of script reform, such as Mirza Fath'ali Akhundzadah (1812–78), Mirza Malkum Khan (1833–1908; see Figure 4.4), and Sayyid Hasan Taqizadah (1878–1970), largely articu-lated their arguments in terms of scientific precision, but their orien-tation towards westernization reveals the fact that their agendas were about culture and identity at least as much as pragmatic issues, if not more so.[42] Discussions of script reform in Iran often focus on a few larger-than-life modernizers like these three, but it is important to see them as part of a much larger trend within Iran, a veritable explosion of script reform proposals.[43] Some advocated Latinization, or the adoption of the Latin script for writing Persian, as was eventually

---

[39] Gilchrist, *The Oriental Fabulist*, preface.
[40] Bose, "Free India and Her Problems," 146.
[41] Azad, *Selected Works of Maulana Abul Kalam Azad*, 3:49–50.
[42] See Algar, "Malkum Khan, Akhūndzada and the Proposed Reform of the Arabic Alphabet"; Perry, "Comparative Perspectives on Language Planning"; and Zia-Ebrahimi, *The Emergence of Iranian Nationalism*, 174–5. Taqizadah later changed his views, abandoning the idea of adopting the Latin script for Persian.
[43] These are summarized in Zuka', *Taghyir-i Khatt-i Farsi*, published in 1329 HS/ 1950–1 CE, and in Ustadi, "Tarikhchah-yi Andishah-yi Taghyir-i Khatt dar Iran."

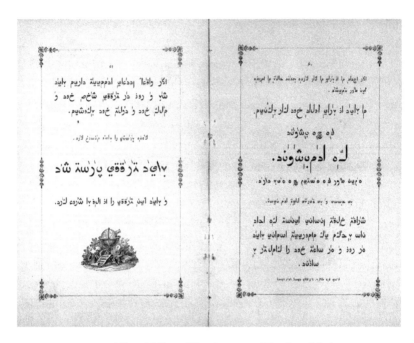

FIGURE 4.4 Mirza Malkum Khan's proposed Persian alphabet.

the case in neighboring Turkey. Others, like Akhundzadah and Mirza Riza Khan Arfaʿ al-Dawlah (1846–1937), invented new alphabets based on Latin, Cyrillic, or even mixtures of the two. Rather than abandoning the Perso-Arabic script altogether, several modernizers proposed to modify it, though some modifications, like Malkum Khan's, stretched the script beyond recognition (Figure 4.4). Still others came up with entirely new writing systems. In 1913, Mirza ʿAli Muhammad Khan Uvaysi (1884–1968/1969), an Iranian consular in Istanbul, published a guide to a truly unique alphabet he had invented for Persian (see Figure 4.5).[44] The Iranian scholar Yahya

[44] Uvaysi, *Khatt-i Naw*. Uvaysi also served as vice consul in Baku, where he wrote and edited the magazine *Haqaʾiq* (Browne, *Press and Poetry*, 77), and as governor of Khuzistan province (Coll 28/67 "Persia. Annual Reports, 1932–") [83r] (165/644), British Library: India Office Records and Private Papers, IOR/L/PS/12/3472A, in Qatar Digital Library <www.qdl.qa/archive/81055/vdc_100056661166.0x0000a6> [accessed 27 June 2020]. His theories on education and race are discussed in Schayegh, *Who Is Knowledgeable Is Strong*, 188 and 191–2 (erroneously transliterated as "Āvisi").

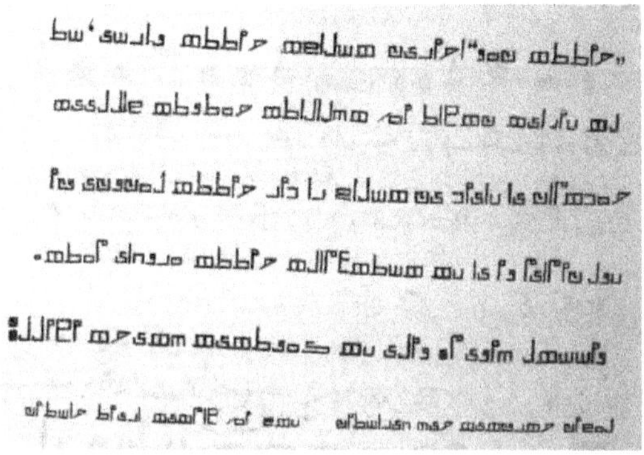

FIGURE 4.5 'Ali Muhammad Khan Uvaysi's "new script" (khatt-i naw).

Zuka' surveys fifty different proposals for changing the Perso-Arabic script from the late nineteenth century until 1950, all from Iran alone.[45] His list reads like a who's who of Iranian intellectuals and litterateurs of the period. Similar replacements for the script were designed by Persian-speakers in Kabul (a place greatly influenced by developments in both Iran and in India and a hub for translation between Persian and Urdu; see Figure 4.6)[46] and Bombay.[47]

These proposals must be viewed as part of a larger trend in Iran, India, other Persianate regions, and indeed throughout the Islamicate world. As discussed above, the late nineteenth and early twentieth

[45] Zuka', Taghyir-i Khatt-i Farsi.

[46] Refer to Figure 4.6 and see Yusufi, "Rasm al-Khatt." Though published in 1953, the journal indicates that the author, Muhammad Akbar Khan Yusufi, had devised this proposal 30–40 years earlier. Yusufi argued that the Perso-Arabic script slowed down the acquisition of knowledge ('ulum) because of the need to learn two or three forms for each letter (i.e.. initial, medial, and final), the absence of short vowels, and other deficiencies. He claimed the Latin script was similarly unsuitable because of the need for digraphs to represent a single sound. Yusufi's script was designed to more adequately represent Persian as well as Pashto and even Arabic, and was fully cursive, so that one would never need to lift their pen from the page while writing. He may have been influenced by the Armenian alphabet, which bears striking resemblance to some of his script's letters. Kabul was home to an Armenian community until well into the twentieth century; see Lee, "The Armenians of Kabul."

[47] Khatt-i Danish va Insaniyat, Bombay 1308 AH. I have been unable to access this lithographed pamphlet.

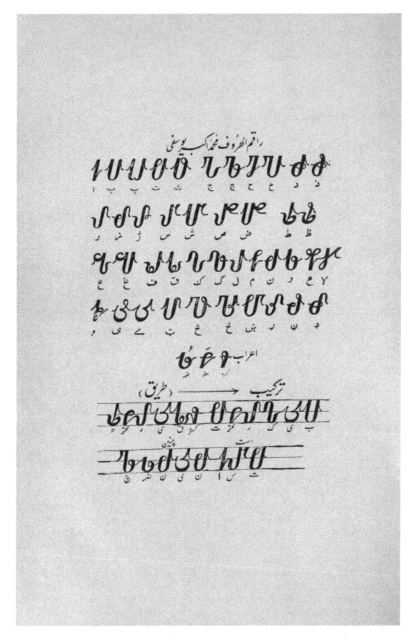

FIGURE 4.6 Muhammad Akbar Khan Yusufi's alphabet for Arabic, Persian, and Pashto.
Courtesy of University of Nebraska Omaha Libraries' Archives and Special Collections.

centuries had witnessed numerous proposals to change the Perso-Arabic script from Turkey to Indonesia. Situating Iran in the context of this global moment of impassioned linguistic reform demonstrates how the endurance of the Perso-Arabic script in Iran cannot be taken for granted; indeed, its use was abandoned for Persian in other countries (Tajikistan and Uzbekistan) more than a century ago. Furthermore, the comparison with Urdu further reveals the historical contingency of the shape that script reform took in Iran. As we saw in Chapter 3, Arabic was a constitutive element of Urdu's identity as a language; the Perso-Arabic script is most often cited as the defining difference between Urdu and Hindi. Therefore, script reform found less traction among Urdu speakers, and where debates over script did emerge, they often took the form of *nasta 'liq* versus *naskh*, or, more rarely, Latinization versus tradition. However, for Iranian nationalists and modernizers who defined their identity *in opposition* to Arabic rather than *through* it, new script proposals offered a third option in addition to Perso-Arabic and Latin. While many Iranian intellectuals identified closely with Europe, with some arguing for westernization and others contending that Iran was already inherently linked to Europe via Aryan heritage,[48] the importance of indigeneity to Iranian nationalism necessitated a third way between Arab-Islamic heritage and the West. Proposing a new script – whether significantly modifying the existing Perso-Arabic script to make it uniquely Iranian, or developing something that is entirely novel – can be understood as an expression of nativist Iranian nationalism, but also as an affective experience.

What motivated modernizers and reformers to direct their creative energies toward script? Nationalism, while undoubtedly an aspect of their worldview, is not a satisfactory explanation on its own. There is a great deal of creative energy and intellectual pleasure

---

[48] Zia-Ebrahimi, *The Emergence of Iranian Nationalism*, 147–68. In what Zia-Ebrahimi terms "dislocative nationalism," Iranian nationalists saw themselves as the Aryan cousins of Europeans and Iran as an essentially European nation in the Middle East. See also Burton, *Genetic Crossroads*, 29–66.

involved in the project of deriving new scripts or writing in a radically new way. Any language student who has learned a new script, or anyone who has invented a secret code for writing private notes, can relate to the pleasures of orthography, the thrill of writing characters that are novel yet intelligible. Moreover, anyone who ever coined a slang term that caught on, even if only among their friends, can understand something of the excitement these modernizers must have felt.

Though proposals to either significantly modify or replace the Perso-Arabic script ultimately failed to gain traction in either Iran or South Asia, nationalists' desires for a unique script found expression instead in the efforts to standardize the script's graphemes, or the particular forms of individual letters. Written in variations of the Perso-Arabic script, many languages developed independent standards which made each language visually distinct. Persian standardized variant forms of letters (in particular its unique *gaf*, distinctive final *kaf*, and undotted final *ya*) which made it more visually dissimilar to Arabic. These letters had existed in the manuscript tradition, but were not used consistently by scribes, who often did not distinguish between *gaf* and *kaf*. Urdu, as discussed above, incorporated elements of *nasta'liq* into its standard *naskh*-based print typefaces (see Figure 4.3). The language was initially written according to Persian orthography, with modifications made over time to differentiate sounds unique to Urdu. Urdu lacked a consistent orthography of its own until the nineteenth or twentieth century. As can be seen from the plethora of orthographic manuals or *imla' namah*s that were produced over the past century or so, the development of the orthographic conventions now more or less standard in Urdu has been an ongoing process that unfolded over a considerable period of time.[49] Urdu orthography underwent several transformations, with individual writers and publishers taking rather idiosyncratic approaches to

---

[49] I thank Walter Hakala for suggesting this avenue for investigating the standardization of Urdu orthography.

the writing system, and different symbols used at different times to represent retroflex consonants (those produced with the tongue curled back in the mouth).

The representation of retroflex consonants was one site where the "narcissism of small differences" manifested itself in the orthographies of South Asian languages written in the Perso-Arabic script like Urdu, Pashto, and Sindhi. The voiceless retroflex stop [ṭ] – put less technically, a "retroflex T" – is pronounced the same but written differently in each of these languages. All three have followed the same principle for creating a new letter to represent this sound by modifying the Arabic letter ت (representing the non-retroflex [t]). However, the three languages have developed three distinctive modifications: ٹ in Urdu (previously written as ٿ), ټ in Pashto, and ٽ in Sindhi.

In 1919, Abdullah Yusuf Ali (1872–1953), the famed Indian translator of the Qur'an into English, published a "Note on Urdu Orthography" in which he lamented inconsistent spelling and orthography in Urdu.[50] He took particular issue with inconsistent spacing between compound words. Ali called for a distinction between final *choti ye* (what he called a "deep and round" shape), *bari ye* ("turned back"), and a third ("shallow and long, left-hand end not turned up").[51] He noted that this distinction was already made by careful writers, but blamed lithographic presses for the "lazy practice" of only distinguishing between the first and second forms – though this tripartite distinction did not ultimately prevail. He further called for the same distinction to be made with the medial *ye*, to distinguish between [ī], [ē], and the diphthong [ai]; this distinction, while also observed by some writers, similarly failed to become standard. His essay discussed other distinctions, some of which became part of the standard conventions of Urdu type (such as calling for discarding the

---

[50] Yusuf Ali was educated in Bombay, in both the reform-oriented Islamic school Anjuman Himayat al-Islam as well as the Scottish mission Wilson College. He was both a personally pious Muslim and a dedicated servant of the British Empire.

[51] Yusuf Ali, "Note on Urdu Orthography," 31.

"antiquated" four dots [ٿ] then used to mark retroflex letters in favor of the superscript *toe* [ٿ]) whereas others failed to gain popularity, such as an idiosyncratic way of writing the letter *waw* to denote the diphthong "au."[52] Elsewhere, Ali clarified that his goal in reforming Urdu orthography was to pave the way for effective movable type in Urdu, lamenting that "no modern language can make progress, or even hold its own, which depends upon lithography and is not able to use the latest resources of the printing-press."[53] However, as we have seen, Urdu lithography endured much longer than Ali predicted.

Such debates demonstrate how orthography was bound up with identitarian concerns and was not simply the outcome of technological changes. Modernizers proposed and adopted new orthographical conventions which would mark their work as modern while also flagging the distinctive identities of their languages. While orthography was a domain in which elements of the manuscript tradition could be retained, albeit standardized, other domains, namely punctuation, were abandoned altogether and replaced entirely with European-style conventions.

4.3   PUNCTUATION BEFORE PRINT

In an article on punctuation published in the final years of his life in 1990, the Iranian writer Muhammad ʿAli Jamalzadah narrates a story which he had read in a book about a comma saving a "dangerous political revolutionary" from Siberian exile. This anecdote appears in a number of English-language journals and books in the first years of the twentieth century, both in didactic contexts emphasizing the importance of proper punctuation and in collections of amusing tidbits and odd facts. An early example, published in *The Typographical Journal* in 1904, reads:

---

[52] Ibid., 33–4. The superscript *toe* may have originally evolved as a shorthand form for quickly writing four dots without lifting the pen. I am grateful to Matt Boutilier for suggesting this possibility.

[53] Yusuf Ali, "Social and Economic Conditions," 361.

On the margin Alexander III had written "Pardon impossible; to be sent to Siberia." The Czarina took up the pen and, striking out the semicolon after "impossible," put it before that word. Then the endorsement read: "Pardon; impossible to be sent to Siberia." The Czar let the correction stand, good husband that he was.[54]

Jamalzadah addresses the issue of punctuation (*nuqtah-guzari*, *'ala-mat-guzari*), explaining that the French call it *"punk tuvasiyun"* (transliterated into Persian), and clarifying, in Latin characters between parentheses, "(Pumctua = tiom)" [*sic*].[55] He explains that not only the French, but "all the people of the West" (*tamam-i mardum-i maghrib zamin*) place great importance on punctuation. By the time he was writing, educated Iranians were familiar with punctuation, but its use was still not entirely naturalized in Persian. As he states, "you must certainly know well that among the Westerners [*farangi-ha*] there are many of these symbols," naming several examples: the period (*nuqtah*), exclamation mark (*nuqtah-yi ta'ajjub*), question mark (*nuqtah-yi istifham*), colon (*du nuqtah*), parenthesis (*parantiz*), comma (*virgul*), semicolon (*nuqtah va virgul*), and dash (*khatt*), among others. Jamalzadah notes that "it is impossible for them to end a sentence without a punctuation mark," whereas Iranians have no such custom, except for the use of blank space in handwritten letters to separate subjects. However, "in the last hundred years" (that is, 1890–1990) younger Iranians who studied European languages had become familiar with the use of punctuation. Early adopters of the form, they used it in their own Persian writing and even in poetry. He goes on to argue for the importance of adopting punctuation, especially in the journal *Kilk* in which his article was published. Worthy of note is that Jamalzadah himself uses

---

[54] Edwards, "Men and Their Methods," 108.

[55] Jamalzadah, "Shivah-yi Nuqtah Guzari." The use of *m* here rather than *n* in spelling "punctuation" may be a misreading of French handwriting wherein *n* resembles an English *m*.

punctuation very sparingly in his article, and some sentences run on for over half a page with nary a comma or period to break them up.

As with print itself, the formal conventions associated with print culture such as punctuation materialized comparatively late in the Arabic-script languages. At the end of his comprehensive *Tarikh Adab al-Lughah al-'Arabiyyah* (*History of Arabic Literature*, 1911–14), the Lebanese historian Jurji Zaydan identifies new developments in Arabic prose during the *nahdah* or Arab "renaissance" in the late nineteenth and early twentieth centuries. Among them are simplified sentence structure, dividing texts into chapters and sections with clear headings indicating their content, indices, the scholarly apparatus in the form of citations and footnotes, and punctuation. He explains the purpose of punctuation: writers "separate sentences with dots (*nuqat*) or marks (*'alamat*) which indicate the objectives of the writer, like stopping, exclamation, questioning, and so on, and marks which surround a parenthetical clause, or distinguish certain circumstances."[56] While European-style punctuation is now used across the Islamicate world – albeit less frequently and consistently than in European languages – few today understand the punctuation system indigenous to the Islamicate manuscript tradition. Indeed, aside from academics and other specialists, contemporary Iranians are often unaware that Persian even had a system of punctuation prior to the European-style period, comma, and so on. In fact, there were many options available to punctuate texts prior to the introduction of print, and an increasingly sophisticated system of manuscript punctuation emerged just before movable type replaced the manuscript tradition in Iran. Some of these pre-print punctuation marks even survived the transition into print, if only briefly.

---

[56] Zaydan, *Tarikh Adab al-Lughah al-'Arabiyyah*, 1470–1. This work was originally published serially as articles in the newspaper *al-Hilal* between 1894–5. On Zaydan's reception in Persian, see Rastegar, "Literary Modernity between Arabic and Persian Prose" and Hanan Hammad, "Relocating a Common Past"; for his impact on historiography in Iran, see Vejdani, *Making History*, 163 and "The Place of Islam," 211.

Traditionally, in Persian writing prior to the advent of print, a page was not broken up by sentences marked by terminal periods as in English but contained extremely long run-on sentences wherein the conjunction *va* ("and") was used to punctuate, serving the role of the comma or period. A list in English of "X, Y, Z" would have been rendered in Persian as "X and Y and Z." Other conventions and paratextual elements were used to separate sections of text, such as a larger and/or bolded heading for the next section appearing on the same line of text, or an image such as a circle or a flower serving the role of a period at the end of a section. These conventions were adopted in some of the earliest Persian typeset publications in Iran. For example, Mirza Salih Shirazi's *Kaghaz-i Akhbar* (*Newspaper*, Figure 4.7), typeset in 1837, makes use of stars to break up text.[57]

Despite the absence of the kinds of print conventions and punctuation we have in English – italics, bold, commas, periods, and so on – there were many options available for breaking up and punctuating text. These were not at all standardized practices and varied significantly from work to work and scribe to scribe. Lines and sections could be demarcated in a variety of ways, including through the use of bold headings and images, among other possibilities.[58] The manuscript tradition also made use of borders (*jadval*), often colored, to separate sections, and sometimes three dots arranged in a triangle (typically in a different color ink than the text) were used to mark the end of a cited couplet of poetry. Rubrication, or the use of colored ink (generally red) in order to highlight words or headings and draw contrast with the otherwise black text, was a ubiquitous practice in the manuscript tradition. It could be found in manuscripts everywhere from German Bibles to Malay Qur'ans, and Persian *tazkirah*s were no exception. There were symbols to indicate quotations of poetry, and symbols that functioned like periods or end-quotes afterwards. Some

---

[57] On this early Persian newspaper, see Izadpanah, "The First Iranian Newspaper"; on its author, Mirza Salih Shirazi, see Green, *The Love of Strangers*.

[58] For additional punctuation strategies deployed in premodern Persian manuscripts see Estaji and Firooziyan Pooresfahani, "The Investigation of Punctuation."

356   PERSIAN NEWSPAPER

اخبار و وقایع شهر محرّم الحرام ۱۲۵۳ ﷼

در دار الخلافهٔ طهرانِ انطباع یافته ﷼

اخبار ممالک شرقیه ﷼

دار الخلافهٔ طهرانْ ٭ عالیجاه مقرب الخاقان خداداد خان انر سفارت
اسلامبول معاودت نمود نامه از اعلیحضرت سلطان محمود بحضور
اعلیحضرت شاهنشاهی آورد انر آنجا که سفارت مشار الیه مستحسن
رای جهان آرای شهریاری افتاد بعد از تبلیغ نامه و عرض مراتب
مامورِیت خود خاطر مبارک ازو خرسند گردید وپایه اعتبار عالیجاه
مشار الیه باعلی مدارج رسید و اورا بوزارت خوی مفتخر و سرافراز
فرمودند بنهجی که شاید و باید با ولایات سرحدیه دولتین علیتین
سعی و جدّ و جهد بلیغ نماید که روز بروز این دوستی و یکجهتی
تزاید پذیرد و رشته اتحاد محکم گردد و امریکه مورث نقار خاطر
و غبار کدورت ضمیر اولیای دولتین است رفع سازد ﷼

ایضا ٭ جناب جلالت مآب شریعت آداب آقا میر محمّد مهدی امام
جمعه و جماعت دار السلطنه اصفهان بدار الخلافه آمدند و با جمعی
کثیرائ علما که در خدمتش بودند بحضور باهر النّور شاهنشاه عدالت
سیر مشرف گشتند و الحق شخص وجودش از جمیع نقایص و ذمایم
پیراسته و بمحاسن اخلاق آراسته و بسبب عدم ریاء و تزویر
و بیساختگی و نجابت ذاتی و فطانت فطری و کمال انسانیت معزی
الیه خاطر مبارک شاهنشاهی خرسند گردید امرا و بزرگان درگاه وسران
و پیشکاران بارگاه با سایر چاکران حضرت دولت علیه و تمامی
اهل دار الخلافه بجنابش دست ارادت دادند دولتخواه و خیراندیش

FIGURE 4.7 *Kaghaz-i Akhbar*, 1837.

of these symbols have been reproduced in typeset Urdu, but not in Persian.

The Qur'an manuscript tradition had its own rich system of punctuation, with divisions made not from sentence to sentence or paragraph to paragraph, but rather verse (*ayah*) to verse and chapter (*surah*) to chapter. A single Qur'anic verse may, therefore, contain what become multiple sentences when translated into English, broken up by conjunction words. *Tajwid*, the rules governing recitation of the Qur'an, offered additional punctuation, including signs that indicate when a pause in reading/reciting is optional, recommended, recommended against, forbidden, and so on. This allows for a good deal of both flexibility and precision. Interestingly, the *tajwid* system has carried on into the print era but remains limited in use only to the text of the Qur'an itself; other modern Arabic texts – including commentaries on the Qur'an – use European-style punctuation.[59]

Strikingly, a symbol similar to an inverted comma appears in some Safavid-era *majmu'ah*s ("collections") of courtly correspondence (*tarassul*), used in place of the aforementioned Arabic formulae to separate poetic quotations (Figure 4.8).[60] The scribes (and authors) of these works are unknown, but given Safavid exchange with Europe,

[59] "Qur'an" literally means "recitation," and despite the well-developed Qur'anic manuscript tradition, it was and remains primarily an oral text to be recited aloud. Timothy Mitchell discusses the ways in which the nineteenth-century Qur'anic scholarly tradition at al-Azhar in Cairo resisted print and saw "the only way to read a text ... was to hear it read aloud, phrase by phrase, by one who had already mastered it, and to repeat and discuss it with such a master" (*Colonising Egypt*, 133). On the "new privileging of formal coherency in language" in nineteenth-century Arabic (Sacks, *Iterations of Loss*, 11) see ibid., 77–145.

[60] See Malik, 3850, *Tarassul*, page 57/folio 28–9. This manuscript is undated, but as it pertains to various individuals in the court of Shah Safi (r. 1629–42), it can be assumed to date from that time. Another example can be found in Malik, 2551, *Munsha'at va Ghayrah Majmu'ah*, 42. Marginalia from this manuscript dates it variously to 1100 AH/1688–9 CE or 1130 AH/1717–18 CE. I thank Shahla Farghadani for bringing these manuscripts to my attention and Kathryn Babayan for sharing the images with me. This symbol deserves further investigation in *majmu'ah*s from the period.

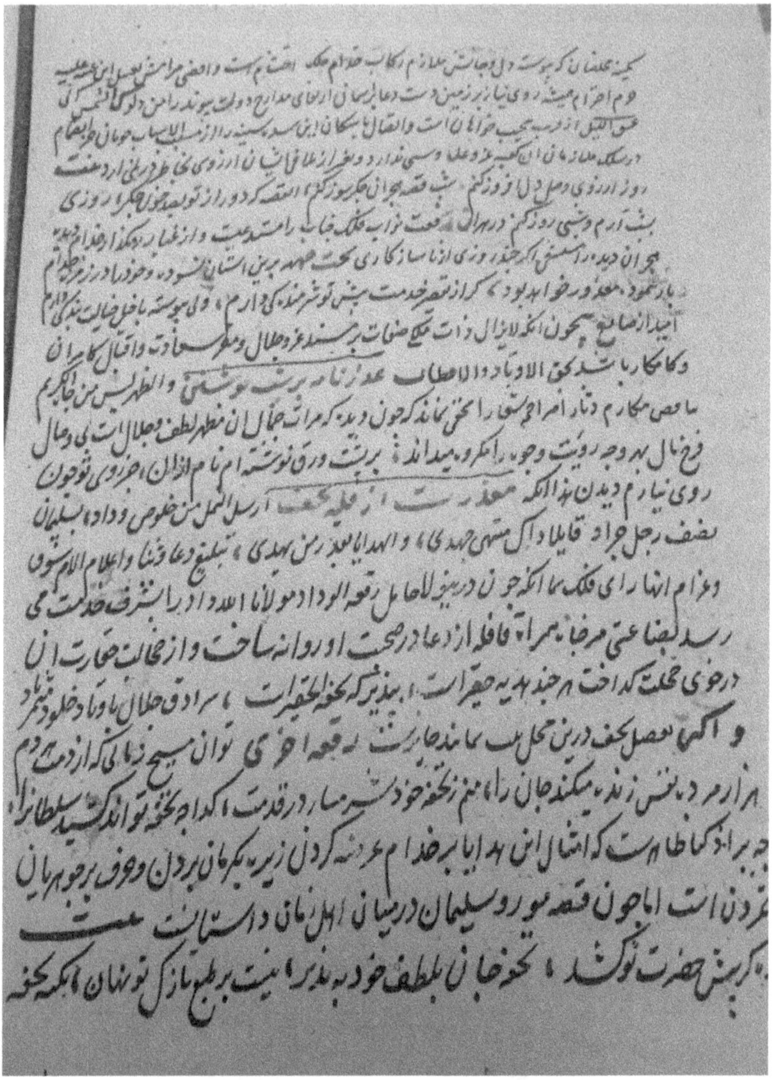

FIGURE 4.8 Note the inverted comma-like symbol used to mark quotations, in slightly lighter ink.

it may be possible that the scribes encountered European-style punctuation.[61] A more likely possibility is that they independently

---

[61] I am grateful to Samuel Hodgkin for suggesting Armenian punctuation, such as the comma-like *storaket*, as another possible source, given the important role of Armenians in Safavid statecraft.

invented a symbol that coincidentally resembles the inverted comma in both form and to some extent usage. In any case, it may have been an idiosyncratic usage, as it otherwise does not appear again in Persian until the European comma is introduced centuries later.

One of the earliest literary histories of Persian, Muhammad-Husayn Furughi 'Zuka' al-Mulk' (1839–1907)'s untitled work, completed posthumously by his sons in 1335 AH/1916–17 CE, makes use of a range of punctuation strategies from both the manuscript tradition and European-style print culture. This unique manuscript achieves a great deal of clarity and precision in its use of punctuation, revealing the full range of possibilities present in the manuscript tradition – possibilities which were ultimately lost in the shift to print culture. The pedagogical nature of Furughi's history informed his scribe's careful attention to punctuation; the text was distributed in the form of *juzvah* or lecture notes to the students of his literature courses at Tehran's School of Political Science.[62]

In Persian or Urdu prose writing, the end of a section could be marked not with a period but by a conventional phrase (or sometimes a religious supplication), often in Arabic.[63] Some examples marking the very end of a work include *tammat bi'l-khayr* "it [the writing] ended well," *faqat* "just [this]," or simply the Persian phrase *tamam shud* "it is finished," sometimes with a combination of phrases as in *tammat tamam shud*. Furughi uses these phrases to separate quotations, and his scribe Mirza Zayn al-'Abidin Sharif Qazvini 'Malik al-Khattatin' ends the text with an Arabic colophon: *tamm al-kitab bi-'awn al-malik al-wahhab* "the book was finished with the aid of [God] the King, the Bestower."[64] His manuscript contains no commas or periods, but spacing is used to demarcate sections. Traditionally,

---

[62] Fani, "Iran's Literary Becoming," 124n30.

[63] This is comparable to the use of the Latin *finis* at the end of an English-language work.

[64] Malik al-Khattatin was an important court scribe of the late Qajar era, and former student of the master calligrapher Mirza Muhammad-Riza Kalhur (1829–92). He also served as a calligrapher for lithographed journals like *Sharaf, Sharafat, Zaban-i Zanan*, and Zuka' al-Mulk Furughi's *Tarbiyat*. See Balaghi, "Nationalism and Cultural Production," 177; Bayani, *Ahval va Asar*, 1:226–7; Faza'ili, *Atlas-i Khatt*, 593–4.

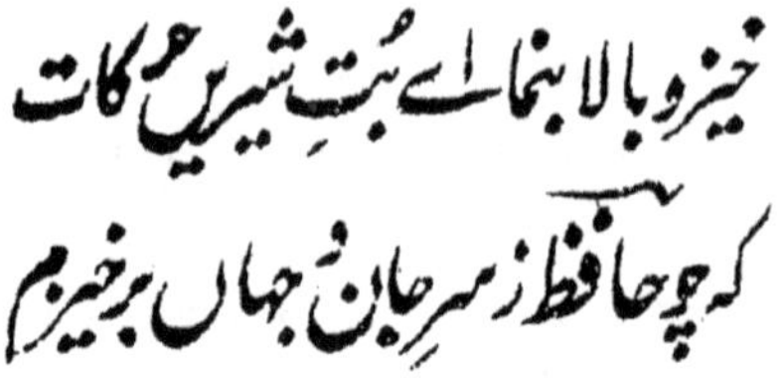

خیزو بالا بنما اے بُتِ شیریں حرکات

که چو حافظ ز سرِ جان و جهاں برخیزم

FIGURE 4.9 Azad uses overlining to mark the *takhallus* of the poet Hafiz.

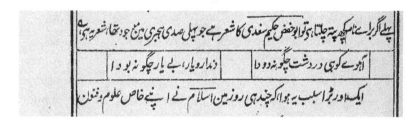

FIGURE 4.10 Overlining as well as *jadval* in a lithograph of Shibli's *Shiʻr al-ʻAjam*.

*tazkirah*s (and other genres such as *bayaz* poetry collections) separated poetic quotations with a line containing the Arabic phrase *wa-lahu* "and to him [is ascribed the following]" or *wa-lahu ayḍan* "and to him also [is ascribed the following]," used throughout Furughi's text as well.[65]

Overlining (rather than underlining) for emphasis or for introducing a new topic is another feature of premodern punctuation, with a long history in the Persian and Arabic manuscript tradition. The overline mark is thought to have developed as an abbreviated form of words or short phrases inserted interlineally to draw attention, such as *qif* (Arabic, "stop"), *babat* (Persian, "concern, matter"), or *batt* (Arabic, "cutting; settling").[66] It is still frequently used in Urdu printed texts to mark the pen-names of poets or other individuals (Figures 4.9 and 4.10), and has even endured into the digital age, with

---

[65] When used in Persian, the phrase is generally fixed and does not become *wa-laha* "and to her" for female poets. See for example Hidayat, *Majmaʻ al-Fusahaʼ*, [1961 CE] 1:3 1334.

[66] Gacek, *Arabic Manuscripts*, 168, 173; Hanaway and Spooner, *Reading Nastaʻliq*, 9–10; Parekh, "Pseudonym."

FIGURE 4.11 "Hafiz" typed in Jameel Noori Nastaleeq font, with Arabic Sign Takhallus.

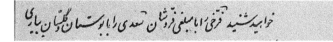

FIGURE 4.12 The names of poets Farrukhi and Saʿdi are marked with bracket-like overlining symbols.

its own dedicated Unicode character, "Arabic Sign Takhallus" (Figure 4.11). Furughi's scribe Qazvini uses a distinct bracket-shaped overlining mark to mark names of poets (Figure 4.12). This bracket-shaped style of overlining can be seen in a number of late nineteenth-century Persian texts from Iran. It served the role of italics, drawing attention to a particular piece of text, marking it as a title or heading of a new section, or sometimes highlighting names.[67] Qazvini uses this mark deliberately, not merely for decoration.

Qazvini makes occasional use of European-style punctuation in the form of quotation marks, using them to mark foreign words in much the same way as English uses italics.[68] Aside from this, he punctuates Furughi's literary history according to the conventions of the Persian manuscript tradition. Qazvini's innovation, however, is his meticulous and systematic application of what had been a largely haphazard method in earlier manuscripts. His extensive use of the bracket-shaped overline, along with spacing to punctuate his handwritten text, give Furughi's sentences the succinct, punchy character of modern European prose. To a large extent, it is this punctuation

[67] The British Orientalist D. C. Phillott's 1919 grammar of Persian notes that this type of overlining is modern, explaining that its use over a word "signifies either that it is a proper noun or that it begins a sentence" (Phillott, *Higher Persian Grammar*, 37).

[68] For example, after mentioning ʿulum-i siyasi, he adds the French term transliterated and encased within parentheses: "(*pulitik*)" (Furughi, *Tarikh-i Adabiyat*, 33).

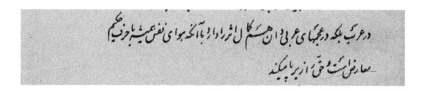

FIGURE 4.13 Furughi's use of this symbol, often decorative, for greater precision.

technique that differentiates Furughi's prose from the endless run-on sentences that typified Persian writing of the time.

Qazvini extends the overline mark to other uses, such as marking quotations. He occasionally doubles up, starting a new section with the phrase *va amma* ("however," which traditionally marked a new clause or section in Persian and Arabic writing), and marking the phrase with the bracket-like overlining he uses for the same purpose.[69] Qazvini's neat, unembellished *nasta 'liq* is made even more lucid and unambiguous by his unusually consistent application of the *tashdid* (gemination mark) and deliberate use of a decorative symbol (Figure 4.13) for greater precision rather than mere decoration.[70] Though often used inconsistently and ornamentally, without meaning, in Persian manuscripts, Qazvini uses the *isharat al-kaf* symbol to indicate a pause, functioning like a comma in Furughi's manuscript.

4.4   PUNCTUATION IN THE PRINT ERA

British Orientalists may have been the first to systematically insert European-style punctuation in Persian and Urdu.[71] They did this for their own educational purposes, in order to make native texts more accessible to British students. For example, the *Gulistan* (*Rose Garden*) of Sa'di had long been a central text of Persianate education. A thirteenth-century work of didactic literature, it was used to teach

---

[69] Ibid., 27.   [70] Ibid., 21.

[71] On the historical development of punctuation in Europe, see Parkes, *Pause and Effect*.

Islamic ethics as well as Persian language and literature throughout the Persianate world for centuries. As such, the *Gulistan* is one of the most influential and widely-read works in the Persian literary canon.[72] It retained its influence and pride of place in new educational curricula, including the *dars-i nizami* syllabus for Indian Muslims which originated in the eighteenth century, and British language training for their own officers in the nineteenth century.[73] Materials prepared for language training ultimately impacted language use outside of the classroom as well.

The *Gulistan* in particular was used for British officers' Persian language exams, and they produced punctuated editions of the text, making it easier to read.[74] Other Persian and Urdu works, like the Urdu *Bagh u Bahar* (*Garden and Spring*, 1803), were similarly prepared. The Scottish Orientalist Duncan Forbes (1798–1868) notes this explicitly in his *Grammar of the Hindūstānī Language*, which includes prose selections printed in *naskh* type and punctuated. He explains:

> I have also inserted a rigid system of punctuation, the same as I should have done in the editing of a Latin Classic. There may be a few individuals so thoroughly wedded to what is foolish or defective, merely because it is old, as to feel shocked at this innovation. They will triumphantly ask, what is the use of punctuation, when the natives have none in their manuscripts? I answer, – the use is, simply to facilitate, for beginners, the acquisition of a knowledge of the language.[75]

Today one can hardly find printed copies of unpunctuated prose works, even those like the *Gulistan* which were composed long before the introduction of punctuation.

---

[72] Kia, "Adab as Ethics of Literary Form." Writing in the *Encyclopædia Iranica*, Franklin Lewis calls it "probably the single most influential work of prose in the Persian tradition" (Lewis, "GOLESTĀN-E SAʿDI").

[73] Metcalf, *Islamic Revival in British India*, 100.

[74] For an example from 1851 see Sprenger, *Gulistan of Saʿdy*.

[75] Forbes, *A Grammar of the Hindūstānī Language*, x.

European punctuation began to haphazardly find its way into Persian in the writings of the first generation of Iranian students who studied in Europe beginning in the early nineteenth century and acquired knowledge of European languages. This was an unsystematic process that continues even today, as the use of punctuation in Persian continues to vary greatly from writer to writer or publication to publication, with some using it sparingly and many unclear as to what standards or rules should guide their use. In Persian as in Urdu punctuation remains inconsistent, having not been codified to the same degree as English or other European languages. Punctuation is thus still used more sparingly and haphazardly in Persian and Urdu than in English.

As Iran entered the era of movable type printing in the twentieth century, some Iranian publishers experimented with native solutions to punctuation and typography. The Berlin-based Persian journal *Kavah* sometimes used *nasta'liq* type for emphasis in place of italics.[76] Given that the journal's editor, Hasan Taqizadah, was a notorious westernizer who called in the pages of *Kavah* for Iran to become thoroughly Europeanized, this use of *nasta'liq* could hardly have arisen out of any nativist resistance to imitating European print norms.[77] Instead, it was a practice which had endured from the conventions of manuscript production. Alternating hands for emphatic effect was often seen in manuscripts, such as works written in *nasta'liq* which quoted from the Qur'an in *naskh* (Figure 4.1). The practice never became widespread in printed Persian, though it is common in Urdu printed works.

Given the Iranian nationalist emphasis on indigeneity, and the South Asian Muslim attachment to the Perso-Arabic script, why did neither Persian nor Urdu develop an indigenous system of punctuation, codifying the conventions to be found in the premodern

[76] For an example see *Kavah* No. 7, Berlin, 1 Zu'l-Qa'dah AH/ July 7, 1921, 2–3 (Universitäts und Landesbibliothek digital collections).

[77] Zia-Ebrahimi, *The Emergence of Iranian Nationalism*, 125.

tradition described above? Other languages ranging from Armenian to Chinese formalized their preexisting punctuation conventions, often complementing them by selective borrowing of punctuation marks from European languages in addition to their native marks.[78] Instead, as detailed earlier by Jamalzadah, Persian and Urdu borrowed their modern system of punctuation wholesale from European languages.

Islamicate systems of punctuation found in the manuscript tradition lacked direct equivalents for many of the European punctuation marks. Why did Iranians and South Asians not simply mix the two systems, retaining (or repurposing) premodern punctuation symbols and adopting European-style symbols to meet their needs? This question can be answered in part with attention to changing social and material circumstances. The old system belonged to the premodern manuscript tradition, developed in a culture that valued orality, when scholarly texts were studied at the foot of a teacher who had mastered, if not authored, the text. The introduction of standardized orthography and punctuation marked the decisive triumph of print over orality. No longer must a text be read together with a teacher; the printed, punctuated text explains itself. But examining the material conditions alone misses the *conventionality* of modernization. Symbols from the manuscript tradition could have been formalized, standardized, and recreated in typography. Instead, reformers considered modern writing to have its own conventions for print and punctuation, and adopting these conventions made them, and their writing, modern. Like so much else in the project of modern literary history, and modernization more broadly, the adoption of European-style punctuation was a historically contingent development, hardly the only possibility.

4.5 CONCLUSION

At the turn of the twentieth century, language reformers and literary innovators were creating a radically new Persian, with simplified

[78] On the history of punctuation in Chinese see Yu, "Learning to Read in Late Imperial China."

prose, Arabic loans replaced with neologisms, classical literary forms replaced with new ones, and a new print culture with typography, standardized orthography, and European-style punctuation.[79] Bahar notes the role of the Dar al-Funun, Iran's first modern institution of higher learning, in "modernizing prose style and simple writing" (*tajdid-i sabk-i nasr va sadah-navisi*) through the study of foreign languages, translation, and reading European books.[80] New proposals for even more drastic changes, down to the very script in which Persian is written, sprang up everywhere.

Yet modern literary histories present Persian literature as a single, stable, continuous tradition from the ninth century to the present day (and often much longer, sometimes beginning as far back as the ancient Achaemenid inscriptions, several centuries before the common era). Literary histories smooth over the transition from manuscript to print, presenting a slick continuity of Persian literature over time and across different scripts and modes of writing and publication. They make it possible to view a medieval courtly *divan*, with its dazzlingly illuminated frontispiece and pages full of *ghazal*s expertly penned in elegant calligraphy, as part of the same tradition as a modern chapbook of free verse poetry, austerely printed with the first clumsy fonts of Persian movable Persian type.

Paradoxically, the changes in Persian writing present themselves as continuity. New technological developments in print, as well as new conventions, were incorporated into the writing of a linear, nationalist literary history. The goal of the modernizers was to shore up the literary heritage, using modern technologies, methodologies, and conventions to protect it and ensure its survival. Persianate modernity covers its tracks, concealing the ways in which

---

[79] On language reform see Ludwig, "Iranian Language Reform."

[80] Bahar, *Sabkshinasi*, 3:337–8. Note that the word Bahar uses for "modernizing," *tajdid*, can also mean "renewal." This is indeed telling of his view, shared with other Iranian modernizers, that the qualities of modernity could be found in the ancient Iranian past and that the modernizer's task was not to create anew but to renew and revivify the ancient.

it transforms the very heritage it seeks to preserve. Scholarship has addressed how the process of producing a modern, national Persian literary canon meant excising many poets from the broader Persianate world who came to be seen as non-national: Turks, Indians, and others from outside the boundaries of the contemporary Iranian nation-state.[81] But the advent of literary history has involved more than the exclusion of these individual poets from the canon. Missing from many accounts of Persian literary modernity is the loss of the manuscript tradition and all that it entailed.

Many contemporary Iranians no longer understand the conventions of the manuscript tradition. While *nasta 'liq* is still frequently used for poetry in Iran today, nearly all other writing is done in *naskh*, and most Iranians are unaware that there was ever any specific significance to many of the marks on a manuscript. Poring over a lithographed manuscript of Furughi's literary history, I also struggled to make sense of these marks. Iranian friends and colleagues I consulted, some of them Persian literary scholars themselves, were quick to dismiss all such symbols as "decorative" (*taz 'ini*). Their instinctive response was not without reason; even many contemporary calligraphers no longer understand the traditional use of these marks and indeed use them decoratively in order to fill space.[82] But Furughi's marks seemed too deliberately placed to be merely decorative, and close reading of his text eventually revealed the systematic logic behind his scribe's punctuation scheme.

Persianate modernizers saw formal conventions, including aspects of typography, orthography, and punctuation, as a kind of technology of modernization. Close attention to such "technologies"

---

[81] Schwartz, *Remapping Persian Literary History*; Sharma, "Redrawing the Boundaries"; Ahmadi, "The Institution of Persian Literature."

[82] For example, the small v-shaped mark (*'alamat al-ihmal*), once used for precision in order to mark unpointed (*muhmal*) letters, is today a favorite of calligraphers who use it decoratively, nescient of its original purpose. On this mark see Witkam, "The Neglect Neglected."

is necessary for making sense of the different strands of Persianate modernity. Without such understanding, one can read too deeply into positions that are merely conventional, as illustrated in Chapter 2, or conversely overlook meaning by assuming everything to be decorative, as we have seen here.

Conclusion

Though I compose my speech in Urdu
my thoughts are indebted to Persian.

(Ziya' Muhammad Ziya', 1928–2009)[1]

The narrativization and nationalization of the *tazkirah*; the disappearance of homoeroticism behind a veil of ersatz Victorianism; the emplotment of linguistic history according to an evolutionary model; the rise of type, standardized orthography, and punctuation. These conventional transformations, I've argued, are central to understanding Persianate modernity and the emergence of the modern genre of literary history. To modernizers, especially in Iran, aesthetic conventions seemed as important as gunpowder. Appearances were everything; Iranian elites were painfully aware of how they were perceived by Europeans.[2] Riza Shah, keen for Iran to appear European, instituted a series of public dress codes beginning in 1928. Ordering men to don European-style headgear in 1935, he also banned the hijab for women in the following year.[3] He even mandated "the Europeanization of eating habits," requiring that patrons of kabab restaurants be seated on chairs rather than on platforms, and eat with

---

[1] *"Misarayam garchah dar urdu sukhan / hast fikr-i man rahin-i farsi"* (Ziya', *Nava-yi Shawq*, 66–7).

[2] Najmabadi, *Women with Mustaches*, chapter 2.

[3] Desouza, *Unveiling Men*, chapter 2; Kashani-Sabet, *Conceiving Citizens*, 152–60; Chehabi, "Staging the Emperor's New Clothes"; Radjavi, *French Hats in Iran*. Sartorial reform, especially headwear, was part of modernizing platforms beyond Iran. See Nereid, "Kemalism on the Catwalk" on similar laws implemented in Turkey in 1925.

utensils rather than their hands.[4] The Shah radically transformed public space, demolishing many of Tehran's old buildings and winding streets, which were replaced with broad, paved boulevards intended to imitate European capital cities.[5] Foreigners were prohibited from photographing visual symbols of "backwardness" in Iran, such as camels or ruined buildings. Riza Shah's modernization program was not only about appearances; it ultimately achieved significant material transformations. But cultivating a modern image – in other words, modern conventions – preceded developing the modern conditions.[6] The same was true of literary history.

Yet the conventions that defined literary history were historically contingent. The era of Persianate modernity was pregnant with alternate possibilities which went unrealized. Key texts which articulated alternative narratives to those that became dominant were overlooked. Muhammad-Husayn Furughi's literary history languished in archives, unknown and unread.[7] Persianate literary history and culture could have developed very different conventions had this not been the case.

One of this book's main interventions has been its attention to conventions in arguing for a Persianate modernity. Scholars rightly recognize the primacy of convention in understanding premodern Persian literature, yet often fail to grasp the conventionality of modern writing. As a consequence, they take modernizers' claims to novelty at face value, overlooking the way Persianate modernity conceals continuities with the early modern period that precedes it in order to present itself as rupture with the past. As we saw with E. G. Browne and Shibli Nu'mani, recognizing the conventions of literary history is vital in order to comprehend the seeming incongruity between these scholars' works and their personal lives.

---

[4] Chehabi, "The Westernization of Iranian Culinary Culture."
[5] Grigor, "The King's White Walls."   [6] Devos, "Engineering a Modern Society?"
[7] Sharma, "Redrawing the Borders of 'Ajam"; Fani, "Iran's Literary Becoming."

I have demonstrated how many of these features are shared between Iranians writing in Persian and Indians writing in Urdu. These include a common set of references, comprising citation of the same premodern and contemporary Muslim scholars as well as European Orientalists; use of texts like *tazkirah*s and the *Shahnamah* as local models for modern literary history; and a convention of Victorian-inspired puritanism on erotic matters. Understanding these shared elements and conventions helps us conceive of the Persianate as a living and evolving complex which continued to connect people across disparate geographies in the modern era. The Persianate framework allowed Iranians and South Asians to draw from their shared heritage, and from each other's experiences, as they sought to transform their respective societies to meet the challenges of modernity.

However, as nationalism became the structuring logic of the Persianate, the shared framework also served – perhaps ironically – for developing divergent national or communal cultures, resulting in different outcomes for Iranians and South Asian Muslims. Divergent relationships to Orientalist philology and to Islam led them to narrate their histories differently; the former emphasized cultural "purity" and the continuity of Iranian identity before and after Islam, while the latter envisioned a composite Muslim culture discontinuous with pre-Islamic traditions. These distinct orientations also led to differing conventions of typography and print; Iranians embraced Persian printed books in *naskh* typesetting, whereas Urdu-speakers rejected this technology in favor of lithography, which could reproduce the calligraphic elegance of *nasta'liq*. These distinctions reveal how Persianate modernity was not always uniform.

Persianate modernity may prove to be a useful framework for other parts of the erstwhile Persianate cosmopolis, beyond Iran and South Asia. My understanding of modern Indo-Iranian connections, one of the main focuses of this book, was facilitated by the work of various centers and scholars to produce archival catalogues, publish print editions, and generally make this history accessible. In places like the Caucasus, where the Persianate textual heritage has been less well preserved, or China, where it faces erasure, this task could be more difficult. I hope that future scholars will explore what Persianate modernity might look like in territories beyond those explored in this book, like Central Asia, the former Ottoman territories, and elsewhere.[8] This book is also a call to extend the Persianate framework into the twentieth century and beyond. Might "Persianate modernity" offer analytical value for understanding the popularity of Ottoman-themed television dramas in Pakistan, or of Bollywood films in Afghanistan? My focus has been on the period from the mid-nineteenth to the mid-twentieth century, but in what follows, I trace the afterlife of the *tazkirah* and literary history, central genres for Persianate modernity, in the second half of the twentieth century, and shed greater light on literary connections between Iran, India, and Pakistan during that time.

C.I LATER *TAZKIRAHS* AND LITERARY HISTORIES

In the twentieth century, *tazkirah* writing petered out in Iran, culminating in Ahmad Gulchin-i Ma'ani (1916–2000)'s *Tarikh-i Tazkirah-ha-yi Farsi* (*History of Persian Tazkirahs*, 1969–71), a veritable meta-*tazkirah* of *tazkirah*s. This massive two-volume work adopts the traditional *tazkirah* format, but each of its entries is about a *tazkirah* rather than a poet. The *tazkirah* genre never completely disappeared in South Asia. By the middle of the twentieth century, while literary history had fully taken the place of the genre in Iran, Urdu-language *tazkirah*s continued to thrive in India and Pakistan, as they do even today. The earliest *tazkirah*s to address Urdu poetry were written in Persian, like Muhammad-Taqi Mir's *Nikat al-Shu'ara* (*Fine Points of the Poets*, 1751–2), Muhammad Qiyam al-Din Qa'im Chandpuri's *Makhzan-i Nikat* (*Treasury of Fine Points*, 1754), or

---

[8] These themes are explored in a special issue of *Philological Encounters*, "The Late Persianate World: Transregional Comparisons and the Question of Language." In other articles I have also considered questions of Persianate modernity in Afghanistan (Jabbari, "From Persianate Cosmopolis to Persianate Modernity") and in China (Jabbari and Tsai, "Sinicizing Islam").

Shafiq Awrangabadi's *Chamanistan* (*Meadowland*, 1761–2).[9] As Urdu grew into its own as a prose language, this trend reversed, seeing the emergence of Urdu-language texts about Persian poetry like Shibli's *Shi'r al-'Ajam* (*Poetry of the Persians*) or Azad's *Nigaristan-i Fars* (*Picture-Gallery of Persia*), along with even greater production of *tazkirah*s of Urdu poetry. Over a century after official efforts to replace Persian with "vernacular" languages in India, Kalim al-Din Ahmad published his *Du Tazkire* (*Two Tazkirahs*, 1959), a traditionally structured *tazkirah* of Urdu poets, written in Persian. The Iranian literary histories made their way into Urdu as well; Rizazadah Shafaq's *Tarikh-i Adabiyat-i Iran* (*History of Iranian Literature*) was translated into Urdu (1955).

As modernizers began to repurpose the *tazkirah* genre to commemorate a newly imagined national community, the genre expanded to accommodate other innovative subjects as well. Female poets had typically received short shrift in *tazkirah*s, but the late nineteenth century witnessed the emergence of elite and influential male reformers like Ashraf 'Ali Thanvi and Sayyid Mumtaz 'Ali in India, alongside feminist activists like Bibi Khanum Astarabadi in Iran, Ruqayyah Sakhavat Husayn in India, and others, all concerned with cultivating modern women.[10] Under the influence of discourses of the "new woman," Indians began to compile *tazkirah*s of women. Muhammad 'Abd al-Razzaq "Bismil" wrote *Tazkirah-i Jamil* (*Beautiful* Tazkirah, 1929), on contemporary women. Shibli's protégé Sayyid Sulayman Nadvi published *Khavatin-i Islam ki Bahaduri* (*The Heroism of the Women of Islam*, 1923; translated into

---

[9] At this earlier stage, "Urdu" was more often identified by other names such as Hindi, Hindvi, Hindustani, or Rekhtah. On Mir's *Nikat al-Shu'ara* see Pritchett, "Long History," 866–70.

[10] On women in pre-nineteenth century *tazkirah*s, see Kia, *Persianate Selves*, 118–21; on nineteenth- and early twentieth-century feminism in the Islamicate world see Ahmed, *Women and Gender in Islam*, part 3; Baron, *Egypt as a Woman*; Kashani-Sabet, *Conceiving Citizens*; Amin, *The Making of the Modern Iranian Woman*; Najmabadi, "Crafting an Educated Housewife"; Mian, "Surviving Modernity," chapter 5.

English by Syed Sabahuddin Abdur Rahman as *Heroic Deeds of Muslim Women*, 1961). Like other texts of its time, Nadvi's work was something between *tazkirah* and narrative history. In Iran, I'timad al-Saltanah's Persian-language *Khayrat al-Hisan* (*Beautiful Maidens*, 1887–9), itself based on an Ottoman Turkish text, was a *tazkirah* of prominent women, not limited to poets. The genre burgeoned in Persian, Urdu, Arabic, and Turkish alike.[11]

Because the *tazkirah* eventually came to represent a deep literary tradition to be mined and reformed in producing modern literary history, it became something of a sine qua non for nationalists in the Persianate world. *Tazkirah*s of Persian and Urdu, as well as Turkish, embodied literary traditions, foundations upon which modern nationalist identities could be established. This left Pashtun nationalists in twentieth-century Afghanistan in a bind. Pashto was rich in oral literature, but had historically not been written, lacking a written tradition before the seventeenth century; it had no *tazkirah* collecting and commemorating its poetry. If literary history made Persian "modern" and "national," it did so by using the *tazkirah* as raw material. At a time when Persian and Pashto vied for national status in Afghanistan, how could Pashto claim to be a national language without a *tazkirah*?[12] Pashtun modernizers and nationalists strived to develop Pashto literature that could compete with Persian, penning Pashto *ghazal*s, establishing literary associations, compiling dictionaries. In the midst of this modernizing project, the Afghan scholar 'Abd al-Hayy Habibi (1910–84) claimed to have discovered just the proof his fellow Pashtun nationalists needed: a manuscript called the *Patah Khazanah* (*Hidden Treasure*). According to Habibi, the manuscript was written in the early eighteenth century and

---

[11] Other examples of biographical dictionaries of prominent women from the period include Mehmet Zihni, *Mashahir al-Nisa'* (Turkish, 1877–8); Maryam al-Nahhas, *Ma'rid al-Hasna'* (Arabic, 1879); 'Abd al-Bari Asi, *Tazkirat al-Khavatin* (Urdu, 1930); for additional Arabic examples see Booth, *Classes of Ladies*.

[12] Green, "Introduction: Afghan Literature"; Nawid, "Language Policy in Afghanistan."

anthologized Pashto poetry dating back to the eighth. If true, it would give Pashto a literary pedigree predating New Persian, whose written tradition begins in the ninth and tenth centuries. Most scholars today see the *Patah Khazanah* as a forgery.[13]

The project of Persian literary history continued in the second half of the twentieth century with Zabihullah Safa's *Tarikh-i Adabiyat dar Iran* (*History of Literature in Iran*; 5 vols., 1953–91). There were also several histories which limited their scope to modern Persian literature, such as Yahya Aryanpur's *Az Saba ta Nima* (*From Saba to Nima*, 3 vols., 1973–95) in Iran. The German *Geschichte und Entwicklung der modernen persischen Literatur* (*History and Development of Modern Persian Literature*, 1964) by the Iranian expatriate Buzurg ʿAlavi remains untranslated into other languages. The Czech Orientalist Jan Rypka (1886–1968)'s *History of Iranian Literature* was a monumental undertaking. First published in Czech as *Dějiny perské a tádžické literatury* (*History of Persian and Tajik Literature*, 1956), it became "Iranian" in Rypka's German translation (*Iranische Literaturgeschichte* or *Iranian Literary History*, 1959) and then in English as well. By this time, the genre had flourished such that Rypka had to acknowledge that "some justification seems to be necessary for the addition of yet another *History of Iranian Literature* to the number of those already in existence."[14] In India, scholarship on Persian literature became largely an Urdu-language enterprise (though the occasional Persian work continued to be written).[15] As a consequence of the shift from Persian to English and "vernacular" languages like Urdu, Persianate literary scholarship took off in English as well.[16] Indian Muslims founded journals like *Islamic Culture*

---

[13] Morgenstierne, "Afghān," 220–1; Andreyev, "Pashto Literature: The Classical Period," 91.

[14] Rypka, *History of Iranian Literature*, v.

[15] For example, Raziyah Akbar's Persian-language study of the poet Baba Fighani, published in Hyderabad in 1974. See Akbar, *Baba Fighani Shirazi*.

[16] This was also true even in the Indian princely states where Persian remained in official use later than in British India. For the case of the princely state of Hyderabad, where Persianate scholarship blossomed in English and Urdu in the

(Hyderabad) and *Islamic Review* (London) to carry on the Persianate tradition in English.

C.2 SUBCONTINENTAL SCHOLARS AND THE PLACE OF URDU IN IRAN

Iran was the first country to recognize Pakistan after the latter declared its independence in 1947. Three years later, Muhammad-Riza Shah became the first head of state to pay Pakistan an official visit, and the two countries established close relations. Pakistani scholars came to Iran to study Persian literature, like Syed Sibte Hasan Rizvi (1927–97), who studied under the literary historian Zabihullah Safa during visits to the University of Tehran in 1956 and 1965.[17] After returning to Pakistan, Rizvi headed the Persian department at Government College in Rawalpindi, and authored a literary history with a novel scope: *Farsi-guyan-i Pakistan* (*Persian Poets of Pakistan*, 1974), on contemporary Pakistani poets who composed in Persian.

Pakistanis were not only visiting to Iran to study; some came to teach as well. The University of Tehran began to offer Urdu classes in 1951, taught by the Pakistani professor Tahsin Firaqi. Urdu instruction continued under the auspices of the Institute of Foreign Languages, established at the university in 1956.[18] In 1971, the Iranian and Pakistani governments signed an agreement to strengthen cultural and linguistic ties, launching the Iran–Pakistan Institute of Persian Studies in Islamabad. The two governments signed an additional accord in 1991 to establish a Department of Urdu at the University of Tehran. This was accomplished the following year with the help of Pakistani scholars like Firaqi who would head the new

---

1880s, see Beverley, "Documenting the World." On the continuation of the Persianate in English see Jabbari, "Sa'di's Gulistan in British India."

[17] Rizvi, *Farsi-guyan-i Pakistan*, ix–x. The author intended to include Shibli Nu'mani in a third volume which never came to fruition (ibid.).

[18] "Asasnamah-yi Mu'assasah-yi Zaban-ha-yi Kharijah," 103.

department, and the first cohort – ten Iranian students – was admitted.

The Department of Urdu initially featured faculty from India and Pakistan, until Iranians trained in Urdu (who had studied in both countries) were able to fill positions in the department. As a result of the 1971 agreement, Pakistan awarded scholarships to Iranian students to complete master's degrees and doctorates in Pakistan. Several Iranian students of Urdu completed degrees at Punjab University, Pakistan, while others chose to study at Jawaharlal Nehru University in New Delhi, India. Today, the department employs mostly Iranian professors of Urdu, and offers undergraduate and postgraduate degrees in Urdu language and literature. At the time of writing, efforts are currently underway to introduce Urdu teaching at the University of Isfahan and Firdawsi University in Mashhad.

In an Urdu-language interview in 2014 with Rekhta Studio in Delhi, ʿAli Bayat, an assistant professor of Urdu at the University of Tehran, laments how little Iranians know about Urdu and about South Asia in general. When asked about translation from Urdu into Persian, he responds that Iranians tend to think that Persian has given Urdu everything and doubt that they would gain from translating in the other direction. "However," he continues, "my position on this is something different: perhaps in classical literature we have contributed a lot to Urdu." Bayat glances to the side conspiratorially and lowers his voice, as if confiding a secret. "But the truth is that in the past two centuries, Urdu [literature] has learned much more from English, Western literature than from Persian. Such great names in poetry and prose have been produced here [in South Asia] – *mashal-lah*."[19] Bayat is hinting at the way Urdu writers were forced to confront colonial modernity earlier, and more directly, than their counterparts in Iran. There was much in Urdu literature that Iranians could learn from as they developed modern literary history. South Asia maintained its importance for Iranian literary critics in the

---

[19] Bayat, "Dr. Ali Bayat Interview."

second half of the twentieth century as well, now aided by the Urdu department at the University of Tehran, and more broadly by cultural and academic ties between Iran and Pakistan cultivated at the state level.

The Urdu department has played an important role in the academic rehabilitation of so-called "Indian style" (sabk-i hindi) poetry in Iran. Faculty in the department worked to translate Urdu literary-critical works into Persian, like Muhammad Iqbal's study of the Indo-Persian poet 'Abd al-Qadir Bidil (1644–1721) in light of the French philosopher Henri Bergson (1859–1941).[20] "Indian style" poetry – more a dismissive catch-all term for several poetic styles dominant in the Safavid–Mughal era than a cohesive poetic movement – had been displaced by an Iran-centric eighteenth-century movement, what Bahar called the bazgasht-i adabi or "literary return."[21] Modernizing literary historians disparaged the "Indian style"; even Indians like Shibli participated in its erasure, effectively writing themselves out of the story of Persian literature. Bahar seemingly dealt it a death blow, coining the term "Indian style" (its practitioners had never identified as such, preferring labels like tazah-gu'i, "fresh-speaking") and consigning it to the dustbin of Persian literary history.[22]

Bahar's terminology – and nationalist framework – caught on, but the fate of this literature started to change by the end of the 1980s, beginning with the works of Muhammad-Riza Shafi'i-Kadkani. Shafi'i-Kadkani, one of Iran's most renowned living literary scholars and poets, had corresponded with the Urdu poet N. M. Rashid during Rashid's second stint in Iran in the 1970s. With his 1987 monograph on Bidil, Shafi'i-Kadkani brought increased attention to an important Indian poet virtually unknown in Iran. As he noted in his preface, while Bidil was revered alongside Hafiz in Afghanistan, Tajikistan, and the subcontinent, in Iran even most people with doctorates in

---

[20] Iqbal, *Haqiqat va Hayrat.*   [21] Schwartz, *Remapping Persian Literary History.*
[22] Smith, "Literary Connnections."

Persian literature had never heard Bidil's name.[23] During the 1990s and 2000s, studies of Indo-Persian literature proliferated in Iranian academia. The devastating eight-year war with Iraq was over, and under President Khatami (r. 1997–2005) an academic culture that was increasingly cosmopolitan and critical blossomed. Even more importantly, South Asian scholars were publishing print editions of crucial Indo-Persian literary works. The Iran Culture House in New Delhi played a central role in preserving Persian manuscripts, which formed the basis for print editions later published in Iran, India, and Pakistan. Rehana Khatoon, professor of Persian at the University of Delhi, prepared print editions of Siraj al-Din 'Ali Khan-i Arzu's works, including his linguistic treatise *Musmir*. The Iran–Pakistan Institute of Persian Studies in Islamabad released a print edition of Arzu's Persian-language *tazkirah*, *Majma' al-Nafa'is* (*Assembly of Subtleties*); the edition was a collaborative effort between Pakistan-based professors and Zeb al-Nisa' 'Alikhan, a professor of Urdu at the University of Tehran who was also of Pakistani origin. The Iran–Pakistan Institute has published numerous print editions of *tazkirah*s, *divan*s, and other texts, prepared catalogues of Persian manuscripts in Pakistani libraries and archives, and published scholarship on Indo-Persian literature. It has also done much to promote Persian language and literature in Pakistan, including publishing numerous literary works in Urdu translation.[24]

These print editions, particularly of *tazkirah*s and *divan*s, and other publications, which bourgeoned in the 1990s, provided the infrastructure for the rediscovery of "Indo-Persian" literature in Iranian academia.[25] Poets unknown to Iranians, their works long confined to crumbling manuscripts held by neglected archives scattered across the subcontinent, became available in modern

---

[23] Shafi'i-Kadkani, *Sha'ir-i Ayinah-ha*, 9.

[24] Naushahi, "Markaz-e Taḥqīqāt."; Iran Pakistan Institute of Persian Studies.

[25] Examples include *Divan-i Rayij Siyalkuti* 1996, ed. Muhammad Sarfraz Zafar; *Divan-i Ghalib* 1998, ed. Kiyani (though collections of Ghalib's Persian poetry had been published in the 1960s and 1970s in the subcontinent).

typesetting, distributed by Iranian presses. The Iranian scholar 'Aliriza Zakavati Qaraguzlu, for example, relied on the Iran–Pakistan Institute's publications, such as its catalogues of Persian literature and its journal *Danish*, in his anthology of "Indian style" poetry.[26] Yet despite the increased attention Iranian academics have paid to this literature in the form of seminars, conferences, articles, scholarly books, and anthologies – a veritable "Indian caravan" as one such anthology is titled – the larger reading public is still largely uninterested in or unfamiliar with the Persian poets of South Asia.[27] The one exception may be Muhammad Iqbal.

C.3 INDIANS IN IRANIAN MEMORY: REMEMBERING IQBAL, FORGETTING GHALIB

Literature continues to be an important symbolic link between Iran and South Asia. During the period of Persianate modernity that I consider in this book, many Iranian writers traveled to India or took up Indian themes in their works. Indian cities and characters feature prominently in short stories by Sadiq Hidayat (1903–51), a fiction writer and descendant of Riza-Quli Khan Hidayat. Sadiq Hidayat was undoubtedly inspired by his experiences in India in the 1930s, where he studied Middle Persian.[28] After the Allied occupation of Iran in the 1940s, Indian characters featured in later Iranian novels set during the war. Indians also appeared onscreen in Iranian films like *Ganj-i Qarun* (*Qarun's Treasure*, 1965). Indian cinema found a major audience in Iran beginning in the 1940s, comprising about a quarter of

---

[26] Qaraguzlu, *Guzidah-yi Ash'ar-i Sabk-i Hindi*.

[27] 'Ali Bayat notes that despite numerous books on Bidil (he lists five published by 2016; several more have been published since), Bidil has still not achieved the popularity in Iran that Bayat feels the poet deserves. Bayat's translation has an unusual trajectory in a country where most "world literature" is translated into Persian from English translations rather than the original languages. In this case, Iqbal wrote "Bedil in the Light of Bergson" in English, which was translated into Urdu by Tahsin Firaqi, and then from Urdu into Persian by Bayat, Firaqi's student (Iqbal, *Haqiqat va Hayrat*, 5).

[28] On Hidayat's time in India and its reflection in his works see Akhtar, "HEDAYAT, SADEQ v."

the foreign films in Iran by the 1970s and influencing Iranian film-making as well.[29] Bollywood films remained popular in Iran even during the years following the 1979 revolution, when they were officially banned or censored by the state.[30]

As the Persianate faded from the Iranian public's memory, South Asian visitors to Iran began to represent the past for Iranians. Afshin Marashi has argued that during the Indian poet Rabindranath Tagore's highly publicized 1932 visit to Iran, Tagore was presented to the Iranian public as a living relic of the ancient Indo-Iranian shared past.[31] Reza Zia-Ebrahimi claims that Manikji Limji Hatariya, an Indian Parsi, had been perceived similarly by Iranians in the late nineteenth century: "as the living memory of Iran's past, as if he had just walked out of a time capsule."[32] A similar dynamic can be observed with the Indian characters of Iraj Pizishkzad's wildly popular novel *Da'i Jan Napil'un* (*Dear Uncle Napoleon*, 1973), set in Iran under the Allied occupation, where the Indian characters haunt the present as specters of the Indo-Iranian past. Marked as outsiders in the novel by their deformed speech and appearance, the Indian characters are forever out of time and out of place, relics of the shared Persianate past.[33] In Indian literature, too, Persianate time was out of joint; Kamleshwar's celebrated Hindi novel *Kitne Pakistan* (*How Many Pakistans?* translated as *Partitions* in English, 2000) features a time-traveling Shibli Nuʿmani.

If Hatariya and Tagore represented the shared Indo-Aryan heritage for Iranians, the eminent South Asian poet Muhammad Iqbal

---

[29] Naficy, *Social History of Iranian Cinema*, 2:161; Partovi, *Popular Iranian Cinema*, 40–1; Cooley, "Soundscape of a National Cinema Industry"; Cooley, "Record with Two Songs"; Rekabtalaei, *Iranian Cosmopolitanism*, 134–83; Sunya, *Sirens of Modernity*, chapter 5.

[30] Zeydabadi-Nejad, "Reception of Banned Films in Iran," 103–6.

[31] Marashi, *Exile and the Nation*, chapter 3.

[32] Zia-Ebrahimi, *The Emergence of Iranian Nationalism*, 82.

[33] I borrow the notion of specter from Derrida's *Specters of Marx*, where the specter is a kind of absence which haunts the present and challenges the binary opposition between past/present, or present/absent. For an expanded version of this reading, see Jabbari, "Race against Time."

(1877–1938), who wrote in both Persian and Urdu, became a symbol of the Islamic tradition. Sayyid Ali Khamenei (then president of the Islamic Republic of Iran, now Supreme Leader, who fancies himself something of an expert on Persian poetry) lauded Iqbal's Persian poetry at significant length.[34] 'Ali Shari'ati, one of the intellectual forebears of the Islamic revolution in Iran, described his project as a continuation of Iqbal's in his *Ma va Iqbal* (*Iqbal and Us*, 1976).[35] Though Iqbal died nearly a decade before the partition of India and the establishment of Pakistan, he lived in territory that eventually became Pakistan. Iqbal's Muslim universalism (sometimes described as pan-Islamism) was seen as an inspiration of Pakistani ideals. The Pakistani state adopted Iqbal as a national figure, celebrating him as the nation's poet and leveraging him in soft power initiatives abroad. In 2010, Pakistan funded the Allama Iqbal Faculty of Arts building at Kabul University in Afghanistan, a $10 million project.[36] Pakistan's general consul in Mashhad, Irfan Mahmood Bokhari, describes Iqbal as a "connecting ring" between Pakistan and Iran.[37] Pakistan was the "land of Iqbal" (*sarzamin-i iqbal*), as one Iranian visitor titled her travelogue.[38]

Mirza Asadullah Khan "Ghalib" (1797–1869) is often held up alongside Iqbal as one of the greatest poets in the Urdu canon. Why is Iqbal known in Iran but not Ghalib? Like Iqbal, Ghalib also wrote in Persian; in fact, Ghalib was most proud of his Persian output, both in poetry and in prose. Unlike Iqbal, however, Ghalib is unknown in Iran, and while Iqbal posthumously became Pakistan's national poet, Ghalib could not be appropriated so easily for national purposes. Aside from a very brief stint in Lahore, Ghalib lived his entire life in cities that remained part of India after partition, making him unsuitable as a national figure in Pakistan. His irreverence, in contrast to Iqbal's

---

[34] Khaminah'i, "Iqbal"; discussed in Adib Moghaddam, "India in the Iranian Imagination," 152–4.

[35] Shari'ati, *Ma va Iqbal*; Saffari, *Beyond Shariati*, 66–8.

[36] "Pak-funded Iqbal Faculty."   [37] "Mashhad ceremony commemorates Iqbal."

[38] Shahsavandi, "Dar Sarzamin-i Iqbal."

piety, would have also disqualified him from representing Islam; on one occasion, Ghalib famously quipped that he was only half Muslim, explaining: "I drink wine, but don't eat pork."[39]

Ghalib was no more appealing to Indian nationalists, as Urdu became increasingly associated with Muslims and Pakistan in the post-partition era. Without a state to promote him, his name did not reach most Iranians. Like his compatriots Shibli Nu'mani, Muhammad Husayn Azad, and others, Ghalib participated in the very trends which ultimately wrote Indians out of Iranian literary history. As Indians and Iranians argued over "proper" Persian – a controversy which had begun earlier, in the early modern *dasatiri* texts and with Arzu – Ghalib did not take the side of his fellow Hindustanis.[40] Instead, he joined Iranians in lambasting the "Indian usage" of Persian. Ghalib claimed to have learned Persian not from Indian teachers as his peers did, but from an Iranian Zoroastrian named 'Abd al-Samad. This story was most likely spurious, but it is revealing in its nationalist association between "pure Persian," Iran, and Zoroastrianism, supposedly undefiled by Arabic. Through his connection to this "pure" source and by writing in "pure" Persian (in *Dastanbu*) and criticizing Indian Persian (in *Qati'-i Burhan*), Ghalib hoped to differentiate himself from other Indian poets and prove his worth and merit as a Persian litterateur in the market for poetic patronage.[41] However, the "pure Persian" trend was one of the developments seized upon by Iranians in the construction of a modern, national identity, with the ironic end result that "Indo-Persian" poetry like Ghalib's was effaced from literary history.

---

[39] Hali, *Yadgar-i Ghalib*, 39.
[40] On the origins of this controversy see Tavakoli-Targhi, *Refashioning Iran*, 77–95; Sheffield, "Language of Heaven."
[41] "Ghalib was a nightingale of the rose garden of Persia / only by mistake I called him a song-bird of India" (cited and translated in Bausani, "Ghalib's Persian Poetry," 74). "Ghalib is not from India; [from] the tune we compose / one would say we're from Isfahan and Herat and Qom" (Ghalib, *Divan-i Ghalib-i Dihlavi*, 103). There are many other examples; for another, see Kirmani, *Evaluation of Ghalib's Persian Poetry*, 60–2.

Similarly unknown to Iranians is N. M. Rashid, the Urdu poet at the center of Iranian literary circles during World War II. Rashid returned to Tehran in 1967, where he lived and directed the U.N. Information Center until 1973, giving lectures and interviews in Persian and publishing poetry in Urdu.[42] He continued to keep company with influential figures in Iranian society, socializing with the likes of Prime Minister Amir-'Abbas Huvayda and Asadullah 'Alam, former prime minister and then-minister of the Pahlavi court.[43] Rashid was a regular fixture in the Iranian literary scene, and met or corresponded with many of the country's greatest contemporary poets, from Ahmad Shamlu to Suhrab Sipihri and many others.[44]

Rashid also contributed to Persian literary history with his Urdu-language *Jadid Farsi Sha'iri* (*Modern Persian Poetry*, 1969), wherein he also translated Persian poetry into Urdu verse. As the national canon of premodern Persian poetry had been more or less settled, literary historians increasingly turned from comprehensive, canon-defining works to narrower topics: contemporary poets, or those belonging to particular groups like Sayyid 'Abdullah's study of Hindus in Persian poetry, *Adabiyat-i Farsi mein Hinduon ka Hissah* (*The Contribution of Hindus to Persian Literature*, 1942). Rashid's critical works touched on all of the themes explored by Iranians and South Asians in this book: tradition, modernity, sexuality (Rashid was also critical of homoerotic classical Urdu poetry), origins and identity, and script.[45] Together with 'Abd al-Hamid 'Irfani and the Pakistani

---

[42] Pue, *I Too Have Some Dreams*, 9.

[43] "Photograph of N. M. Rashed with Prime Minister Hoveyda, Tehran," Noon Meem Rashed Archive; "Photograph of N. M. Rashed with Prime Minister Hoveyda of Iran on right," Noon Meem Rashed Archive.

[44] These included Mahmud Kiyanush, Nadir Nadirpur, Ahmad Shamlu, Yadullah Ruyayi, Manuchihr Atashi, Isma'il Khu'i, Muhammad-Riza Shafi'i-Kadkani, Riza Barahini, Suhrab Sipihri, Ahmadriza Ahmadi, Parviz Natal-Khanlari, Isma'il Nuri 'Ala, 'Abd al-'Ali Dastghayb, and Colonel Farrukhzad, father of the famed poet Furugh Farrukhzad.

[45] On orthography, see Rashid, *Maqalat-i Rashid*, 170–8; on modernity, ibid., 179–84.

embassy, Rashid contributed to Iqbal's growing popularity in Iran, organizing Iqbal Day celebrations in Tehran.[46]

Despite his legacy as an important connection between Iran and South Asia, Rashid remains "a stranger in Iran," as he titled one of his poems, unknown by Iranians. During the academic rise in attention to literature of the subcontinent in the 1990s, some of his poetry was finally translated into Persian, published posthumously in an issue of the journal *Shi'r* (*Poetry*) alongside other Urdu poets like Faiz Ahmad 'Faiz,' as well as Afghan and Tajik poets.[47] This obscure publication is perhaps the only recognition Rashid received in Iran. For most Iranians today the era of Persianate modernity, like Rashid himself, is yet unknown.

---

[46] Ibid., 302–13. [47] Rashid, "Ayandagan va Dard-i Hushyari."

Bibliography

ARCHIVES

British Library, London. Additional Manuscripts. India Office Records and Private
Papers.
University of Cambridge. Browne Archive.
Institute of Islamic Studies, McGill University. The Noon Meem Rashed Archive.
Malik National Library and Museum, Tehran.
National Library of Iran, Tehran.
Salar Jung Museum Library, Hyderabad.
Universitäts und Landesbibliothek, Bonn. Digital Collections.
Yasmin Rashed Hassan. Personal collections.

OTHER PRIMARY AND SECONDARY SOURCES

Abdi, Kamyar. "Nationalism, Politics, and the Development of Archaeology in
Iran." *American Journal of Archaeology* 105, no. 1 (January 2001): 51–76.
Adib-Moghaddam, Arshin. "India in the Iranian Imagination: Between Culture and
Strategic Interest." In *Competing Visions of India in World Politics: India's
Rise beyond the West*, edited by Kate Sullivan, 145–59. London: Palgrave
Macmillan, 2015.
——— *Psycho-nationalism: Global Thought, Iranian Imaginations*. Cambridge:
Cambridge University Press, 2017.
Ahanchi, Azar. "Reflections of the Indian Independence Movement in the Iranian
Press." *Iranian Studies* 42, no. 3 (2009): 423–43.
Ahmad, Aziz. "Ṣafawid Poets and India." *Iran* 14 (1976): 117–32.
Ahmad, Rizwan. "Urdu in Devanagari: Shifting Orthographic Practices and Muslim
Identity in Delhi." *Language in Society* 40, no. 3 (June 2011): 259–84.
Ahmad, Saifuddin. "*Bas ke samjhe hain isko sare 'awam*: The Emergence of Urdu
Literary Culture in North India." *Social Scientist* 42, no. 3/4 (March–April
2014): 3–23.
Ahmadi, Wali. "The Institution of Persian Literature and the Genealogy of Bahar's
'Stylistics.'" *British Journal of Middle Eastern Studies* 31, no. 2 (November
2004): 141–52.

Ahmed, Leila. *Women and Gender in Islam: Historical Roots of a Modern Debate.* New Haven: Yale University Press, 1992.

Ahmed, Shahab. *What Is Islam? The Importance of Being Islamic.* Princeton: Princeton University Press, 2016.

Akbar, Raziyah. *Sharh-i Ahval va Sabk-i Ash'ar-i Baba Fighani Shirazi* [*Biography and Poetic Style of Baba Fighani Shirazi*]. Hyderabad: Shalimar Publications, 1974.

Akhtar, Jan-Nisar. *Khak-i Dil* [*Dust of the Heart*]. Amroha: Idarah-i Isha'at-i Urdu, 1974.

Akhtar, M. Saleem. "DĀʿĪ-AL-ESLĀM, SAYYED MOḤAMMAD ʿALĪ." *Encyclopædia Iranica*, vol. 6.6, 594–5. Available online at <iranicaonline.org/articles/dai-al-eslam-sayyed-mohammad-ali-persian-scholar-preacher-and-lexicographer-born-1295-1878-at-larijan>. Accessed August 30, 2020.

Akhtar, Nadeem. "HEDAYAT, SADEQ v. Hedayat in India." *Encyclopædia Iranica.* Available online at <https://iranicaonline.org/articles/hedayat-sadeq-v>. Accessed August 30, 2020.

Alatas, Syed Hussein. *The Myth of the Lazy Native: A Study of the Image of the Malays, Filipinos and Javanese from the 16th to the 20th Century and Its Function in the Ideology of Colonial Capitalism.* London: Routledge, 1977.

Alavi, Bozorg. *Geschichte und Entwicklung der modernen persischen Literatur* [*History and Development of Modern Persian Literature*]. Berlin: Akademie-Verlag, 1964.

Algar, Hamid. "Malkum Khan, Akhūndzada and the Proposed Reform of the Arabic Alphabet." *Middle Eastern Studies* 5, no. 2 (1969): 116–30.

Ali, Zulfikar. *Persian Tadkira Writing in India during the 18th Century with Special Reference to Azad Bilgrami.* New Delhi: Indian Council for Cultural Relations, 2006.

Allan, Michael. *In the Shadow of World Literature: Sites of Reading in Colonial Egypt.* Princeton: Princeton University Press, 2016.

Amanat, Abbas. "From Peshawar to Tehran: An Anti-Imperialist Poet of the Late Persianate Milieu." In *The Persianate World: The Frontiers of a Eurasian Lingua Franca*, edited by Nile Green, 279–99. Oakland: University of California Press, 2019.

"Legend, Legitimacy and Making a National Narrative in the Historiography of Qajar Iran (1785–1925)." In *A History of Persian Literature, vol. 10, Persian Historiography*, edited by Charles Melville, 292–366. London: I. B. Tauris, 2012.

Ameer Ali, Syed. *The Spirit of Islam: The Life and Teachings of Mohammed.* Calcutta: S. K. Lahiri, 1902.

Amin, Camron Michael. *The Making of the Modern Iranian Woman: Gender, State Policy, and Popular Culture 1865–1946*. Gainesville: University Press of Florida, 2009.

Amman, Mir. *Bagh u Bahar, ya'ni Qissah-i Chahar Darvesh* [*The Garden and the Spring: The Tale of the Four Dervishes*]. Edited by Maulvi 'Abdul Haq. Delhi: Anjuman-i Taraqqi-i Urdu (Hind), 1944.

Amstutz, Andrew McKinney. "Finding a Home for Urdu: Islam and Science in Modern South Asia." PhD diss., Cornell University, 2017.

Anderson, Benedict. *Imagined Communities: Reflections on the Origin and Spread of Nationalism*. New York: Verso, 2006.

Andrews, Walter G., and Mehmet Kalpaklı. *The Age of Beloveds: Love and the Beloved in Early-Modern Ottoman and European Culture and Society*. Durham: Duke University Press, 2005.

Andreyev, Sergei. "Pashto Literature: The Classical Period." In *A History of Persian Literature XVIII: Oral Literature of Iranian Languages*, edited by Philip G. Kreyenbroek and Ulrich Marzolph, 89–113. London: I. B. Tauris, 2010.

Anjuman-i Asar-i Milli (Iran). *Majmu'ah-yi Intisharat-i Qadim-i Anjuman* [*Collection of the Society's Old Publications*]. Tehran: Silsilah-yi Intisharat-i Anjuman-i Asar-i Milli, 1351 HS/1972 CE.

Ansari, Ali M. "Nationalism and the Question of Race." In *Constructing Nationalism in Iran: From the Qajars to the Islamic Republic*, edited by Meir Litvak, 101–16. London: Routledge, 2017.

Anushiravani, Alireza. "Comparative Literature in Iran." *Comparative Studies of South Asia, Africa and the Middle East* 32, no. 3 (2012): 484–91.

Arberry, A. J., M. Minovi, and E. Blochet. *The Chester Beatty Library: A Catalogue of the Persian Manuscripts and Miniatures*. Edited by J. V. S. Wilkinson. 3 vols. Dublin: Hodges Figgis, 1959–62.

Arjomand, Saïd Amir. "From the Editor: Defining Persianate Studies." *Journal of Persianate Studies* 1, no. 1 (2008): 1–4.

Arondekar, Anjali R. *For the Record: On Sexuality and the Colonial Archive in India*. Durham: Duke University Press, 2009.

Aryanpur, Yahya. *Az Saba ta Nima: Tarikh-i 150 Sal-i Adab-i Farsi* [*From Saba to Nima: The History of 150 Years of Persian Literature*]. 3 vols. Tehran: Zavvar, 1387 hs/2008–9 CE.

Arzu, Siraj al-Din 'Ali Khan. *Muthmir* [*Fruitful*]. Edited by Rehana Khatoon. Karachi: The Institute of Central and West Asian Studies, University of Karachi, 1991.

——— . *Tazkirah-yi Majma' al-Nafa'is* [*Assembly of Subtleties*]. 3 vols. Edited by Zayb al-Nisa' 'Ali Khan and Mihr Nur Muhammad Khan. Islamabad: Iran-Pakistan Institute of Persian Studies, 2004.

"Asasnamah-yi Mu'assasah-yi Zaban-ha-yi Kharijah" [Charter of the Foreign Languages Institute]. *Majallah-yi Danishkadah-yi Adabiyat [Danishgah-i Tihran]* 3, no. 4 (Tir 1335/June–July 1956): 103–5.

Ashraf, Ahmad. "CONSPIRACY THEORIES." *Encyclopædia Iranica*, vol. 6.2, 138–47. Available online at <https://iranicaonline.org/articles/conspiracy-theo ries>. Accessed August 30, 2020.

Ashraful Hukk, Mohammed, Hermann Ethé, and Edward Robertson. *A Descriptive Catalogue of the Arabic and Persian Manuscripts in Edinburgh University Library.* Hertford: Austin, 1925.

Asif, Manan Ahmed. *A Book of Conquest: The Chahnama and Muslim Origins in South Asia.* Cambridge: Harvard University Press, 2016.

Atabaki, Touraj. "Far from Home, But at Home: Indian Migrant Workers in the Iranian Oil Industry." *Studies in History* 31, no. 1 (2015): 85–114.

'Awfi, Muhammad. *Tazkirah-yi Lubab al-Albab [The Piths of Intellects].* Edited by Edward Browne. Leiden: Brill, 1906.

Awhadi Balyani, Taqi al-Din. *'Arafat al-'Ashiqin va 'Arasat al-'Arifin [Mount Arafat of the Lovers and Arasat of the Gnostics].* Edited by Zabihullah Sahibkar, Aminah Fakhr Ahmad, and Muhammad Qahraman. 8 vols. Tehran: Miras-i maktub, 2010.

Aytürk, İlker. "Attempts at Romanizing the Hebrew Script and Their Failure: Nationalism, Religion and Alphabet Reform in the Yishuv." *Middle Eastern Studies* 43, no. 4 (June 2007): 625–45.

"Editorial Introduction: Romanisation in Comparative Perspective." *Royal Asiatic Society of Great Britain and Ireland* Third Series 20, no. 1 (January 2010): 1–9.

Ayub Khan, Mohammad. *Speeches and Statements.* 8 vols. Karachi: Pakistan Publications, 1959–66.

Azad, Abu'l Kalam. *Selected Works of Maulana Abul Kalam Azad.* Edited by Ravindra Kumar. Vol. 3. New Delhi: Atlantic, 1991.

Azad, Muhammad-Husayn. *Ab-i Hayat [Water of Life].* Lahore: Naval Kishor, 1907.

Āb-e ḥayāt: Shaping the Canon of Urdu Poetry. Translated and edited by Frances Pritchett and Shamsur Rahman Faruqi. New Delhi: Oxford University Press, 2001.

Nigaristan-i Fars [Picture-Gallery of Persia]. Lahore: Karimi Press, 1922.

Sayr-i Iran [Travels in Iran]. Lahore: Karimi Press, n.d.

Azar, Lutf 'Ali Bayg bin Aqakhan Baygdili Shamlu. *Atashkadah: bakhsh-i duvvum [Fire-Temple: Part Two].* Edited by Hasan Sadat Nasiri. Tehran: Amir Kabir, 1338 HS/1959 CE.

ʿAzimabadi, Shad. *Furugh-i Hasti* [*Splendor of Existence*]. Darbhanga: Hamidiyyah Barqi Press, 1957.

Azimi, Fakhreddin. "Historiography in the Pahlavi Era." In *A History of Persian Literature. Volume X: Persian Historiography*, edited by Charles Melville, 367–435. London and New York: I. B. Tauris, 2012.

Babayan, Kathryn. *Mystics, Monarchs, and Messiahs: Cultural Landscapes of Early Modern Iran*. Cambridge: Harvard University Press, 2002.

Bahar, Muhammad-Taqı. *Bahar va Adab-i Farsi* [*Bahar and Persian Literature*]. 2 vols. Tehran: Kitabha-yi jibi, 1382 HS/2003–4 CE.

——. *Divan-i Ashʿar-i Shadravan-i Muhammad-Taqi Bahar Malik al-Shuʿara* [*Divan of Poetry of the Late Poet-Laureate Muhammad-Taqi Bahar*]. Second ed. 3 vols. Tehran: Amir Kabir, 1344–5 HS/1965–6 CE.

——. *Sabkshinasi: ya Tarikh-i Tatavvur-i Nasr-i Farsi* [*Stylistics: or the History of the Evolution of Persian Prose*]. Third ed. 3 vols. Tehran: Zavvar, 1388 HS/2009–10 CE.

Bahar, Parvanah. *Murgh-i Sahar: Khatirat-i Parvanah Bahar* [*Bird of Dawn: Memoirs of Parvaneh Bahar*]. Tehran: Shahab, 1382 HS/2003 CE.

Bailey, T. Grahame. *A History of Urdu Literature*. Lahore: Al-Biruni, 1977.

Balaghi, Shiva. "Nationalism and Cultural Production in Iran, 1848–1906." PhD diss., University of Michigan, 2008.

Balsley, Sivan. *Iranian Masculinities: Gender and Sexuality in Late Qajar and Early Pahlavi Iran*. Cambridge: Cambridge University Press, 2019.

Banani, Amin. *The Modernization of Iran, 1921–1941*. Stanford: Stanford University Press, 1961.

Bandy, Hunter Casparian. "Building a Mountain of Light: Niẓām al-Dīn Gīlānī and Shīʿī Naturalism Between Safavid Iran and the Deccan." PhD diss., Duke University, 2019.

Baron, Beth. *Egypt as a Woman: Nationalism, Gender, and Politics*. Berkeley: University of California Press, 2005.

Bashir, Elena. "INDO-IRANIAN FRONTIER LANGUAGES." *Encyclopædia Iranica*. Available online at <https://iranicaonline.org/articles/indo-iranian-frontier-languages-and-the-influence-of-persian>. Accessed August 30, 2020.

Bausani, A[lessandro]. "Ghalib's Persian Poetry." In *Ghalib: The Poet and his Age*, edited by Ralph Russell, 70–104. Cambridge: George Allen & Unwin, 1972.

Bayani, Mahdi. *Ahval va Asar-i Khvushnivisan* [*Lives and Works of Calligraphers*]. 2 vols. Tehran: Intisharat-i ʿIlmi, 1363 HS/1985 CE.

Bayat, Ali. "Dr. Ali Bayat Interview at Rekhta Studio." Rekhta. November 24, 2014. YouTube video, 18:18. <https://youtu.be/QUaLCHJSOJw>.

Bayevsky, Solomon. "ḠĪĀṮ AL-LOḠĀT." *Encyclopædia Iranica*. Available online at <https://iranicaonline.org/articles/gia-al-logat-1>. Accessed August 30, 2020.

Beg, Mirza Khalil A. "The Standardization of Script for Urdu." In *Standardization and Modernization: Dynamics of Language Planning*, edited by S. I. Hasnain, 227–41. New Delhi: Bahri Publications, 1995.

Bergne, Paul. *The Birth of Tajikistan: National Identity and the Origins of the Republic*. New York: I. B. Tauris, 2007.

Beverley, Eric Lewis. "Documenting the World in Indo-Persianate & Imperial English: Idioms of Textual Authority in Hyderabad." *Journal of the Economic and Social History of the Orient* 62, no. 5–6 (2019): 1046–78.

Bhajiwalla, Rustom Pestonji. *Maulana Shibli and Ûmar Khayyam*. Surat: I. P. Mission Press, 1932.

"Bicchu ki Paida'ish [The Birth of the Scorpion]." *The Daily Roshni*, December 30, 2017, <http://thedailyroshni.com/>بچھو-کی-پیدائش. Accessed August 30, 2020.

Bihruz, Zabih. *Khatt va Farhang [Script and Culture]*. Tehran: Rushdiyyah, 1373 HS/1994 CE.

 Zaban-i Iran: Farsi ya 'Arabi? [The Language of Iran: Persian or Arabic?] Tehran: Chapkhanah-yi Mihr, 1313 HS/1934–5 CE.

Bonakdarian, Mansour. "Edward G. Browne and the Iranian Constitutional Struggle: From Academic Orientalism to Political Activism." *Iranian Studies* 26, no. 1/2 (1993): 7–31.

 "Iranian Nationalism and Global Solidarity Networks 1906–1918: Internationalism, Transnationalism, Globalization, and Nationalist Cosmopolitanism." In *Iran in the Middle East: Transnational Encounters and Social History*, edited by H. E. Chehabi, Peyman Jafari, and Maral Jefroudi, 77–119. London: I. B. Tauris, 2015.

Bondarev, Dmitry. "Qur'anic Exegesis in Old Kanembu: Linguistic Precision for Better Interpretation." *Journal of Qur'anic Studies* 15, no. 3 (October 2013): 56–83.

Bondarev, Dmitry, and Abba Tijani. "Performance of Multilayered Literacy: Tarjumo of the Kanuri Muslim Scholars." In *African Literacies: Ideologies, Scripts, Education*, edited by Kasper Juffermans, Yonas Mesfun Asfaha, and Ashraf Abdelhay, 115–42. Newcastle upon Tyne: Cambridge Scholars Publishing, 2014.

Boone, Joseph Allen. *The Homoerotics of Orientalism*. New York: Columbia University Press, 2014.

Booth, Marilyn. *Classes of Ladies of Cloistered Spaces: Writing Feminist History through Biography in Fin-de-siècle Egypt*. Edinburgh: Edinburgh University Press, 2015.

Boroujerdi, Mehrzad. "Contesting Nationalist Constructions of Iranian Identity." *Critique: Critical Middle Eastern Studies* 7, no. 12 (Spring 1998): 43–55.

Bose, Subhas Chandra. "Free India and Her Problems." In *Azad Hind: Writings and Speeches, 1941–43*, edited by Sisir K Bose and Sugata Bose, 140–8. London: Anthem Press, 2004.

Boyce, Mary. "Manekji Limji Hataria in Iran." In *K. R. Cama Oriental Institute Golden Jubilee Volume*, edited by N. D. Minochehr-Homji and M. F. Kanga, 19–31. Bombay: K. R. Cama Oriental Institute, 1969.

Browne, Edward G. *A Literary History of Persia*. 4 vols. Cambridge: Cambridge University Press, 1929.

———. *The Press and Poetry of Modern Persia: Partly Based on the Manuscript Work of Mírzá Muḥammad 'Alí Khán "Tarbiyat" of Tabríz*. Cambridge: Cambridge University Press, 1914.

———. "Some Notes on the Poetry of the Persian Dialects." *Journal of the Royal Asiatic Society of Great Britain and Ireland* (October 1895): 773–825.

Bukhari, Shohrat. "Obituary." *Iqbal Review* 30.31, no. 3.1 (October 1989–April 1990): 225–6.

Burney, Fatima. "Locating the World in Metaphysical Poetry: The Bardification of Hafiz." *Journal of World Literature* 4, no. 2 (2019): 149–68.

Burton, Elise K. "Evolution and Creationism in Middle Eastern Education: A New Perspective." *Evolution: International Journal of Organic Evolution* 65, no. 1 (January 2011): 301–4.

———. *Genetic Crossroads: The Middle East and the Science of Human Heredity*. Stanford: Stanford University Press, 2021.

Busch, Allison. *Poetry of Kings: The Classical Hindi Literature of Mughal India*. Oxford: Oxford University Press, 2011.

Chehabi, Houchang E. "The Paranoid Style in Iranian Historiography." In *Iran in the 20th Century: Historiography and Political Culture*, edited by Touraj Atabaki, 155–76. London: I. B. Tauris, 2009.

———. "Staging the Emperor's New Clothes: Dress Codes and Nation-Building under Reza Shah." *Iranian Studies* 26, no. 3/4 (Summer–Autumn 1993): 209–29.

———. "The Westernization of Iranian Culinary Culture." *Iranian Studies* 36, no. 1 (March 2003): 43–61.

Cooley, Claire. "Record with Two Songs from the Iranian Film *Qarun's Treasure* (1965) Found in India." *Film History* 32, no. 3 (Fall 2020): 210–14.

———. "Soundscape of a National Cinema Industry: *Filmfarsi* and Its Sonic Connections with Egyptian and Indian Cinemas, 1940s–1960s." *Film History* 32, no. 3 (Fall 2020): 43–74.

Cooper, Frederick. *Colonialism in Question: Theory, Knowledge, History.* Berkeley: University of California Press, 2005.

Chung, Karen Steffen. "Some Returned Loans: Japanese Loanwords in Taiwan Mandarin." In *Language Change in East Asia,* edited by T. E. McAuley, 161–79. Richmond, UK: Curzon, 2001.

Cohn, Bernard S. *Colonialism and Its Forms of Knowledge: The British in India.* Princeton: Princeton University Press, 1996.

Cole, Juan R. I. "Iranian Culture and South Asia, 1500–1900." In *Iran and the Surrounding World: Interactions in Culture and Cultural Politics,* edited by Nikki R. Keddie and Rudi Matthee, 15–35. Seattle: University of Washington Press, 2002.

Conrad, Sebastian. *What Is Global History?* Princeton: Princeton University Press, 2016.

Cook, Nilla Cram. "The Theater and Ballet Arts of Iran." *Middle East Journal* 3, no. 4 (October 1949): 406–20.

Da'i al-Islam, Iran Banu. "Din-i Babi va Hajji Husayn-Quli [The Babi Religion and Hajji Husayn-Quli]," *A'in-i Islam* 17 (25 Shahrivar 1328/ September 16, 1949): 4–4.

Da'i al-Islam, Sayyid Muhammad-'Ali. *Farhang-i Nizam: Farsi bah Farsi [Nizam Dictionary: Persian to Persian].* 5 vols. Tehran: Danish, 1362 HS/1983–4 CE.

Daneshgar, Majid. "Uninterrupted Censored Darwin: From the Middle East to the Malay-Indonesian World." *Zygon: Journal of Religion & Science* 55, no. 4 (December 2020): 1041–57.

Darwin, Charles. *The Origin of Species by Means of Natural Selection, or the Preservation of Favored Races in the Struggle for Life, and the Descent of Man and Selection in Relation to Sex.* New York: The Modern Library, 1957.

Davis, Dick. *Faces of Love: Hafez and the Poets of Shiraz.* New York: Penguin, 2013.

Dayal, Subah. "Vernacular Conquest? A Persian Patron and His Image in the Seventeenth-Century Deccan." *Comparative Studies of South Asia, Africa and the Middle East* 37, no. 3 (December 2017): 549–69.

De Blois, François. *Persian Literature: A Bio-Bibliographical Survey. Volume V: Poetry of the Pre-Mongol Period.* 2nd ed. New York: Routledge, 2004.

De Bruijn, J. P. T. "Arabic Influences on Persian Literature." In *General Introduction to Persian Literature,* edited by J. T. P. de Bruijn, 369–84. London: I. B. Tauris, 2009.

DeSouza, Wendy. "The Love That Dare Not Be Translated: Erasures of Premodern Sexuality in Modern Persian Mysticism." In *Rethinking Iranian Nationalism and Modernity*, edited by Kamran Scot Aghaie and Afshin Marashi, 67–86. Austin: University of Texas Press, 2014.

  Unveiling Men: Modern Masculinities in Twentieth-Century Iran. Syracuse: Syracuse University Press, 2019.

Devos, Bianca. "Engineering a Modern Society? Adoptions of New Technologies in Early Pahlavi Iran." In *Culture and Cultural Politics under Reza Shah: The Pahlavi State, New Bourgeoisie and the Creation of a Modern Society in Iran*, edited by Bianca Devos and Christoph Werner, 266–87. New York: Routledge, 2014.

Dihlavi, Sayyid Ahmad. *Farhang-i Asafiyyah [Asafiyyah Dictionary].* 4 vols. Lahore: Matbaʿ rifah-i ʿamm, 1908.

Doğan, Atila. *Osmanlı Aydınları ve Sosyal Darwinizm [Ottoman Intellectuals and Social Darwinism].* Istanbul: İstanbul Bilgi Üniversitesi Yayınları, 2006.

Dubrow, Jennifer. *Cosmopolitan Dreams: The Making of Modern Urdu Literary Culture in Colonial South Asia.* Honolulu: University of Hawaiʻi Press, 2018.

Dudney, Arthur. *India in the Persian World of Letters: Ḵhān-i Ārzū among the Eighteenth-Century Philologists.* Oxford: Oxford University Press, 2022.

  "Going Native: Iranian Émigré Poets and Indo-Persian." *Comparative Studies of South Asia, Africa and the Middle East* 37, no. 3 (December 2017): 531–48.

  "Sabk-e Hendi and the Crisis of Authority in Eighteenth-Century Indo-Persian Poetics." *Journal of Persianate Studies* 9, no. 1 (2016): 60–82.

  "Urdu as Persian: Some Eighteenth-Century Evidence on Vernacular Poetry as Language Planning." In *Text and Tradition in Early Modern North India*, edited by Tyler Williams, Anshu Malhotra, and John Stratton Hawley, 40–57. New Delhi: Oxford University Press, 2018.

Eagleton, Terry. *Marxism and Literary Criticism.* Berkeley: University of California Press, 1976.

Eaton, Richard M. *India in the Persianate Age: 1000–1765.* London: Penguin Books, 2019.

  "The Persian Cosmopolis (900–1900) and the Sanskrit Cosmopolis (400–1400)." In *The Persianate World: Rethinking a Shared Sphere*, edited by Abbas Amanat and Assef Ashraf, 63–83. Leiden: Brill, 2019.

Edwards, John. "Men and Their Methods." Edited by J. M. Bramwood. *Typographical Journal* 24, no. 2 (February 1904): 107–11.

Elhalaby, Esmat. "The Arab Rediscovery of India." PhD diss., Rice University, 2019.

Elling, Rasmus Christian. *Minorities in Iran: Nationalism and Ethnicity after Khomeini.* New York: Palgrave Macmillan, 2013.

Ellis, Alexander John. "Phonetic Literature." *Phonotypic Journal* 3, no. 29 (May 1844): 133–44.

El-Rouayheb, Khaled. *Before Homosexuality in the Arab-Islamic World, 1500–1800.* Chicago: University of Chicago Press, 2005.

Elshakry, Marwa. *Reading Darwin in Arabic, 1860–1950.* Chicago: University of Chicago Press, 2013.

Elwell-Sutton, L. P. "ARABIC LANGUAGE iii. Arabic influences in Persian literature." *Encyclopædia Iranica*, vol. 2.3, 233–7. Available online at <https://iranicaonline.org/articles/arabic-iii>. Accessed August 30, 2020.

Estaji, Azam, and Ailin Firooziyan Pooresfahani. "The Investigation of Punctuation in Photographic Copies of Persian Writing." *Theory and Practice in Language Studies* 2, no. 5 (May 2012): 1090–7.

Ethé, Hermann. "Neupersische Litteratur [New Persian Literature]." In *Grundriss der Iranischen Philologie [Outline of Iranian Philology]*, Vol. 2. Strassburg: K. J. Trübner, 1904.

Fallon, S. W. *A New Hindustani-English Dictionary, with Illustrations from Hindustani Literature and Folk-Lore.* London: Trubner and Co., 1879.

Fani, Aria. "Becoming Literature: The Formation of Adabiyāt as an Academic Discipline in Iran and Afghanistan (1895–1945)." PhD diss., University of California, Berkeley, 2019.

"Iran's Literary Becoming: Zokā᾽ ol-Molk Forughi and the Literary History That Wasn't." *Iran Namag* 5, no. 3 (Fall 2020): 114–44.

Farghadani, Shahla. "A History of Style and a Style of History: The Hermeneutic of *Tarz* in Persian Literary Criticism." *Iranian Studies* 55, no. 2 (2022): 501–19.

Faruqi, Shamsur Rahman. "Unprivileged Power: The Strange Case of Persian (and Urdu) in Nineteenth-Century India." *Annual of Urdu Studies* 13 (1998): 3–30.

Faruqi, Shamsur Rahman. *Early Urdu Literary Culture and History.* New Delhi: Oxford University Press, 2001.

Faza᾽ili, Habibullah. *Atlas-i Khatt: Tahqiq dar Khutut-i Islami [Atlas of Script: An Inquiry into Islamic Scripts].* Isfahan: Intisharat-i Mash῾al, 1362 HS/1983–4 CE.

Firdawsi. *Shahnamah-yi Firdawsi, az ru-yi nuskhah-yi khatti-yi baysunghuri [Firdawsi's Shahnamah, from the Baysunghurid manuscript].* Tehran: Shura-yi Markazi-yi Jashn-i Shahanshahi-yi Iran, 1350 HS/1971 CE.

"Firdousī." *Encyclopædia Britannica.* New York: The Encyclopædia Britannica Company, 1911.

Fischel, Roy S. *Local States in an Imperial World: Identity, Society and Politics in the Early Modern Deccan.* Edinburgh: Edinburgh University Press, 2020.

Fish, Laura. "The Bombay Interlude: Parsi Transnational Aspirations in the First Persian Sound Film." *Trasnational Cinemas* 9, no. 2 (2018): 197–211.

Fisher, Michael H. "Conflicting Meanings of Persianate Culture: An Intimate Example from Colonial India and Britain." In *The Persianate World: The*

Frontiers of a Eurasian Lingua Franca, edited by Nile Green, 225–41. Oakland: University of California Press, 2019.

Flatt, Emma J. *The Courts of the Deccan Sultanates: Living Well in the Persian Cosmopolis*. Cambridge: Cambridge University Press, 2019.

Floor, Willem. *Encyclopædia Iranica*, vol. 4.7, 760-4. Available online at <https://iranicaonline.org/articles/cap-print-printing-a-persian-word-probably-derived-from-hindi-chapna-to-print-see-turner-no>. Accessed August 30, 2020.

Foltz, Richard C. "Islam." In *The Oxford Handbook of Religion and Ecology*, edited by Roger S. Gottlieb, 207–19. Oxford: Oxford University Press, 2006.

Forbes, Duncan. *A Grammar of the Hindūstānī Language, in the Oriental and Roman Character, with Numerous Copper-Plate Illustrations of the Persian and Devanāgarī Systems of Alphabetic Writing: to which is Added, a Copious Selection of Easy Extracts for Reading, in the Persi-Arabic and Devanāgarī Characters, Forming a Complete Introduction to the Bagh-o-Bahar, Together with a Vocabulary, and Explanatory Notes*. London: Wm. H. Allen & Co., 1846.

Foucault, Michel. *The History of Sexuality*. 3 vols. New York: Vintage, 1990.

"What Is Enlightenment?" In *The Foucault Reader*, edited by Paul Rabinow, 32–50. New York: Pantheon, 1984.

Friedman, Susan Stanford. "Why Not Compare?" *PMLA* 126, no. 3 (May 2011): 753–62.

Fuchs, Simon Wolfgang. *In a Pure Muslim Land: Shi'ism between Pakistan and the Middle East*. Chapel Hill: University of North Carolina Press, 2019.

Furughi, Muhammad-'Ali. *Sayr-i Hikmat dar Urupa* [*History of Philosophy in Europe*]. 3 vols. Tehran: Intisharat-i Zavvar, 1344 HS/1965–6 CE.

Khatirat-i Muhammad-'Ali Furughi bah hamrah-i Yaddasht-ha-yi Ruzanah az Sal-ha-yi 1293 ta 1320 [*Memoirs of Muhammad-'Ali Furughi together with Diary from 1293 to 1320*]. Edited by Muhammad Afshin-Vafa'i and Pazhman Firuzbakhsh. Tehran: Sukhan, 1396 HS/2017 18 CE.

Yaddasht-ha-yi Ruzanah-yi Muhammad-'Ali Furughi az safar-i kunfirans-i sulh-i paris, disambr-i 1918– ut-i 1920 [*Diary of Muhammad-'Ali Furughi from travel to Paris Peace Conference, December 1918 to August 1920*]. Tehran: Sukhan, 1394 HS/2017–18 CE.

Furughi, Muhammad-Husayn Khan. [*Tarikh-i Adabiyat*]. N.p.: Matba'ah Mirza 'Ali-Asghar, 1335 AH/1916–17 CE. National Library of Iran, Tehran, Cat. No. 13157.

Furuzanfar, Badi' al-Zaman. *Sukhan va Sukhanvaran* [*Poetry and Poets*]. Tehran: Zavvar, 1387 HS/2008–9 CE.

Tarikh-i Adabiyat-i Iran: Ba'd az Islam ta Payan-i Timuriyan [*History of Iranian Literature: After Islam to the End of the Timurids*]. Tehran: Sazman-i Chap va Intisharat, Vizarat-i Farhang va Irshad-i Islami, 1383 HS/2004 CE.

Gabrieli, F. "ʿAdjam." In *The Encyclopedia of Islam, Second Edition*, volume 1, edited by H. A. R. Gibb, J. H. Kramers, E. Lévi-Provençal, and J. Schacht, 206. Leiden: Brill, 1986.

Gacek, Adam. *Arabic Manuscripts: A Vademecum for Readers*. Leiden: Brill, 2009.

Gelvin, James L. and Nile Green, eds. *Global Muslims in the Age of Steam and Print*. Berkeley: University of California Press, 2013.

Ghalib Dihlavi, Mirza Asadullah Khan. *Divan-i Ghalib-i Dihlavi* [Divan of *Ghalib*]. Edited by Muhammad-Hasan Haʾiri. Tehran: Miras-i maktub, 1386 HS/2007–8 CE.

Gheissari, Ali. *Iranian Intellectuals in the 20th Century*. Austin: University of Texas Press, 1998.

Gilchrist, John Borthwick. *Hindoostanee Philology; Comprising a Dictionary, English and Hindoostanee; with a Grammatical Introduction*. London: Kingsbury, Parbury, and Allen, 1825.

Gilchrist, John Borthwick. *The Oriental Fabulist, or polyglot translations of Esop's and other ancient fables from the English language into Hindoostanee, Persian, Arabic, Brij B'hak'ha, Bongla, and Sun[s]krit, in the Roman character, by various hands, under the direction and superintendence of John Gilchrist, for the use of the College of Fort William*. Calcutta: Hurkaru Office, 1803.

Gould, Rebecca. "How Newness Enters the World: The Methodology of Sheldon Pollock." *Comparative Studies of South Asia, Africa, and the Middle East* 28, no. 3 (2008): 533–57.

Green, Nile. *Bombay Islam: The Religious Economy of the Western Indian Ocean, 1840–1915*. New York: Cambridge University Press, 2011.

"Introduction: Afghan Literature between Diaspora and Nation." In *Afghanistan in Ink: Literature between Diaspora and Nation*, edited by Nile Green and Nushin Arbabzadah, 1–30. Oxford: Oxford University Press, 2012.

"Introduction: The Frontiers of the Persianate World (ca. 800–1900)." In *The Persianate World: The Frontiers of a Eurasian Lingua Franca*, edited by Nile Green, 1–71. Oakland: University of California Press, 2019.

"Journeymen, Middlemen: Travel, Transculture, and Technology in the Origins of Muslim Printing." *International Journal of Middle East Studies* 41, no. 2 (2009): 203–24.

The Love of Strangers: What Six Muslim Students Learned in Jane Austen's London. Princeton and Oxford: Princeton University Press, 2016.

"New Histories for the Age of Speed: The Archaeological-Architectural Past in Interwar Afghanistan and Iran." *Iranian Studies* 54, no. 3-4 (2021): 349–97.

"Persian Print and the Stanhope Revolution: Industrialization, Evangelicalism, and the Birth of Printing in Early Qajar Iran." *Comparative Studies of South Asia, Africa and the Middle East* 30, no. 3 (December 2010): 473–90.

"Spacetime and the Muslim Journey West: Industrial Communications in the Making of the 'Muslim World.'" *American Historical Review* 118, no. 2 (April 2013): 401–29.

Greenberg, Robert D. *Language and Identity in the Balkans: Serbo-Croatian and Its Disintegration.* Oxford: Oxford University Press, 2004.

Grigor, Talinn. *Building Iran: Modernism, Architecture, and National Heritage under the Pahlavi Monarchs.* New York: Periscope, 2010.

"The King's White Walls: Modernism and Bourgeois Architecture." In *Culture and Cultural Politics under Reza Shah: The Pahlavi State, New Bourgeoisie and the Creation of a Modern Society in Iran*, edited by Bianca Devos and Christoph Werner, 95–118. New York: Routledge, 2014.

"Persian Architectural Revivals in the British Raj and Qajar Iran." *Comparative Studies of South Asia, Africa, and the Middle East* 36, no. 3 (December 2016): 384–97.

Guimbretière, A. "Āzād." In *Encyclopaedia of Islam, Second Edition*, edited by P. Bearman, et al. Brill Online, 2015. <http://referenceworks.brillonline.com/entries/encyclopaedia-of-islam-2/a-za-d-SIM_8374>.

Gulchin-i Maʿani, Ahmad. *Tarikh-i Tazkirah-ha-yi Farsi* [History of Persian Tazkirahs]. 2 vols. Tehran: Kitabkhanah-yi sanaʾi, 1363 ᴴꜱ/1984–5 ᴄᴇ.

Haag-Higuchi, Roxane. "Modernization in Literary History: Malek al-Shoʿara Bahar's Stylistics." In *Culture and Cultural Politics under Reza Shah: The Pahlavi State, New Bourgeoisie and the Creation of a Modern Society in Iran*, edited by Bianca Devos and Christoph Werner, 19–36. New York: Routledge, 2014.

Hakala, Walter N. *Negotiating Languages: Urdu, Hindi, and the Definition of Modern South Asia.* New York: Columbia University Press, 2016.

Hali, Altaf Husayn. *Yadgar-i Ghalib* [Remembering Ghalib]. Kanpur: Nami Press, 1897.

Hammad, Hanan. "Relocating a Common Past and the Making of East-centric Modernity: Islamic and Secular Nationalism(s) in Egypt and Iran." In *Rethinking Iranian Nationalism and Modernity*, edited by Kamran Scot Aghaie and Afshin Marashi, 275–96. Austin: University of Texas Press, 2014.

Hammer-Purgstall, Joseph von. *Geschichte der schönen redekünste Persiens, mit einer blüthenlese aus zweyhundert persischen dichtern* [History of the Beautiful Oratory of Persia, with a chrestomathy of two hundred Persian poets]. Vienna: Heubner und Volke, 1818.

Hanaway, William L. and Brian Spooner. *Reading Nasta'liq: Persian and Urdu Hands from 1500 to the Present*. Costa Mesa: Mazda, 2007.

Haneda, Masashi. "Emigration of Iranian Elites to India during the 16th–18th Centuries." *Cahiers d'Asie Centrale* 3/4 (1997): 129–43.

Hanioğlu, M. Şükrü. "Blueprints for a Future Society: Late Ottoman Materialists on Science, Religion, and Art." In *Late Ottoman Society: The Intellectual Legacy*, edited by Elisabeth Özdalga, 27–116. New York: Routledge, 2005.

Hazin Lahiji, Muhammad ʿAli. *Tarikh-i Hazin* [*Hazin's History*]. Isfahan: Kitabfurushi-yi Taʾid, 1332 HS/1953–4 CE.

Hemmat, Kaveh. "Completing the Persianate Turn." *Iranian Studies* 54, no. 3–4 (2021): 633–46.

Henley, David. "Hybridity and Indigeneity in Malaya, 1900–70." In *Belonging across the Bay of Bengal: Religious Rites, Colonial Migrations, National Rights*, edited by Michael Laffan, 181–92. London: Bloomsbury Academic, 2017.

Hidayat, Riza-Quli Khan. *Majmaʿ al-Fusahaʾ* [*Assembly of the Eloquent*]. Edited by Mazahir Musaffa. 6 vols. Tehran: Muʾassasah-i Matbuʿati-i Amir Kabir [chap-i musavi], 1336-40 HS/1957–61 CE.

———. *Majmaʿ al-Fusahaʾ* [*Assembly of the Eloquent*]. Edited by Mazahir Musaffa. 6 vols. Tehran: Muʾassasah-i Intisharat-i Amir Kabir, 1382 HS/2003 CE.

"Hikayat-i Saʿdi [Anecdote from Saʿdi]." *Roznama 92 News*, June 9, 2018, <https://roznama92news.com/9-6-2018حکایت-سعدی.>

Hikmat, ʿAli-Asghar. *Naqsh-i Parsi bar Ahjar-i Hind* [*Persian Inscriptions on Indian Stones*]. Tehran: Ibn Sina, 1337 HS/1958–9 CE.

———. *Rah-Avard-i Hikmat* [*Hikmat's Gift*]. Edited by Sayyid Muhammad Dabiri-Siyaqi. 2 vols. Tehran: Anjuman-i Asar va Mafakhir-i Farhangi, 1379 HS/2000–1 CE.

Hodgkin, Samuel Gold. "Classical Persian Canons of the Revolutionary Press: Abū al-Qāsim Lāhūtī's Circles in Istanbul and Moscow." In *Persian Literature and Modernity: Production and Reception*, edited by Hamid Rezaei Yazdi and Arshavez Mozafari, 185–212. New York: Routledge, 2019.

———. "Lāhūtī: Persian Poetry in the Making of the Literary International, 1906–1957." PhD diss., University of Chicago, 2018.

Hodgson, Marshall G. S. *The Venture of Islam: Conscience and History in a World Civilization*. 3 vols. Chicago: University of Chicago Press, 1974.

"HOMOSEXUALITY iii. IN PERSIAN LITERATURE." *Encyclopædia Iranica*, vol. 12.4, 445–8, and 12.5, 449–54. Available online at <http://iranicaonline.org/articles/homosexuality-iii>. Accessed August 30, 2020.

Humaʾi, Jalal al-Din. *Tarikh-i Adabiyat-i Iran* [*History of Iranian Literature*]. Tehran: Vizarat-i Irshad, 1383 HS/2004–5 CE.

Yaddasht-ha-yi Ustad 'Allamah Huma'i dar Hashiyah-yi Majma' al-Fusaha'-i hidayat [*Notes of the Learned Professor Huma'i in the Margins of Hidayat's Majma' al-Fusaha'*]. Edited by Nasir al-Din Shah Husayni. 2 vols. Tehran: Huma, 1385 HS/2006–7 CE.

Hurani, Ibrahim. *Manahij al-Hukama' fi Nafy al-Nushu' wa al-Irtiqa'* [*A Philosophical Approach to Refuting Evolution*]. Beirut: n.p., 1884.

Ibn 'Abidin, Muhammad Amin. *Radd al-Muhtar 'ala al-Durr al-Mukhtar* [*Guiding the Baffled to The Exquisite Pearl*]. Edited by 'Adil Ahmad 'Abd al-Mawjud and 'Ali Muhammad Mu'awwad. 14 vols. Riyadh: Dar 'Alam al-Kutub, 2003.

Ingenito, Domenico. *Beholding Beauty: Sa'di of Shiraz and the Aesthetics of Desire in Medieval Persian Poetry*. Leiden: Brill, 2021.

Iqbal, Muhammad. *Bang-i Dara* [*The Call of the Marching Bell*]. Hyderabad: Ghulam Muhy al-Din, 1900.

———. *Javid-Namah* [*The Book of Eternity*]. Hyderabad: Intizami Machine Press, 1945.

———. *Javid-Nama*. Translated by Arthur J. Arberry. New York: Routledge, 2011.

———. *Haqiqat va Hayrat: Mutala'ah-yi Bidil dar Partaw-i Andishah-ha-yi Birgsun* [*Truth and Astonishment: A Study of Bidil in the Light of Bergson's Thought*]. Edited by Tahsin Firaqi. Translated by 'Ali Bayat. Tehran: Parniyan-i Khayal, 1395 HS/2016–17 CE.

Iraj Mirza, [Jalal al-Mamalik]. *Tahqiq dar Ahval va Asar va Afkar va Ash'ar-i Iraj Mirza va Khandan va Niyagan-i U* [*Biography, Works, Thought, and poetry of Iraj Mirza and his Family and Ancestors*]. Edited by Mahmud Ja'far Mahjub. Tehran: Rushdiyyah, 1353 HS/1974–5 CE.

Iran Pakistan Institute of Persian Studies. n.d. <http://ipips.ir>. Accessed August 30, 2020.

'Irfani, 'Abd al-Hamid. *Sharh-i Ahval va Asar-i Malik al-Shu'ara Muhammad-Taqi Bahar* [*Biography and Works of Poet-Laureate Muhammad-Taqi Bahar*]. Tehran: Ibn Sina, 1956.

Ishaque, Mohammad. *Modern Persian Poetry*. Calcutta: Mohammad Israil, 1943.

———. *Sukhanvaran-i Iran dar 'Asr-i Hazir* [*Iranian Poets in the Present Age*]. 2 vols. Delhi: Chapkhanah-yi Jami'ah, 1351 HS/1932–3 CE.

Izadpanah, Borna. "Early Persian Printing and Typefounding in Europe." *Journal of the Printing Historical Society* 29 (Winter 2018): 87–123.

———. "The first Iranian newspaper: Mirza Salih Shirazi's Kaghaz-i akhbar." *Asian and African studies blog, British Library*, July 18, 2019. <https://blogs.bl.uk/asian-and-african/2019/07/the-first-iranian-newspaper-mirza-salih-shirazis-kaghaz-i-akhbar.html>.

Jabbari, Alexander. "From Persianate Cosmopolis to Persianate Modernity: Translating from Urdu to Persian in Twentieth-Century Iran and Afghanistan." *Iranian Studies* 55, no. 3 (July 2022): 611–30.

——— "The Introduction to Mohammad-Taqi Bahār's Sabkshenāsi." *Journal of Persianate Studies*, 2023.

——— "Race against Time: Racial Temporality and Sexuality in Modern Iran." *Journal of Middle East Women's Studies*, 2023.

——— "Sa'di's Gulistan in British India: A Provocation." In *The Routledge Handbook of Persian Literary Translation*, edited by Pouneh Shabani-Jadidi, Michelle Quay, and Patricia J. Higgins (London: Routledge, 2022): 131–42.

——— "The Sound of Persianate Modernity: Gendered Soundscapes in Modern Iran." *Philological Encounters*, 2023.

Jabbari, Alexander and Tiffany Yun-Chu Tsai. "Sinicizing Islam: Translating the *Gulistan* of Sa'di in Modern China." *International Journal of Islam in Asia* 1, no. 1 (2020): 6–26.

Jackson, Ashley. *Persian Gulf Command: A History of the Second World War in Iran and Iraq*. New Haven: Yale University Press, 2018.

Jaffrelot, Christophe and Laurence Louër, eds. *Pan-Islamic Connections: Transnational Networks between South Asia and the Gulf*. New York: Oxford University Press, 2019.

Jamalzadah, Sayyid Muhammad 'Ali. "Shivah-yi Nuqtah Guzari va ... [Manner of Punctuation and ...]" *Kilk* 4, no.1 (Tir 1369 HS/June–July 1990): 126–9.

Jawhar Aftabchi, *Tazkirat al-Vaqi'at* [*Memoir of Events*], 1610, Additional Manuscripts 16711, folio 76r, Asian & African Studies Reading Room, British Library.

Jenkins, Jennifer. "Iran in the Nazi New Order, 1933–1941." *Iranian Studies* 49, no. 5 (2016): 727–51.

Jones, Sir William. *The Works of Sir William Jones*. 6 vols. London: G. G. and J. Robinson, 1799.

Jusserand, Jean Jules. *A Literary History of the English People: From the Origins to the Renaissance*. London: T. F. Unwin, 1909.

Karimi-Hakkak, Ahmad. *Recasting Persian Poetry: Scenarios of Poetic Modernity in Iran*. Salt Lake City: University of Utah Press, 1995.

Kashani-Sabet, Firoozeh. *Conceiving Citizens: Women and the Politics of Motherhood in Iran*. Oxford: Oxford University Press, 2011.

——— "Cultures of Iranianness: The Evolving Polemics of Iranian Nationalism." In *Iran and the Surrounding World: Interactions in Culture and Cultural Politics*, edited by Nikki R. Keddie and Rudi Matthee, 162–81. Seattle: University of Washington Press, 2002.

Frontier Fictions: Shaping the Iranian Nation, 1804–1946. Princeton: Princeton University Press, 1999.

Kasravi, Ahmad. *Pindar-ha [Suppositions].* Tehran: Payman, 1324 HS/1945–6 CE.

Tarikhchah-yi Shir va Khvurshid [Brief History of the Lion and the Sun]. Tehran: Mu'assasah-yi Khavar, 1309 HS/1930–1 CE.

Katouzian, Homa. "The Poet-Laureate Bahār in the Constitutional Era." *Iran* 40 (2002): 233–47.

Keshavmurthy, Prashant. "Finitude and the Authorship of Fiction: Muhammad Awfis [sic] Preface to his Chronicle, Lubab al-Albab (The Piths of Intellects)." *Arab Studies Journal* 19, no. 1 (Spring 2011): 94–120.

Key, Alexander. "Translation of Poetry from Persian to Arabic: 'Abd al-Qāhir al-Jurjānī and Others." *Journal of Abbasid Studies* 5, no. 1–2 (2018): 146–76.

Khabarguzari-yi IRNA (@IRNA_1313). 2019. "'Imran Khan, Nukhist Vazir-i Pakistan … [Imran Khan, Prime Minister of Pakistan …]" Twitter, April 22, 2019. <https://twitter.com/IRNA_1313/status/1120249590488469504>.

Khaleghi Motlagh, Dj., and T. Lentz. "BĀYSONĠORĪ ŠĀH-NĀMA." *Encyclopædia Iranica*, vol. 4.1, 9–11. Available online at <www.iranicaonline.org/articles/baysongori-sah-nama>. Accessed August 30, 2020.

Khamah'i, Anvar. *Chahar Chihrah [Forty Faces].* Tehran: Kitab Sara, 1368 HS/ 1989 CE.

Khaminah'i, Sayyid 'Ali. "Iqbal, Sitarah-yi Buland-i Sharq [Iqbal, the High Star of the East]." In *Mahtab-i Sham-i Sharq: Guzarah va Guzinah-yi Andishah-Shinasi-yi Iqbal [Evening Moonlight of the East: Commentary and Selection of Iqbal's Thought]*, edited by Muhammad-Husayn Sakit, 141–70. Tehran: Miras-i Maktub, 1385 HS/2005–6 CE.

Khan, Pasha M. "Marvellous Histories: Reading the *Shahnamah* in India." *Indian Economic Social History Review* 49, no. 4 (2012): 527–56.

"What Storytellers Were Worth in Mughal India." *Comparative Studies of South Asia, Africa and the Middle East* 37, no. 3 (2017): 570–87.

Khazeni, Arash. *The City and the Wilderness: Indo-Persian Encounters in Southeast Asia.* Oakland: University of California Press, 2020.

Kia, Mana. "Adab as Ethics of Literary Form and Social Conduct: Reading the *Gulistān* in Late Mughal India." In *No Tapping around Philology: A Festschrift in Honor of Wheeler McIntosh Thackston Jr.'s 70th Birthday*, edited by Alireza Korangy and Daniel J. Sheffield, 281–308. Wiesbaden: Harrassowitz Verlag, 2014.

"Imagining Iran before Nationalism: Geocultural Meanings of Land in Azar's Atashkadeh." In *Rethinking Iranian Nationalism and Modernity*, edited by

Kamran Scot Aghaie and Afshin Marashi, 89–112. Austin: University of Texas Press, 2014.

"Indian Friends, Iranian Selves, Persianate Modern." *Comparative Studies of South Asia, Africa and the Middle East* 36, no. 3 (2016): 398–417.

"Muhammad 'Ali 'Hazin' Lahiji (1692–1766), *Tazkirat al-Ahval* (1742)." Accessing Muslim Lives. <https://accessingmuslimlives.org/uncategorized/tazkirat-al-ahwal>. Accessed August 30, 2020.

Persianate Selves: Memories of Place and Origin before Nationalism. Stanford: Stanford University Press, 2020.

Kia, Mana and Afshin Marashi. "Introduction: After the Persianate." *Comparative Studies of South Asia, Africa, and the Middle East* 36, no. 3 (December 2016): 379–83.

Kia, Mehrdad. "Persian Nationalism and the Campaign for Language Purification." *Middle Eastern Studies* 34, no. 2 (April 1998): 9–36.

King, Christopher R. *One Language, Two Scripts: The Hindi Movement in Nineteenth Century North India.* New Delhi: Oxford University Press, 1994.

King, Ross. "Nationalism and Language Reform in Korea." In *Nationalism and the Construction of Korean Identity,* edited by Hyung Il Pai and Timothy R. Tangherlini, 33–69. Berkeley: Institute of East Asian Studies, University of California, 1998.

Kinra, Rajeev. "Make It Fresh: Time, Tradition, and Indo-Persian Literary Modernity." In *Time, History and the Religious Imaginary in South Asia,* edited by Anne Murphy, 12–39. London: Routledge, 2011.

Kirmani, Waris. *Evaluation of Ghalib's Persian Poetry.* Aligarh: Aligarh Muslim University Press, 1972.

Kłagisz, Mateusz. "Hints on French Loanwords in Modern New Persian." *Romanica Cracoviensia* 13, no. 1 (2013): 38–51.

Kotwal, Firoze M., Jamsheed K. Choksy, Christopher J. Brunner, and Mahnaz Moazami. "HATARIA, MANEKJI LIMJI." *Encyclopædia Iranica.* Available online at <www.iranicaonline.org/articles/hataria-manekji-limji>. Accessed August 30, 2020.

Kovacs, Hajnalka. "The Role of Persian Language and Literature in Muhammad Husain Azad's Modernist Thought." Paper presented at the 39th Annual Conference on South Asia, Madison, WI, October 2010.

Koyagi, Mikiya. "Drivers across the Desert: Infrastructure and Sikh Migrants in the Indo-Iranian Borderlands, 1919–31." *Comparative Studies of South Asia, Africa and the Middle East* 39, no. 3 (2019): 375–88.

"Moulding Future Soldiers and Mothers of the Iranian Nation: Gender and Physical Education under Reza Shah, 1921–41." *International Journal of the History of Sport* 26, no. 11 (September 2009): 1668–96.

"Tribes and Smugglers in Iran's Eastern Borderlands, 1921–41." *Iranian Studies* 55, no. 2 (2022): 405–22.

Kugle, Scott. "Sultan Mahmud's Makeover: Colonial Homophobia and the Persian–Urdu Literary Tradition." In *Queering India: Same-Sex Love and Eroticism in Indian Culture and Society*, edited by Ruth Vanita, 30–46. New York: Routledge, 2002.

Kuru, Selim S. "Generic Desires: Homoerotic Love in Ottoman Turkish Poetry." In *Mediterranean Crossings: Sexual Transgressions in Islam and Christianity (10th–18th Centuries)*, edited by Umberto Grassi, 43–63. Rome: Viella, 2020.

Lee, Jonathan L. "The Armenians of Kabul and Afghanistan." In *Cairo to Kabul: Afghan and Islamic Studies*, edited by Warwick Ball and Leonard Harrow, 157–62. London: Melisende, 2002.

Leese, Simon. "Longing for Salmá and Hind: (Re)producing Arabic Literature in 18th- and 19th-Century North India." PhD diss., SOAS, University of London, 2019.

Lefebvre, Henri. *Introduction to Modernity: Twelve Preludes, September 1959–May 1961*. Translated by John Moore. New York: Verso, 1995.

Lelyveld, David. "*Naichari* Nature: Sir Sayyid Ahmad Khan and the Reconciliation of Science, Technology, and Religion." In *The Cambridge Companion to Sayyid Ahmad Khan*, edited by Yasmin Saikia and M. Raisur Rahman, 69–85. Cambridge: Cambridge University Press, 2019.

"Sir Sayyid's Public Sphere: Urdu Print and Oratory in Nineteenth Century India." In *Islamicate Traditions in South Asia: Themes from Culture & History*, edited by Agnieszka Kuczkiewicz-Fraś, 97–128. New Delhi: Manohar, 2013.

Lewis, Bernard. "Watan." *Journal of Contemporary History* 26, no. 3 (July 1991): 523–33.

Lewis, Franklin. "GOLESTĀN-E SAʿDI." *Encyclopædia Iranica*, vol. 11.1, 79–86. Available online at <www.iranicaonline.org/articles/golestan-e-sadi>. Accessed August 30, 2020.

Rumi: Past and Present, East and West. The Life, Teachings and Poetry of Jalâl al-Din Rumi. Oxford: Oneworld Publications, 2011.

Lewis, Geoffrey. *The Turkish Language Reform: A Catastrophic Success*. New York: Oxford University Press, 1999.

Lockman, Zachary. *Field Notes: The Making of Middle East Studies in the United States*. Stanford: Stanford University Press, 2016.

Loeb, Laurence D. *Outcaste: Jewish Life in Southern Iran.* New York: Routledge, 2011.

Loraine, Michel B. "Bahār in the Context of Persian Constitutional Revolution." *Iranian Studies* 5, no. 2–3 (Spring–Summer 1972): 79–87.

Loraine, M. B., and J. Matīnī. "BAHĀR, MOḤAMMAD-TAQĪ." *Encyclopædia Iranica,* vol. 3.5, 476–9. Available online at <www.iranicaonline.org/articles/bahar-mohammad-taqi>. Accessed August 30, 2020.

Losensky, Paul. "Biographical Writing: *Tadhkere* and *Manâqeb.*" In *A History of Persian Literature, Volume V: Persian Prose,* edited by Bo Utas, 339–78. London: I. B. Tauris, 2021.

———. *Welcoming Fighani: Imitation and Poetic Individuality in the Safavid–Mughal Ghazal.* Costa Mesa: Mazda, 1998.

Ludwig, Paul. "Iranian Language Reform in the Twentieth Century: Did the First Farhangestān (1935–40) Succeed?" *Journal of Persianate Studies* 33, no. 1 (2010): 78–103.

"Madari Zaban [Mother Tongue]," Urdu Lughat, accessed August 30, 2020, <http://udb.gov.pk/result_details.php?word=50567>.

Maggi, Mauro and Paola Orsatti. "From Old to New Persian." In *The Oxford Handbook of Persian Linguistics,* edited by Anousha Sedighi and Pouneh Shabani-Jadidi, 7–51. Oxford: Oxford University Press, 2018.

Mahfouz, Naguib. *The Cairo Trilogy: Palace Walk, Palace of Desire, Sugar Street.* Translated by William Maynard Hutchins, Olive E. Kenny, Lorne M. Kenny, and Angele Botros Samaan. 3 vols. New York: Everyman's Library, 2001.

———. *Al-Sukkariyyah [Sugar Street].* Cairo: Dar al-Shuruq, 2015.

Maldonado Garcia, María Isabel. "A Corpus Based Quantitative Survey of the Persian and Arabic Elements in the Basic Vocabulary of Urdu Language." *Pakistan Vision* 16, no. 1 (2015): 63–95.

Mamdani, Mahmood. *Define and Rule: Native as Political Identity.* Cambridge: Harvard University Press, 2012.

Marashi, Afshin. *Exile and the Nation: The Parsi Community of India and the Making of Modern Iran.* Austin: University of Texas Press, 2020.

———. *Nationalizing Iran: Culture, Power, and the State 1870–1940.* Seattle: University of Washington Press, 2008.

———. "Print Culture and Its Publics: A Social History of Bookstores in Tehran, 1900–1950." *International Journal of Middle East Studies* 47, no. 1 (February 2015): 89–108.

Marcus, Steven. *The Other Victorians: A Study of Sexuality and Pornography in Mid-Nineteenth-Century England.* New Brunswick: Transaction, 2009.

Marzolph, Ulrich. *Narrative Illustration in Persian Lithographed Books*. Leiden: Brill, 2001.

⸻. *The Printing Press as an Agent of Tradition in Iran*. 2014. Video. <www.loc.gov/item/webcast-6511>.

"Mashhad Ceremony Commemorates Iqbal Lahori." *Mehr News Agency* (Tehran, Iran), November 10, 2015. <https://en.mehrnews.com/news/111819/Mashhad-ceremony-commemorates-Iqbal-Lahori>.

"Mashriqiyat." *Daily Mashriq Peshawar*, November 10, 2020. <https://mashriqtv.pk/latest/81936/>.

Massad, Joseph Andoni. *Desiring Arabs*. Chicago: University of Chicago Press, 2007.

Matthee, Rudi. "Transforming Dangerous Nomads into Useful Artisans, Technicians, Agriculturalists: Education in the Reza Shah Period." In *The Making of Modern Iran: State and Society under Riza Shah, 1921–1941*, edited by Stephanie Cronin, 128–51. London and New York: Routledge, 2005.

Matthews, David. "URDU." *Encyclopædia Iranica*. Available online at <https://iranicaonline.org/articles/urdu>. Accessed August 30, 2020.

Mayeur-Jaouen, Cathérine. "Introduction." In *Adab and Modernity: A "Civilising Process"? (Sixteenth–Twenty-First Century)*, edited by Cathérine Mayeur-Jaouen, 1–45. Leiden: Brill, 2020.

McDonough, Sheila. "Shibli Nuʿmani: A Conservative Vision of Revitalized Islam." In *Religion in Modern India*, edited by Robert D. Baird, 564–88. New Delhi: Manohar, 1995.

McFarland, Stephen Lee. "The Crises in Iran, 1941–1947: A Society in Change and the Peripheral Origins of the Cold War." PhD diss., University of Texas, Austin, 1981.

Meisami, Julie Scot. "Genres of Court Literature." In *General Introduction to Persian Literature*, edited by J. T. P. de Bruijn, 233–69. London: I. B. Tauris, 2009.

⸻. "Iran." In *Modern Literature in the Near and Middle East 1850–1970*, edited by Robin Ostle, 45–62. New York: Routledge, 1991.

⸻. *Persian Historiography to the End of the Twelfth Century*. Edinburgh: Edinburgh University Press, 1999.

Metcalf, Barbara Daly. *Islamic Revival in British India: Deoband, 1860–1900*. Princeton: Princeton University Press, 1982.

⸻. *Moral Conduct and Authority: The Place of Adab in South Asian Islam*. Berkeley: University of California Press, 1984.

Mian, Ali Altaf. "Surviving Desire: Reading Ḥāfiẓ in Colonial India." *Journal of Urdu Studies* 2, no. 1 (2021): 31–67.

"Surviving Modernity: Ashraf ʿAli Thanvi (1863–1943) and the Making of Muslim Orthodoxy in Colonial India." PhD diss., Duke University, 2015.

Mikkelson, Jane. "Of Parrots and Crows: Bidil and Ḥazin in Their Own Words." *Comparative Studies of South Asia, Africa and the Middle East* 37, no. 3 (2017): 510–30.

Miller, Matthew Thomas. "Embodying the Beloved: Embodiment, (Homo)eroticism, and the Straightening of Desire in the Hagiographic Tradition of Fakhr al-Dīn ʿIrāqī." *Middle Eastern Literatures* 21, no. 1 (2018): 1–27.

Mir, Farina. "Imperial Policy, Provincial Practices: Colonial Language Policy in Nineteenth-Century India." *Indian Economic and Social History Review* 43, no. 4 (2006): 395–427.

Mir, Mir Taqi. *Kulliyat-i Mir [Collected Works of Mir]*. Edited by Mirza Kazim ʿAli Javan, and Mirza Jan Tapish. Calcutta: Hindustani Press, 1811.

Mitchell, Lisa. *Language, Emotion, and Politics in South India: The Making of a Mother Tongue*. New Delhi: Permanent Black, 2010.

Mitchell, Timothy. *Colonising Egypt*. Berkeley and Los Angeles: University of California Press, 1991.

Mojtabāʾī, Fatḥ-Allāh. "DABESTĀN-E MAḌĀHEB." *Encyclopædia Iranica*, vol. 6.5, 532–4. Available online at <http://iranicaonline.org/articles/dabestan-e-madaheb>. Accessed August 30, 2020.

Morgenstierne, G. "Afghān." In *The Encyclopedia of Islam, Second Edition*, volume 1, edited by H. A. R. Gibb, J. H. Kramers, E. Lévi-Provençal, and J. Schacht, 216–21. Leiden: Brill, 1986.

Morton, Alexander H. "Some ʿUmarian Quatrains from the Lifetime of ʿUmar Khayyām." In *The Great ʿUmar Khayyām: A Global Reception of the Rubáiyát*, edited by A. A. Seyed-Gohrab, 55–65. Leiden: Leiden University Press, 2012.

Motter, T. H. Vail. *The Persian Corridor and Aid to Russia*. Washington, DC: Office of the Chief of Military History, Department of the Army, 1952.

Muʾazzini, ʿAli-Muhammad and Baharah Fazli-Darzi. "Maqam-i Shamikh-i Bahar dar Pakistan [The Lofty Status of Bahar in Pakistan]." *Danish* 118 (1393 ʜs/2014 ᴄᴇ), 58–63.

Mufti, Aamir R. *Forget English! Orientalisms and World Literatures*. Cambridge: Harvard University Press, 2016.

Muʿtaman, Zayn al-ʿAbidin. *Shiʿr va Adab-i Farsi [Persian Poetry and Literature]*. Tehran: Tabish, 1953.

Nadvi, ʿAbd al-Salam. *Shiʿr al-Hind [Poetry of India]*. Azamgarh: Maʿarif, 1949.

Naficy, Hamid. *A Social History of Iranian Cinema*. 4 vols. Durham: Duke University Press, 2011–12.

Naim, C. M. *Urdu Texts and Contexts: The Selected Essays of C. M. Naim*. New Delhi: Permanent Black, 2004.

Al-Najafi al-Isfahani, Abi al-Majd al-Shaykh Muhammad al-Rida. *Naqd Falsafat Darwin [Critique of Darwin's Philosophy]*. Edited by Hamid Naji al-Isfahani. Beirut: Mu'assasat al-Tarikh al-'Arabi, 2015.

Najmabadi, Afsaneh. "Crafting an Educated Housewife in Iran." In *Remaking Women: Feminism and Modernity in the Middle East*, edited by Lila Abu-Lughod, 91–125. Princeton: Princeton University Press, 1998.

——. *Women with Mustaches and Men without Beards: Gender and Sexual Anxieties of Iranian Modernity*. Berkeley: University of California Press, 2005.

Nasr, Seyyed Hossein. *Islamic Philosophy from Its Origin to the Present: Philosophy in the Land of Prophecy*. Albany: State University of New York Press, 2006.

Naushahi, Arif. "MARKAZ-E TAḤQIQĀT-E FĀRSI-E IRĀN WA PĀKESTĀN." *Encyclopædia Iranica*. Available online at <https://iranicaonline.org/articles/markaz-e-tahqiqat>. Accessed August 30, 2020.

Nava'i, Mir Nizam al-Din 'Ali Shir. *Tazkirah-yi Majalis al-Nafa'is [Assembly of Subtleties]*. Edited by 'Ali-Asghar Hikmat. Tehran: Manuchihri, 1363 HS/ 1984–5 CE.

Nawid, Senzil. "Language Policy in Afghanistan: Linguistic Diversity and National Unity." In *Language Policy and Language Conflict in Afghanistan and Its Neighbors: The Changing Politics of Language Choice*, edited by Harold F. Schiffman, 31–52. Leiden: Brill, 2012.

Nereid, Camilla T. "Kemalism on the Catwalk: The Turkish Hat Law of 1925." *Journal of Social History* 44, no. 3 (Spring 2011): 707–28.

Nizam, al-Shaykh. *Al-Fatawa al-Hindiyyah [Indian Fatwas]*. Edited by 'Abd al-Latif Hasan 'Abd al-Rahman. 6 vols. Beirut: Dar al-Kutub al-'Ilmiyyah, 2015.

Olender, Maurice. *The Languages of Paradise: Aryans and Semites, a Match Made in Heaven*. Translated by Arthur Goldhammer. New York: Other Press, 1992.

Omidsalar, Mahmoud. *Poetics and Politics of Iran's National Epic, the Shahnameh*. New York: Palgrave Macmillan, 2011.

——. "Review: Epic and Sedition: The Case of Ferdowsi's Shāhnāmeh." *British Journal of Middle Eastern Studies* 20, no. 2 (1993): 237–43.

Overton, Keelan, ed. *Iran and the Deccan: Persianate Art, Culture, and Talent in Circulation, 1400–1700*. Bloomington: Indiana University Press, 2020.

Özkan, Behlül. *From the Abode of Islam to the Turkish Vatan: The Making of a National Homeland in Turkey*. New Haven: Yale University Press, 2012.

"Pak-Funded Iqbal Faculty Building Handed over to Kabul University." *News International* (Karachi, Pakistan), July 29, 2010.

Parekh, Rauf. "Pseudonym, or takhallus, in Urdu: Some Interesting Facts," *Dawn*, June 6, 2016, <https://dawn.com/news/1262981>.

Parkes, M. B. *Pause and Effect: An Introduction to the History of Punctuation in the West.* Berkeley and Los Angeles: University of California Press, 1993.

Partovi, Pedram. *Popular Iranian Cinema before the Revolution: Family and Nation in Fīlmfārsī.* London: Routledge, 2017.

Pazargad, B. "*Pishahangi-yi Iran [Iranian Scouting].*" *Tehran: Kitabkhanah-yi Markazi*, 1315 HS/1936 CE.

Pellò, Stefano. "A Linguistic Conversion: Mīrzā Muḥammad Ḥasan Qatīl and the Varieties of Persian (ca. 1790)." In *Borders: Itineraries on the Edges of Iran,* edited by Stefano Pellò, 203–40. Venice: Edizioni Ca' Foscari.

Perkins, David. *Is Literary History Possible?* Baltimore: The Johns Hopkins University Press, 1992.

Perry, John R. "ARABIC LANGUAGE v. Arabic Elements in Persian." *Encyclopædia Iranica.* Available online at <https://iranicaonline.org/articles/arabic-v>. Accessed August 30, 2020.

——— "Comparative Perspectives on Language Planning in Iran and Tajikistan." In *Language and Society in the Middle East and North Africa: Studies in Variation and Identity,* edited by Yasir Suleiman, 154–74. London: Curzon, 1999.

——— *Form and Meaning in Persian Vocabulary: The Arabic Feminine Ending.* Costa Mesa: Mazda Publishers, 1991.

——— "Language Reform in Turkey and Iran." *International Journal of Middle East Studies* 17, no. 3 (August 1985): 295–311.

——— "Persian during the Safavid Period: Sketch for an Etat de Langue." In *Safavid Persia: The History and Politics of an Islamic Society,* edited by Charles Melville, 269–83. New York: I. B. Tauris, 1996.

——— "The Historical Role of Turkish in Relation to Persian of Iran." *Iran & the Caucasus* 5 (2001): 193–200.

Phillott, D. C. *Higher Persian Grammar.* Calcutta: Baptist Mission Press, 1919.

Pishavari, Adib. *Divan-i Qasa'id va Ghazaliyat-i Farsi va 'Arabi [Divan of Persian Qasidahs and Ghazals].* Edited by 'Ali 'Abd al-Rasuli. Tehran: Majlis, 1312 HS/1933–4 CE.

Pizzi, Italo. *Manuale di letteratura persiana [Manual of Persian Literature].* Milan: Ulrico Hoepli, 1887.

——— *Storia della poesia persiana [History of Persian Poetry].* 2 vols. Turin: Unione tipografico-editrice, 1894.

Pollock, Sheldon. *The Language of the Gods in the World of Men: Sanskrit, Culture, and Power in Premodern India*. Berkeley: University of California Press, 2006.

Pritchett, Frances W. "A Long History of Urdu Literary Culture, Part 2: Histories, Performances, and Masters." In *Literary Cultures in History: Reconstructions from South Asia*, edited by Sheldon Pollock, 864–911. Berkeley: University of California Press, 2003.

——— *Nets of Awareness: Urdu Poetry and Its Critics*. Berkeley: University of California Press, 1994.

Pue, A. Sean. *I Too Have Some Dreams: N. M. Rashed and Modernism in Urdu Poetry*. Oakland: University of California Press, 2014.

Qaraguzlu, ʿAliriza Zakavati. *Guzidah-yi Ashʿar-i Sabk-i Hindi [Selected Poems of the Indian Style]*. Tehran: Markaz-i Nashr-i Danishgahi, 1372 HS/1993–4 CE.

Qidwai, Sarah A. "Darwin or Design? Examining Sayyid Ahmad Khan's Views on Human Evolution." In *The Cambridge Companion to Sayyid Ahmad Khan*, edited by Yasmin Saikia and M. Raisur Rahman, 214–32. Cambridge: Cambridge University Press, 2019.

Radjavi, Heydar. *French Hats in Iran*. Washington, DC: Mage, 2011.

Raghavan, Srinath. *India's War: World War II and the Making of Modern South Asia*. New York: Basic Books, 2016.

Rahman, M. "AŠRAF GĪLĀNĪ." *Encyclopædia Iranica*, vol. 2.8, 795–6. Available online at <https://iranicaonline.org/articles/asraf-gilani-poet>. Accessed August 30, 2020.

Rahman, Munibur. "RAŠHĪD YĀSIMĪ." In *The Encyclopedia of Islam, Second Edition*, volume 8, edited by C. E. Bosworth, E. van Donzel, W. P. Heinrichs, and G. Lecomte, 448. Leiden: Brill, 1986.

Rahman, S. M. "Sufism and Islam." *Islamic Culture: Hyderabad Quarterly Review* 1, no. 4 (October 1927): 640–4.

Rahman, Tariq. *From Hindi to Urdu: A Social and Political History*. New Delhi: Orient Blackswan, 2011.

——— *Language and Politics in Pakistan*. New Delhi: Orient Longman, 1997.

Ramezannia, Mehrdad. "Persian Print Culture in India, 1780–1880." PhD diss., Jawaharlal Nehru University, 2010.

Rashid, N. M. "Ayandagan va Dard-i Hushyari ['The Future Ones' and 'The Pain of Sobriety]." *Shiʿr [Poetry]* 8 (Day 1372 HS/January 1994 CE): 26–7.

——— *Jadid Farsi Shaʿiri [Modern Persian Poetry]*. Lahore: Majlis-i Taraqqi-i Adab, 1987.

——— *Maqalat-i Rashid [Articles by Rashid]*. Edited by Shima Majid. Islamabad: Alhamra, 2002.

Rastegar, Kamran. "Literary Modernity between Arabic and Persian Prose: Jurji Zaydan's *Riwayat* in Persian Translation." *Comparative Critical Studies* 4, no. 3 (2007): 359–78.

Literary Modernity between Middle East and Europe: Textual Transactions in Nineteenth-Century Arabic, English and Persian Literatures. London: Routledge, 2010.

"*Mashruteh* and *al-Nahda*: The Iranian Constitutional Revolution in the Iranian Diaspora Press of Egypt and in Arab Reformist Periodicals." In *Iran's Constitutional Revolution: Popular Politics, Cultural Transformations and Transnational Connections*, edited by H. E. Chehabi and Vanessa Martin, 357–68. New York: I. B. Tauris, 2010.

Rastigar Fasa'i, "'Ali-Asghar Khan Hikmat Mard-i Farhang ['Ali-Asghar Khan Hikmat, Man of Culture]." *Namah-yi Anjuman* 18 (Summer 1384 HS/2005 CE): 4–30.

Razi, Amin Ahmad. *Tazkirah-yi Haft Iqlim* [*The Seven Climes*]. Edited by Sayyid Muhammad-Riza Tahiri. 3 vols. Tehran: Surush, 1378 HS/1999–2000 CE.

Reis, Seydi Ali. *Mir'âtü'l-Memâlik* [*The Mirror of Countries*]. Edited by Necdet Akyıldız. Istanbul: Tercüman 1001 Temel Eser, 1975.

"The Mirror of Countries, or, The Adventures of Sidi Ali Reis." In *The Sacred Books and Early Literature of the East, Volume VI: Medieval Arabic, Moorish, and Turkish*, edited by Charles F. Horne, 332–95. New York: Parke, Austin, and Lipscomb, 1917.

Rekabtalaei, Golbarg. *Iranian Cosmopolitanism: A Cinematic History*. Cambridge: Cambridge University Press, 2019.

Ricci, Ronit. *Islam Translated: Literature, Conversion, and the Arabic Cosmopolis of South and Southeast Asia*. New Delhi: Permanent Black, 2011.

Ringer, Monica. *Pious Citizens: Reforming Zoroastrianism in India and Iran*. Syracuse: Syracuse University Press, 2011.

Rizvi, Kishwar. "Between the Human and the Divine: The *Majālis al-'ushshāq* and the Materiality of Love in Early Safavid Art." In *Ut pictura amor: The Reflexive Imagery of Love in Artistic Theory and Practice, 1500–1700*, edited by Walter Melion, Michael Zell, and Joanna Woodall, 229–63. Leiden: Brill, 2017.

Rizvi, Sayyid Sibt-i Hasan. *Farsi-guyan-i Pakistan* [*Persian-Speakers of Pakistan*]. Rawalpindi: Markaz-i Tahqiqat-i Farsi-yi Iran va Pakistan, 1974.

Robinson, Francis. "Technology and Religious Change: Islam and the Impact of Print." *Modern Asian Studies* 27, no. 1 (1993): 229–51.

Rypka, Jan. *History of Iranian Literature*. Edited by Karl Jlahn. Dordrecht: D. Reidel, 1968.

Sachau, Ed[uard] and Hermann Ethé. *Catalogue of the Persian, Turkish, Hindûstânî, and Pushtû Manuscripts in the Bodleian Library. Part 1: The Persian Manuscripts*. Oxford: Clarendon Press, 1954.

Sacks, Jeffrey. *Iterations of Loss: Mutilation and Aesthetic Form, al-Shidyaq to Darwish*. New York: Fordham University Press, 2015.

Sa'di, Muslih al-Din. *Gulistan-i Sa'di* [*Sa'di's Rose-Garden*]. Edited by Ghulam-Husayn Yusufi. Tehran: Intisharat-i Khwarazmi, 1394 HS/2015–16 CE.

   Kulliyat-i Sa'di [*The Collected Works of Sa'di*]. Edited by Muhammad-'Ali Furughi. Tehran: Intisharat-i Hirmis, 1385 HS/2006 CE.

   The Persian and Arabick Works of Sâdee in Two Volumes. Edited by John Herbert Harington. Vol. 2. Calcutta: Honourable Company's Press, 1795.

Sadiq, Muhammad. *A History of Urdu Literature*. Oxford: Oxford University Press, 1985.

"Safar-i shahanshah ba-pakistan [The King's Trip to Pakistan]." *Danish* 1, no. 10–11 (Day-Bahman 1328 HS/February 1949 CE): 516–23.

Saffari, Siavash. *Beyond Shariati: Modernity, Cosmopolitanism, and Islam in Iranian Political Thought*. Cambridge: Cambridge University Press, 2017.

Salim, Vahid al-Din. *Vaz'-i Istalahat* [*Coining Terms*]. Aligarh: Aligarh Muslim University Press, 1931.

Samarqandi, Dawlatshah. *Tazkirat al-Shu'ara'* [*Memorial of the Poets*]. Edited by Edward Browne. Leiden: Brill, 1900.

Sarwar, Hafiz Ghulam. *Philosophy of the Qur-an* [*sic*]. Lahore: Sh. Muhammad Ashraf, 1946.

Schayegh, Cyrus. *Who Is Knowledgeable Is Strong: Science, Class, and the Formation of Modern Iranian Society, 1900–1950*. Berkeley: University of California Press, 2009.

Schimmel, Annemarie. *Mystical Dimensions of Islam*. Chapel Hill: University of North Carolina Press, 2011.

   The Triumphal Sun: A Study of the Works of Jalāloddin Rumi. Albany: State University of New York Press, 1993.

Schwartz, Kevin L. *Remapping Persian Literary History, 1700–1900*. Edinburgh: Edinburgh University Press, 2020.

Seidel, Roman. "The Reception of European Philosophy in Qajar Iran." In *Philosophy in Qajar Iran*, edited by Reza Pourjavady, 313–71. Leiden: Brill, 2018.

Sen, Madhurima. "Contested Sites: The Prison, Penal Laws, and the 1857 Revolt." In *The Great Rebellion of 1857 in India: Exploring Transgressions, Contests, and Diversities*, edited by Biswamoy Pati, 82–94. New York: Routledge, 2010.

Seyed-Gohrab, Ali-Asghar. "Modern Persian Prose and Fiction between 1900 and 1940." In *Literature of the Early Twentieth Century: From the Constitutional Period to Reza Shah*, edited by Ali-Asghar Seyed Gohrab, 133–60. London: I. B. Tauris, 2015.

Shafieioun, Saeid. "Some Critical Remarks on the Migration of Iranian Poets to India in the Safavid Era." *Journal of Persianate Studies* 11, no. 2 (2019): 155–74.

Shafi'i-Kadkani, Muhammad-Riza. *Sha'ir-i Ayinah-ha: Barrasi-yi Sabk-i Hindi va Shi'r-i Bidil [The Poet of Mirrors: A Study of the Indian Style and the Poetry of Bidil]*. Tehran: Intisharat-i Agah, 1371 HS/1992–3 CE.

"Talaqqi-yi Qudama az Vatan [The Ancients' Understanding of 'Homeland']." *Bukhara* 75 (Farvardin-Tir 1389 HS/March–July 2010 CE): 16–45.

Shahsavandi, Shahla. "Dar Sarzamin-i Iqbal [In the Land of Iqbal]." *Shi'r* 8 (Day 1372 HS/January 1994 CE): 5.

Shakespear, John. *A Dictionary, Hindustani and English, with a Copious Index, Fitting the Work to Serve, Also, as a Dictionary of English and Hindustani.* London: Parbury, Allen, & Co., 1834.

A Grammar of the Hindustani Language. London: Cox & Baylis, 1826.

Shamisa, Sirus. *Shahidbazi dar Adabiyat-i Farsi [Witness-Play in Persian Literature].* Tehran: Intisharat-i Firdaws, 1381 HS/2002 CE.

Shamisa, Sirus and Shahla Farghadani. "Tahlil-i Didgah-ha-yi Intiqadi-yi Khan-i Arzu dar Tazkirah-yi Majma' al-Nafa'is [Analysis of Khan-i Arzu's Critical Views in Assembly of Subtleties]." *Faslnamah-yi Mutala'at-i Shibh-i Qarah [Journal of Subcontinental Studies]* 2, no. 5 (Winter 1389 HS/2011 CE): 7–28.

Shams, Alex. "From Guests of the Imam to Unwanted Foreigners: The Politics of South Asian Pilgrimage to Iran in the Twentieth Century." *Middle Eastern Studies* 4, no. 57 (2021): 581–605.

Shari'ati, 'Ali. *Majmu'ah-yi Asar [Collected Works]. Vol. 5, Iqbal va Ma [Iqbal and Us].* Tehran: Husayniyyah-yi Irshad, 1356 HS/1977–8 CE.

Sharma, Sunil. *Mughal Arcadia: Persian Literature in an Indian Court.* Cambridge: Harvard University Press, 2017.

"Redrawing the Boundaries of 'Ajam in Early Modern Persian Literary Histories." In *Iran Facing Others: Identity Boundaries in a Historical Perspective*, edited by Abbas Amanat and Farzin Vejdani, 51–64. New York: Palgrave Macmillan, 2012.

"Translating Gender: Āzād Bilgrāmī on the Poetics of the Love Lyric and Cultural Synthesis." *The Translator* 15, no. 1 (2009): 87–103.

"Wandering Quatrains and Women Poets in the 'Khulāsāt al-ash'ār fī al-rubā'īyāt.'" In *The Treasury of Tabriz: The Great Il-Khanid Compendium,* edited by A. A. Seyed-Gohrab and S. McGlinn, 153–69. Amsterdam: Rozenberg, 2007.

Sheffield, Daniel J. "Exercises in Peace: Āzar Kayvānī Universalism and Comparison in the *School of Doctrines.*" *Modern Asian Studies* 56, no. 3 (2022): 959–92.

"Iran, the Mark of Paradise or the Land of Ruin? Historical Approaches to Reading Two Parsi Travelogues." In *On the Wonders of Land and Sea: Persianate Travel Writing*, edited by Roberta Micallef and Sunil Sharma, 14–43. Cambridge: Harvard University Press, 2013.

"The Language of Heaven in Safavid Iran: Speech and Cosmology in the Thought of Āzar Kayvān and His Followers." In *No Tapping Around Philology: A Festschrift in Honor of Wheeler McIntosh Thackston Jr.'s 70th Birthday*, edited by Alireza Korangy and Daniel J. Sheffield, 161–83. Wiesbaden: Harrassowitz Verlag, 2014.

Shibli Nu'mani, Muhammad. *Kitabkhanah-yi Iskandariyyah* [*The Library of Alexandria*]. Translated by Muhammad-Taqi Fakhr-i Da'i Gilani. Tehran: Armaghan, 1315 ah/1936–7 ce.

Safarnamah-i Rum va Misr va Sham [*Travelogue of Turkey, Egypt, and Syria*]. Delhi: Qawmi Press, 1319 ah/1901–2 ce.

Savanih-i Mawlana Rum [*Biography of Rumi*]. Kanpur: Nami Press, 1906.

Shi'r al-'Ajam [*Poetry of the Persians*]. 5 vols. Azamgarh: Ma'arif Press, 1920.

Shi'r al-'Ajam [*Poetry of the Persians*]. Translated by Muhammad-Taqi Da'i Gilani. 5 vols. Tehran: Ibn Sina, 1335 hs/1956 ce.

Turkey, Egypt, and Syria: A Travelogue. Translated by Gregory Maxwell Bruce. Syracuse: Syracuse University Press, 2020.

Al-Shidyaq, Ahmad Faris. *Leg over Leg.* Edited and translated by Humphrey Davies. 4 vols. New York: New York University Press, 2014.

Shraybom Shivtiel, Shlomit. "The Question of Romanisation of the Script and the Emergence of Nationalism in the Middle East." *Mediterranean Language Review* 10 (1998): 179–96.

Shumayyil, Shibli. *Al-haqiqah: wa-hiya risalah tatadamman rududan li-ithbat madhhab Darwin fi al-nushu' wa'l-irtiqa'* [*The Truth: being a Treatise including Responses to Prove the Doctrine of Darwin on Evolution*]. Cairo: al-Muqtataf, 1885.

Falsafat al-nushu' wa'l-irtiqa' [*The Philosophy of Evolution*]. Cairo: al-Muqtataf, 1910.

Simon, Maurya. "A Brief History of Punctuation." *Georgia Review* 53, no. 3 (Fall 1999): 513–28.

Sinha, Sachchidananda. *Iqbal: The Poet and His Message.* Allahabad: Ram Narain Lal, 1947.

Smith, Matthew C. "Literary Connections: Bahār's *Sabkshenāsi* and the *Bāzgasht-e Adabi.*" *Journal of Persianate Studies* 2, no. 2 (2009): 194–209.

———. "Literary Courage: Language, Land, and the Nation in the Works of Malik al-Shu'ara Bahar." PhD diss., Harvard University, 2006.

Spear, Thomas. "Early Swahili History Reconsidered." *International Journal of African Historical Studies* 33, no. 2 (2000): 257–90.

Spooner, Brian. "Epilogue: The Persianate Millennium." In *The Persianate World: The Frontiers of a Eurasian Lingua Franca*, edited by Nile Green, 301–16. Oakland: University of California Press, 2019.

Spooner, Brian, and William L. Hanaway, eds. *Literacy in the Persianate World: Writing and the Social Order*. Philadelphia: University of Pennsylvania Museum of Archaeology and Anthropology, 2012.

———. "*Siyaq*: Numerical Notation and Numeracy in the Persianate World." In *The Oxford Handbook of the History of Mathematics*, edited by Eleanor Robinson and Jacqueline Stedall, 429–47. Oxford: Oxford University Press, 2009.

Sprachman, Paul. "BEHRŪZ, ḌABĪḤ." *Encyclopædia Iranica*, vol. 4.1–2, 111–13. Available online at <www.iranicaonline.org/articles/behruz-dabih-1889-1971-persian-satirist-son-of-the-physician-and-calligrapher-abul-fazl-savaji>. Accessed August 30, 2020.

———. *Suppressed Persian: An Anthology of Forbidden Literature*. Costa Mesa: Mazda Publishers, 1995.

Sprenger, A[loys]. *A Catalogue of the Arabic, Persian and Hindústány Manuscripts of the Libraries of the King of Oudh*. Calcutta: J. Thomas, 1854.

———. *Gulistan of Sa'dy: Edited in Persian, with Punctuation and the Necessary Vowel-Marks, for the Use of the College of Fort William*. Calcutta: J. Thomas, 1851.

Stark, Ulrike. *An Empire of Books: The Naval Kishore Press and the Diffusion of the Printed Word in Colonial India*. Ranikhet: Permanent Black, 2008.

Stewart-Robinson, J. "Tadhkira." In Encyclopaedia of Islam, Second Edition, edited by P. Bearman, et al. Brill Online, 2015. <http://referenceworks.brillonline.com/entries/encyclopaedia-of-islam-2/tadhkira-COM_1140>.

Storey, C. A. and François de Blois. *Persian Literature: A Bio-Bibliographical Survey*. 5 vols. London: Luzac & Company, 1927–2004.

Subrahmanyam, Sanjay. "Connected Histories: Notes towards a Reconfiguration of Early Modern Eurasia." *Modern Asian Studies* 31, no. 3 (July 1997): 735–62.

———. "Iranians Abroad: Intra-Asian Elite Migration and Early Modern State Formation." *Journal of Asian Studies* 51, no. 2 (May 1992): 340–63.

Sunya, Samhita. *Sirens of Modernity: World Cinema via Bombay*. Oakland: University of California Press, 2022.

Syed, Muhammad Aslam. "How Could Urdu Be the Envy of Persian [rashk-i-Fārsi]!" In *Literacy in the Persianate World: Writing and the Social Order*, edited by Brian Spooner and William L. Hanaway, 279–310. Philadelphia: University of Pennsylvania Museum of Archaeology and Anthropology, 2012.

Talattof, Kamran. "Early Twentieth-Century Journals in Iran: Response to Modernity in Literary Reviews." In *Literature of the Early Twentieth Century: From the Constitutional Period to Reza Shah*, edited by Ali-Asghar Seyed Gohrab, 411–47. London: I. B. Tauris, 2015.

Tavakoli-Targhi, Mohamad. *Refashioning Iran: Orientalism, Occidentalism, and Nationalist Historiography*. New York: Palgrave Macmillan, 2001.

"The Homeless Texts of Persianate Modernity." *Cultural Dynamics* 13, no. 3 (November 2001): 263–91.

"Tarikh-pardazi va iran-ara'i: baz-sazi-yi huviyyat-i irani dar guzarish-i tarikh." *Iran Nameh* 12, no. 4 (1994): 583–628.

Thiesen, Finn. *A Manual of Classical Persian Prosody: With Chapters on Urdu, Karakhanidic and Ottoman Prosody*. Wiesbaden: Otto Harrassowitz, 1982.

Thompson, Levi. "Re-Orienting Modernism: Mapping East–East Exchanges between Arabic and Persian Poetry." *Alif: Journal of Comparative Poetics* 40 (2020): 115–38.

Toirov, Urvatullo, Mirzo Solehov, and Rajab Sharifov. *Adabiyoti Tojik: Baroi Sinfi 10 [Tajik Literature: For Grade 10]*. Dushanbe: n.p., 2007.

Tolz, Vera. *Russia's Own Orient: The Politics of Identity and Oriental Studies in the Late Imperial and Early Soviet Periods*. Oxford: Oxford University Press, 2011.

Toutant, Marc. "De-Persifying Court Culture: The Khanate of Khiva's Translation Program." In *The Persianate World: The Frontiers of a Eurasian Lingua Franca*, edited by Nile Green, 243–58. Oakland: University of California Press, 2019.

Türkmen, Erkan. "The Turkish Elements in Urdu." *Journal of Ottoman Studies* VI (1986): 1–30.

Uluç, Lâle. "The Majālis al-'Ushshāq: Written in Herat, Copied in Shiraz, Read in İstanbul." In *M. Uğur Derman 65 Yaş Armağanı*, edited by İrvin C. Schick, 569–602. Istanbul: Sabancı University, 2000.

UNESCO. "Adult and Youth Literacy: National, Regional and Global Trends, 1985–2015." UNESCO Institute for Statistics, June 2013. <www.uis.unesco.org/Education/Documents/literacy-statistics-trends-1985-2015.pdf>.

Ustadi, Kazim. "Tarikhchah-yi Andishah-yi Tahghyir-i Khatt dar Iran [Brief History of the Idea of Script Change in Iran]." *Ayinah-yi Pazhuhish* 23, no. 2 (Khurdad-Tir 1391 HS/2012 CE): 22–38.

Uvaysi, Mirza 'Ali-Muhammad Khan. *Khatt-i Naw: Tarh-i Asasi dar Islah-i Alifba-ha-yi Islami* [New Script: A Blueprint for Reforming Islamic Alphabets]. Istanbul: Chapkhanah-yi Shams, 1331 HS/1913 CE.

Vajid 'Ali Shah. *Mubahasah bayn al-Nafs va al-'Aql [Debate between the Ego and the Intellect]*. Calcutta: Matba'-i Sultani, 1291 AH/1874 CE.

Valih Daghistani, 'Ali-Quli. *Tazkirah-yi Riyaz al-Shu'ara'* [Garden of the Poets]. 5 vols. Edited by Sayyid Muhsin Naji Nasrabadi. Tehran: Asatir, 1382 HS/2003–4 CE.

Vaziri, Mostafa. *Iran as Imagined Nation: The Construction of National Identity.* Piscataway: Gorgias Press, 2013.

Vejdani, Farzin. "Indo-Iranian Linguistic, Literary, and Religious Entanglements: Between Nationalism and Cosmopolitanism, ca. 1900–1940." *Comparative Studies of South Asia, Africa, and the Middle East* 36, no. 3 (2016): 435–54.

———. *Making History: Education, Nationalism, and Print Culture.* Stanford: Stanford University Press, 2015.

———. "The Place of Islam in Interwar Iranian Nationalist Historiography." In *Rethinking Iranian Nationalism and Modernity*, edited by Kamran Scot Aghaie and Afshin Marashi, 205–18. Austin: University of Texas Press, 2014.

Versteegh, Kees. "The Myth of the Mixed Languags." In *Advances in Maltese Linguistics*, edited by Benjamin Saade and Mauro Tosco, 217–38. Berlin and New York: De Gruyter Mouton, 2017.

Warren, Allen. "Sir Robert Baden-Powell, the Scout Movement and Citizen Training in Great Britain, 1900–1920." *English Historical Review* 101, no. 399 (April 1986): 376–98.

Wasif Khan, Maryam. *Who Is a Muslim? Orientalism and Literary Populisms.* New York: Fordham University Press, 2021.

Williams, Raymond. *Marxism and Literature.* Oxford: Oxford University Press, 1977.

Windfuhr, Gernot. "FĀRS viii. Dialects." *Encyclopædia Iranica*, vol. 9.4, 362–73. Available online at <https://iranicaonline.org/articles/fars-viii>. Accessed August 30, 2020.

Witkam, Jan Just. "The Neglect Neglected: To Point or Not to Point, That is the Question." *Journal of Islamic Manuscripts* 6, no. 2–3 (January 2015): 376–408.

Witzel, Michael. "Indocentrism: Autochthonous Visions of Ancient India." In *The Indo-Aryan Controversy: Evidence and Inference in Indian History*, edited by Edwin F. Bryant and Laurie L Patton, 341–404. New York: Routledge, 2005.

Wright, Elaine. *The Look of the Book: Manuscript Production in Shiraz, 1303–1452.* Washington, DC: Freer Gallery of Art Occasional Papers and Seattle: University of Washington Press, 2012.

Yacoob, Saadia. "Hermeneutics of Desire: Ontologies of Gender and Desire in Early Ḥanafī Law." PhD diss., Duke University, 2016.

Yasami, Rashid. *Divan-i Rashid Yasami, 1314–1331* [*Divan of Rashid Yasami, 1314–1331*]. Tehran: Amir Kabir, 1362 ʜs/1983–4 ᴄᴇ.

Yilmaz, Huseyin. "The Eastern Question and the Ottoman Empire: The Genesis of the Near and Middle East in the Nineteenth Century." In *Is There a Middle East? The Evolution of a Geopolitical Concept*, edited by Michael E. Bonne, Abbas Amanat, and Michael Ezekiel Gasper, 11–35. Stanford: Stanford University Press, 2012.

Yu, Li. "Learning to Read in Late Imperial China." *Studies on Asia: Series III* 1, no. 1 (2004): 7–28.

Yūsofī, Ḡolām-Ḥosayn. "CALLIGRAPHY." *Encyclopædia Iranica*, vol. 4.7, 680–704. Available online at <www.iranicaonline.org/articles/calligraphy>. Accessed August 30, 2020.

Yusuf Ali, A. "Note on Urdu Orthography." *Bulletin of the School of Oriental Studies, University of London* 1, no. 3 (1920): 29–34.

"Social and Economic Conditions During the Middle Ages of Indian History." *Islamic Culture* 2, no. 3 (July 1928): 360–75.

Yusufi, Muhammad Akbar Khan. "Rasm al-Khatt [Orthography]." *Aryana* 126, no. 6 (Saratan 1332 ʜs/June–July 1953 ᴄᴇ): 6–7.

Zaman, Muhammad Qasim. "Arabic, the Arab Middle East, and the Definition of Muslim Identity in Twentieth Century India." *Journal of the Royal Asiatic Society* 8, no. 1 (1998): 59–81.

Zarrinkub, ʿAbd al-Hosayn. "EVOLUTION." *Encyclopædia Iranica*, vol. 9.1, 86–7. Available online at <https://iranicaonline.org/articles/evolution>. Accessed August 30, 2020.

Zaheer, Ibtisam Elahi. "Hikayat-i Saʿdi [Anecdote from Saʿdi]." *Dunya* (Pakistan), November 3, 2016. <https://dunya.com.pk/index.php/author/allama-ibtisam-elahi-zaheer/2016-11-03/17395/40203844>.

Zaydan, Jurji. *Tarikh Adab al-Lughah al-ʿArabiyyah* [*History of Arabic Literature*]. Cairo: Muʾassasat al-Hindawi, 2012.

Zeʾevi, Dror. *Producing Desire: Changing Sexual Discourse in the Ottoman Middle East, 1500–1900*. Berkeley: University of California Press, 2006.

Zehra, Khushnood. "Hikayat-i Saʿdi [Anecdote from Saʿdi]." *Express News* (Pakistan), October 3, 2015. <www.express.pk/story/395996>.

Zeydabadi-Nejad, Saeed. "Watching the Forbidden: Reception of Banned Films in Iran." In *The State of Post-Cinema: Tracing the Moving Image in the Age of Digital Dissemination*, edited by Malte Hagener, Vinzenz Hediger, and Alena Strohmaier, 99–113. London: Palgrave Macmillan, 2016.

Zhong, Yurou. *Chinese Grammatology: Script Revolution and Literary Modernity, 1916–1958.* New York: Columbia University Press, 2019.

Zia-Ebrahimi, Reza. "'Arab Invasion' and Decline, or the Import of European Racial Thought by Iranian Nationalists." *Ethnic and Racial Studies* 37, no. 6 (2014): 1043–61.

——. "An Emissary of the Golden Age: Manekji Limji Hataria and the Charisma of the Archaic in Pre-Nationalist Iran." *Studies in Ethnicity and Nationalism* 10, no. 3 (December 2010): 377–90.

——. *The Emergence of Iranian Nationalism: Race and the Politics of Dislocation.* New York: Columbia University Press, 2016.

——. "Self-Orientalization and Dislocation: The Uses and Abuses of the 'Aryan' Discourse in Iran." *Iranian Studies* 44, no. 4 (2011): 445–72.

Zipoli, Riccardo. *Irreverent Persia: Invective, Satirical and Burlesque Poetry from the Origins to the Timurid Periode (10th to 15th Centuries).* Leiden: Leiden University Press, 2015.

Ziya', Ziya' Muhammad. *Nava-yi Shawq* [*Melody of Desire*]. Edited by Muhammad-Husayn Tasbihi. Sialkot: Anjuman-i Farsi, 1977.

Zubairi, Muhammad Amin. *Shibli ki Rangin Zindagi* [*Shibli's Colorful Life*]. Lahore: Faruq 'Umar Publishers, 1952.

Zuckermann, Ghil'ad. "A New Vision for Israeli Hebrew: Theoretical and Practical Implications of Analyzing Israel's Main Language as a Semi-Engineered Semito-European Hybrid Language." *Journal of Modern Jewish Studies* 5, no. 1 (March 2006): 57–71.

Zuka', Yahya. *Dar Piramun-i Taghyir-i Khatt-i Farsi* [*On Changing the Persian Script*]. Tehran: n.p., 1329 HS/1950–1 CE.

Zutshi, Chitralekha. *Languages of Belonging: Islam, Regional Identity, and the Making of Kashmir.* Oxford: Oxford University Press, 2004.

Index

Printed in the USA
CPSIA information can be obtained
at www.ICGtesting.com
LVHW012012100124
768605LV00006B/377